TRIUMPH
Production Testers' Tales – from the Meriden Factory

Hughie Hancox

Other great books from Veloce –

RAC handbooks
Caring for your scooter – How to maintain & service your 49cc to 125cc twist & go scooter (Fry)
How your motorcycle works – Your guide to the components & systems of modern motorcycles (Henshaw)
Motorcycles – A first-time-buyer's guide (Henshaw)

Enthusiast's Restoration Manual Series
Beginner's Guide to Classic Motorcycle Restoration, The (Burns)
Classic Large Frame Vespa Scooters, How to Restore (Paxton)
Ducati Bevel Twins 1971 to 1986 (Falloon)
How to restore Honda CX500 & CX650 (Burns)
How to restore Honda Fours (Burns)
Triumph Trident T150/T160 & BSA Rocket III, How to Restore (Rooke)
Yamaha FS1-E, How to Restore (Watts)

Essential Buyer's Guide Series
BSA 350 & 500 Unit Construction Singles (Henshaw)
BSA 500 & 650 Twins (Henshaw)
BSA Bantam (Henshaw)
Choosing, Using & Maintaining Your Electric Bicycle (Henshaw)
Ducati Bevel Twins (Falloon)
Ducati Desmodue Twins (Falloon)
Ducati Desmoquattro Twins – 851, 888, 916, 996, 998, ST4 1988 to 2004 (Falloon)
Harley-Davidson Big Twins (Falloon)
Hinckley Triumph triples & fours 750, 900, 955, 1000, 1050, 1200 – 1991-2009 (Henshaw)
Honda CBR FireBlade (Henshaw)
Honda CBR600 Hurricane (Henshaw)
Honda SOHC Fours 1969-1984 (Henshaw)
Kawasaki Z1 & Z900 (Orritt)
Moto Guzzi 2-valve big twins (Falloon)
Norton Commando (Henshaw)
Royal Enfield Bullet (Henshaw)
Triumph 350 & 500 Twins (Henshaw)
Triumph Bonneville (Henshaw)
Triumph Thunderbird, Trophy & Tiger (Henshaw)
Velocette 350 & 500 Singles (Henshaw)
Vespa Scooters – Classic 2-stroke models 1960-2008 (Paxton)

Those Were The Days ... Series
Café Racer Phenomenon, The (Walker)
Drag Bike Racing in Britain – From the mid '60s to the mid '80s (Lee)

Auto-Graphics Series
Lambretta Li Series Scooters (Sparrow)

Biographies
A Chequered Life – Graham Warner and the Chequered Flag (Hesletine)
A Life Awheel – The 'auto' biography of W de Forte (Skelton)
Amédée Gordini ... a true racing legend (Smith)
André Lefebvre, and the cars he created at Voisin and Citroën (Beck)
Chris Carter at Large – Stories from a lifetime in motorcycle racing (Carter & Skelton)
Cliff Allison, The Official Biography of – From the Fells to Ferrari (Gauld)
Edward Turner – The Man Behind the Motorcycles (Clew)
Driven by Desire – The Desiré Wilson Story
First Principles – The Official Biography of Keith Duckworth (Burr)
Inspired to Design – F1 cars, Indycars & racing tyres: the autobiography of Nigel Bennett (Bennett)
Jack Sears, The Official Biography of – Gentleman Jack (Gauld)
Jim Redman – 6 Times World Motorcycle Champion: The Autobiography (Redman)
John Chatham – 'Mr Big Healey' – The Official Biography (Burr)
The Lee Noble Story (Wilkins)
Mason's Motoring Mayhem – Tony Mason's hectic life in motorsport and television (Mason)
Raymond Mays' Magnificent Obsession (Apps)

Pat Moss Carlsson Story, The – Harnessing Horsepower (Turner)
'Sox' – Gary Hocking – the forgotten World Motorcycle Champion (Hughes)
Tony Robinson – The biography of a race mechanic (Wagstaff)
Virgil Exner – Visioneer: The Official Biography of Virgil M Exner Designer Extraordinaire (Grist)

General
BMW Boxer Twins 1970-1995 Bible, The (Falloon)
BMW Cafe Racers (Cloesen)
BMW Custom Motorcycles – Choppers, Cruisers, Bobbers, Trikes & Quads (Cloesen)
BMW – The Power of M (Vivian)
Bonjour – Is this Italy? (Turner)
British 250cc Racing Motorcycles (Pereira)
British Café Racers (Cloesen)
British Custom Motorcycles – The Brit Chop – choppers, cruisers, bobbers & trikes (Cloesen)
BSA Bantam Bible, The (Henshaw)
BSA Motorcycles – the final evolution (Jones)
Ducati 750 Bible, The (Falloon)
Ducati 750 SS 'round-case' 1974, The Book of the (Falloon)
Ducati 860, 900 and Mille Bible, The (Falloon)
Ducati Monster Bible (New Updated & Revised Edition), The (Falloon)
Ducati 916 (updated edition) (Falloon)
Fine Art of the Motorcycle Engine, The (Peirce)
From Crystal Palace to Red Square – A Hapless Biker's Road to Russia (Turner)
Funky Mopeds (Skelton)
Italian Cafe Racers (Cloesen)
Italian Custom Motorcycles (Cloesen)
Japanese Custom Motorcycles – The Nippon Chop – Chopper, Cruiser, Bobber, Trikes and Quads (Cloesen)
Kawasaki Triples Bible, The (Walker)
Kawasaki Z1 Story, The (Sheehan)
Lambretta Bible, The (Davies)
Laverda Twins & Triples Bible 1968-1986 (Falloon)
Lea-Francis Story, The (Price)
Little book of trikes, the (Quellin)
Moto Guzzi Sport & Le Mans Bible, The (Falloon)
Motorcycle Apprentice (Cakebread)
Motorcycle GP Racing in the 1960s (Pereira)
Motorcycle Road & Racing Chassis Designs (Noakes)
MV Agusta Fours, The book of the classic (Falloon)
Off-Road Giants! (Volume 1) – Heroes of 1960s Motorcycle Sport (Westlake)
Off-Road Giants! (Volume 2) – Heroes of 1960s Motorcycle Sport (Westlake)
Off-Road Giants! (volume 3) – Heroes of 1960s Motorcycle Sport (Westlake)
Racing Line – British motorcycle racing in the golden age of the big single (Guntrip)
Scooter Lifestyle (Grainger)
SCOOTER MANIA! – Recollections of the Isle of Man International Scooter Rally (Jackson)
Singer Story: Cars, Commercial Vehicles, Bicycles & Motorcycle (Atkinson)
Triumph Bonneville Bible (59-83) (Henshaw)
Triumph Bonneville!, Save the – The inside story of the Meriden Workers' Co-op (Rosamond)
Triumph Motorcycles & the Meriden Factory (Hancox)
Triumph Speed Twin & Thunderbird Bible (Woolridge)
Triumph Tiger Cub Bible (Estall)
Triumph Trophy Bible (Woolridge)
TT Talking – The TT's most exciting era – As seen by Manx Radio TT's lead commentator 2004-2012 (Lambert)
Velocette Motorcycles – MSS to Thruxton – New Third Edition (Burris)
Vespa – The Story of a Cult Classic in Pictures (Uhlig)
Vincent Motorcycles: The Untold Story since 1946 (Guyony & Parker)

For post publication news, updates and amendments relating to this book please visit www.veloce.co.uk/books/V4441

www.veloce.co.uk

First published in November 2012 by Veloce Publishing Limited, Veloce House, Parkway Farm Business Park, Middle Farm Way, Poundbury, Dorchester, Dorset, DT1 3AR, England. Fax 01305 250479/e-mail info@veloce.co.uk/web www.veloce.co.uk or www.velocebooks.com. Reprinted July 2016.
ISBN: 978-1-845844-41-7 UPC: 6-36847-04441-1
© Hughie Hancox and Veloce Publishing 2012 and 2016. All rights reserved. With the exception of quoting brief passages for the purpose of review, no part of this publication may be recorded, reproduced or transmitted by any means, including photocopying, without the written permission of Veloce Publishing Ltd. Throughout this book logos, model names and designations, etc, have been used for the purposes of identification, illustration and decoration. Such names are the property of the trademark holder as this is not an official publication.
Readers with ideas for automotive books, or books on other transport or related hobby subjects, are invited to write to the editorial director of Veloce Publishing at the above address.
British Library Cataloguing in Publication Data – A catalogue record for this book is available from the British Library.
Typesetting, design and page make-up all by Veloce Publishing Ltd on Apple Mac. Printed and bound by CPI Group (UK) Ltd, Croydon, CR0 4YY.

TRIUMPH

Production Testers' Tales – from the Meriden Factory

Hughie Hancox

Veloce Publishing
THE PUBLISHER OF FINE AUTOMOTIVE BOOKS

THE BEST MOTORCYCLE IN THE WORLD

Contents

Acknowledgements 5
Foreword 6
Initiation 7
The first ride out 18
The Cubs 21
One out, one in 40
The C range 46
Bill's story 62
The six fifties 70
The new models 90
The Tiger 100S/S 104
Summer of '62 121
The new unit twins 127
Christmas '62 142
Reflections 146
Index
   Technical 159
   General 159

Acknowledgements

I would first of all like to mention the chaps who have gone to the big factory in the sky since I started on this book in 2001, without whose help and permission to say what I do about them, I could not have possibly completed it. If it helps to keep their names and memories alive, then I – and I am sure they – will be happy.

The chaps we have lost are Bill Letts, Eddie Dent, Jim Brown, Dennis Peacock, Norris Harrison, Stan Whitcomb, and Bill Hemmings, and from the sections adjoining the test, Roger Bryant, Eric Miller; both from the Rectification section, or 'Knacker Gang' as it was called. I am also sad to say we have lost Geoff Price whilst I have been writing this book.

I would also like to say thank you to my old army chums Les Williams and Jock Copland. Also to Pete West, Jim Lee, Bert Watmore, and Dennis Griffin.

I shall be forever in debt to my old boss, Mr John R Nelson, Patron of the Triumph Owners Club of Great Britain, for his readiness to help with illustrations and advice. Without him I could not have managed, and also to Roy Shilling, President of the Triumph Owners Club.

I would also like to thank my son, Simon Hancox, for his patience and technical help on scanning and printing, generally getting me out of trouble on some of the illustrations, and ordering off the internet the equipment required, and especially to Fiona, who changed my two handwritten manuscript books into electronic form so efficiently.

A big thank you to my old friend Percy 'Sam' Tait; his escapades are legendary. Lastly, to one of my old Triumph colleagues, Alex Scobie, who is no longer with us. If you're up there listening, Alex, know that you are always in my thoughts; you were probably the greatest tester of them all.

So, finally we come to it, the one person without whose agreement and support I could not have taken up the post of road tester, my wife, Gloria. For her tireless efforts in drying out my wet kit night after night, and putting up with me during this period in my motorcycling life, thank you.

Hughie Hancox

Foreword

During my time at Meriden, the home of Triumph motorcycles – and possibly the finest place to be if you were a motorcyclist back in the 1950s and 1960s – I spent a couple of years on Production Test.

This was back when every single machine to come off the end of either the 'Cub' track, or the main production assembly dealing with all the twins, was checked over by a keen motorcyclist and taken out for an extensive test run. I say keen motorcyclist because all the chaps on Production Test knew that should they not fulfil their responsibilities, the quality of the product would suffer.

At this particular moment in the twentieth century, Triumph could do no wrong; riding on the crest of a manufacturing wave, it could literally sell anything sporting two wheels. This period was briefly touched upon in my previous book about Meriden in the chapter headed, *A testing time*. In this book, I will attempt to fill in, expand upon and describe in more detail that particular, very happy time in my life.

The machines we had to road test in the course of a day's work, between 1960 and the winter of 1962, were considered by many to be the finest machines Meriden ever made. As a new boy on test, I was restricted to riding the Tiger Cub models only, until both the Chief Tester and Finishing Shop Foreman thought I was ready for the 'big stuff.'

To say that this was the most glamorous job at Meriden is something of an understatement. On a fine summer's day, motorcyclists from miles around would congregate on the grass verge opposite the main factory gate, just to sit and watch the black-suited riders come and go on a variety of exotic American variants of the Bonneville and Trophy models.

The job, however, did have its downside; the weather, namely fog, rain, snow and ice.

When the testers finally came in from the cold in the late 1960s, and all the machines were run-up on rolling roads, many thought this was a retrograde step, taken in the interest of speed of process, and not at all beneficial to quality control. It was the start of the slippery slope.

It's been fifty years since I rode those new machines, yet I still occasionally dream of those days and remember vividly the times we had.

I count myself very lucky indeed to have been there.

Hughie Hancox

Sadly, Hughie Hancox passed away in 2011, shortly after checking the proofs for this book. May the book be a lasting tribute to Hughie, a fascinating character who was always a great pleasure to work with.

Rod Grainger, Publisher

Initiation

As with all new testers, the crash helmet had to be inspected to make sure it was in good condition, and not damaged in any way. My own helmet was the popular ACU-approved type of the 1950s and 1960s, gloss white with the Royal Corps of Signals Motorcycle Display Team transfer.

During the years before my army service, I had initially worn a Corker helmet, as used by police motorcyclists of the day, going backwards and forwards to Ripon in North Yorkshire each weekend on my Tiger 100, JRW 405, whilst I was going through the three months training to be a Despatch Rider, and learning how to ride the army way.

Riding the big, clumsy BSA M20, with girder forks and a big, red, prominent letter 'L' on the front mudguard, and wearing the army tin helmet seemed a bit silly, especially as I was thrashing to and from camp on a 100mph-plus Triumph twin.

The army tin helmets were truly awful, and I certainly was glad when I eventually got posted to the Display Team. This was 1957, and Arthur Lampkin, BSA works rider and Pinhard prize winner, slept in the next barrack room with none other than Peter Fletcher, works Royal Enfield team member. These blokes, especially Arthur, had lots of friends in the 'trade' with motorcycle shops. One of these was Tom Ellis, whose shop happened to be in Ripon town centre. Arthur arranged for Tom to supply me with a nice new ACU-approved, low crown helmet, as worn by Geoff Duke, Bob Mac, et al. Needless to say, this was soon painted gloss white, the colour of the Display Team's helmets, the coveted RSDT transfer affixed front and centre. It was this same helmet that was now inspected and approved for use on Production Test, and it proved up to another stint.

My riding coat, however, was not acceptable, as I had to have the same riding gear as the rest of the

The ACU-approved helmet, as worn by the author when in the Royal Signals Display Team and on Production Test at Meriden. This is now in the Signals Museum at Blandford.

Author on board JRW 405 at a 1957 race meeting during training. Note the 'Corker' helmet.

Triumph Production Testers' Tales – from the Meriden Factory

The 'Hill,' looking down towards the village in 1980 (top), and in 2011.

chaps, who wore the black, waxed cotton Belstaff two-piece suit, so a works order and a quick ride of thirty or so miles to Stone in Staffordshire was necessary to pick up my suit. For this, I was given a 'mileage' T100A so was soon back with my new attire, looking very posh.

As I had gone to work that morning on my own bike, I somehow had to get JRW and my old riding coat home. That evening, when the knocking off bell sounded, home I went wearing my new suit and my old coat folded and secured to the tank parcel grid with a couple of Dunlop rubber bands.

The following morning, my father-in-law dropped me off at the factory gates at ten minutes to eight. Wearing my new riding suit and carrying my crash helmet and gloves, I walked up the inclined drive into the main yard. By this time it was five minutes to eight, and workers – mainly on solos and combos – were streaming in. Amongst them, I noted the occasional new machine wearing the obligatory red and white trade plates. Where the workers turned left into the main car park, the testers swung right and up the inclined ramp off the yard, through the rubber swing doors, and into the finishing shop.

Before my call-up, the main yard down the right-hand side of the factory – a long lean-to against the outside wall of the finishing shop – had covered solo motorcycle sheds, with the cars and combos in the main car park.

However, whilst I had been away, the bike sheds had been moved into the main car park, so now all went into the car park, leaving the main yard traffic-free.

At the top of the ramp into the finishing shop was a pair of stout rubber swing doors. Although both doors had small 'peek-a-boo' windows in them, I often thought, as a tester roared up the ramp and smacked the doors open with his front tyre, that I wouldn't like to be coming the other way ...

The Time Office, at the head of the drive off the main road, was the domain of 'Pop' Wright, the long-standing works timekeeper and gateman. Sharing his office was his daughter, a lovely lady called Joan, who used to be married to one of the testers who, unfortunately, was killed.

Dick Pinfold, Joan's husband, was a very experienced motorcyclist, but he met his fate along the Berkswell Lane, when a lorry loaded with alloy castings headed for the Standard Motor car factory, pulled across in front of him. Going too fast and with no chance of avoiding such a long vehicle broadside on, Dick stood no chance at all. They do say that at the speed Dick hit the trailer, the impact caused it to move sideways about a foot.

The only other tester to lose his life was Peter Cooper, a close friend of Bill Letts (one of the testers I write about later on). Peter was heading down Meriden Hill when, again, a vehicle turned across in front of him, this time a Brooke Bond tea van. The driver had simply misjudged Peter's speed, and that was that. His helmet was brought back into the finishing shop, and it remained on a desk outside the Manager's office as a reminder for all to see.

I'm happy to say, no one else lost their life on test, but plenty came a cropper, resulting in broken bones, gravel rash, and other injuries associated with

Initiation

Looking up the Hill in 1980 (top), and in 2011. Very little has changed, except for the speed limit.

Church Lane and the 'banks.' Riding up and onto the top, a commanding view of the main road could be had – plus you were out of sight if you wanted a quiet ten minutes.

motorcycling mishaps. In fact, there were so many broken bones – and not just those of the testers, but people from other parts of the factory as well – that the local hospital in Gulson Road, Coventry, unofficially named one of its wards 'Triumph Ward.'

Those testers who had small children came in for special treatment from Joan. She made it her business to know when their birthdays were, so they always got a card, and usually a box of Maltesers, too. At Easter, it was always a chocolate rabbit.

Well, it was into this illustrious fraternity that I found myself propelled, not so much against my will, but with a certain amount of trepidation on this, the first morning.

After clocking-in, I went and sat on the testers' bench. This was their private little patch; just an ordinary empty work bench in the main finishing area that was not being used, and which the testers had commandeered. This was where they would leave their WWII gas mask cases, satchel-type khaki canvas bags, with a top flap held closed by a couple of press-studs, and an adjustable over-the-shoulder strap. These were sold in their millions by army surplus stores after the war, and I should think just about every motorcyclist in the land had one slung over his shoulder on a work day. Used now for sandwich tins and other personal belongings, every tester had one, which he placed on the bench to mark his spot. Thus it was I had to wait until they were all present to see if there was a little space that I could call my own.

In quick order, every minute or so, there would be a mighty roar as another rider banged through the rubber swing doors, pulling up, putting the bike on the centre stand, removing helmet, gloves and lunch bag, before strolling up to the time clock and 'dinging' his clock card.

It wasn't long before I was amongst a group of blokes who, although I knew them, now somehow seemed strangers, and even slightly hostile toward this new, young interloper. The 'getting ready for the day's work' performances of both the Experimental and Repair Shops where I had previously worked seemed so different. Those areas were full of talk and banter, but the testers were quiet, simply moving around the lines of new machines, not saying much at all.

The test card – which came with each new machine – was tucked under the edge of the rubber knee-pad on the side of the petrol tank. When going out on test, or going home, the card was carefully folded and carried in one of the capacious pockets of the Belstaff jacket. These cards would be completed on their 'going home' bike, the machine they had just

Triumph Production Testers' Tales – from the Meriden Factory

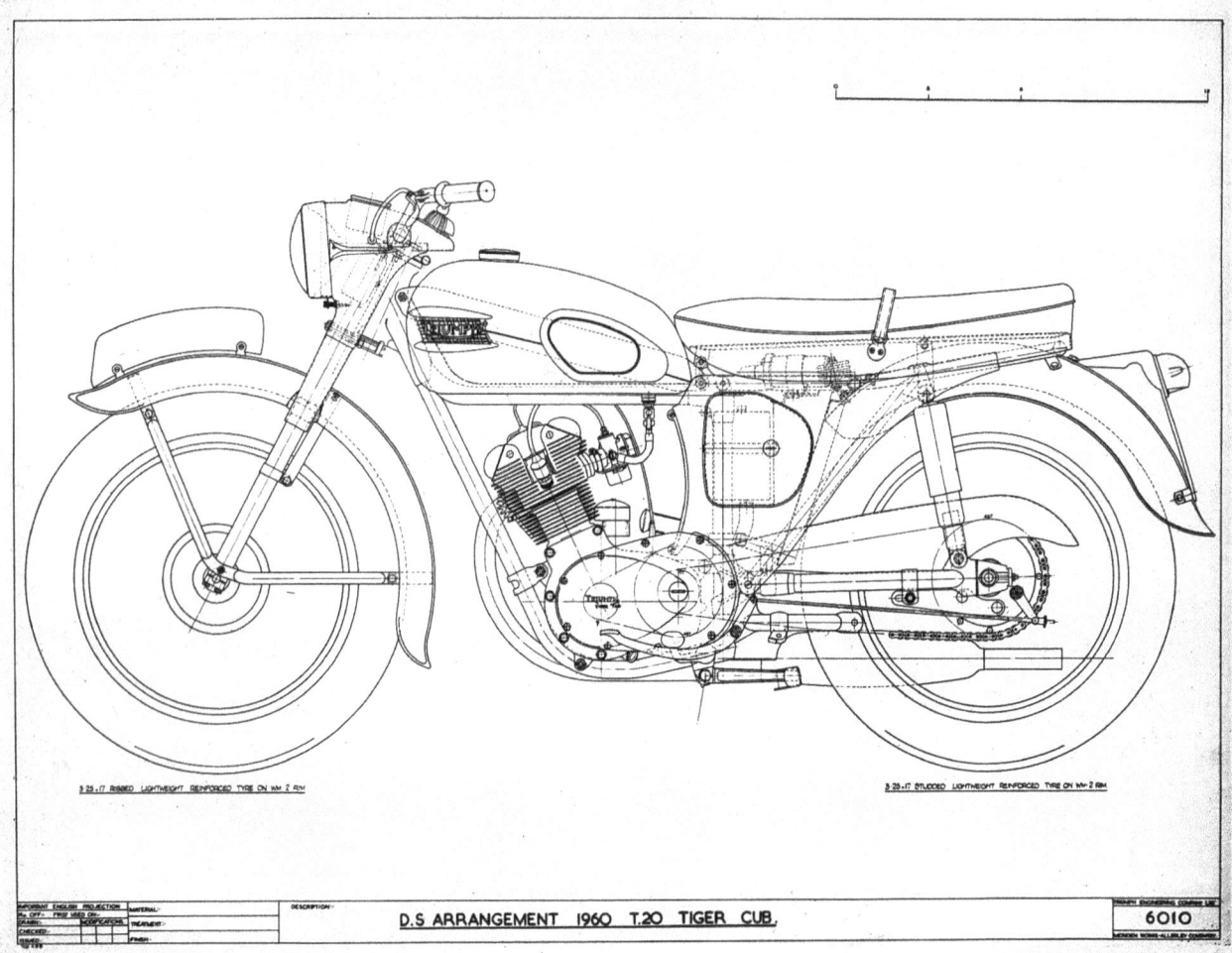

Original schematic of a 1960 standard T20 'Cub' from the drawing office.

arrived on. After carefully checking over the bike, the trade plates would be removed, the completed card tucked behind the knee-pad, and the bike wheeled up to whichever rectification section was required. The tester's individual trade plates would be placed on the tester's spot on the bench with their bag, crash helmet and gloves. The chaps who had gone home the previous evening on Tiger Cubs took them to the 'Tiddler' knacker gang, comprising Eric Miller, Dennis Griffin, Fred Watson, and Stan Hawkins, who took care of all adjustments or rectifications, and indeed any work necessary to satisfactorily 'pass off' the little models.

Those who had gone home on any of the twin cylinder models took their mounts to the big rectification section, headed by Roger Bryant and his gang of reprobates. The 'Cub' and 'Twin' boys were very skilled, and adept at dealing with the testers' remarks and notations on the test cards. They did the required work, crossing it off the card and initialling this, and would finish off by checking tappets, timing, carburettor, and chains to see if any required a final adjustment.

Mostly, the jobs were only niggles; maybe a control cable would catch, or become entrapped when the handlebars were turned. On the occasion that something more serious was necessary, such as tightening of the motor, indicating a slight piston seize, the barrel and piston would be removed speedily and a new version of each fitted.

The machine would then be brought to the attention of the particular tester who had rejected the bike in the first place, who, after refitting his trade plates, and running the motor for a few minutes outside in the main yard to ensure all was well, would take out the bike again. If all was satisfactory, the bike would go for

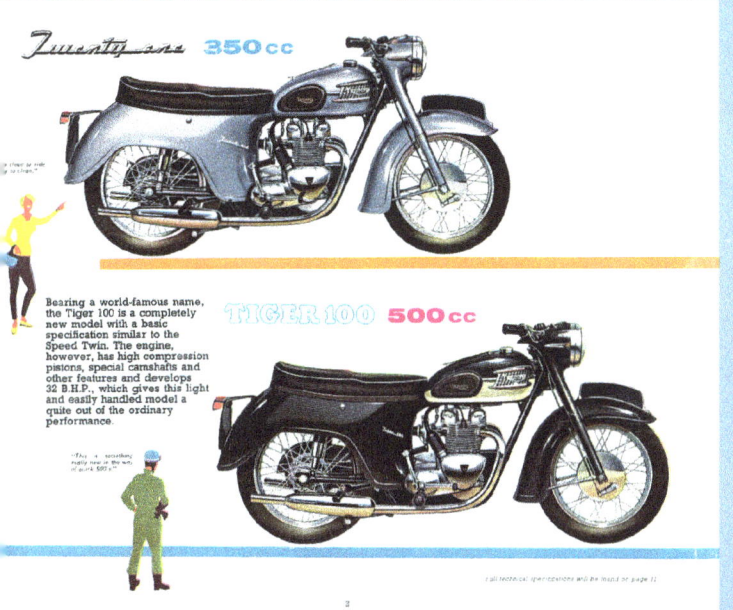

The 1960 T21 350 twin and its bigger brother, the 500 T100A sports.

The 1960 5TA 500 speed twin, a nice smooth-running tourer.

The 1960 TR6 650 Trophy, a favourite with all the chaps on test (the two-into-one exhaust made a glorious noise). Finished in Aztec Red and Ivory: very attractive.

The much-lauded 'Bonnie' with the remote-float carburettor setup. This could be a pain when slow running was required.

The trusty 6T Thunderbird for 1960, with 'softer' camshafts than the T110, made a nice tourer or sidecar machine.

A sports-touring 650 – the Tiger 110. Some people said you did not need a Bonneville; this would do all that was required.

TECHNICAL DATA
(All Models)

MODEL	Tiger Cub (T20)	Tiger Cub (T20S)	Twenty-One (3TA)	Speed Twin (5TA)	Tiger 100 (T100A)	Thunder-bird (6T)	Tiger 110 (T110)	Trophy (TR6)	Bonneville 120 (T120)
ENGINE TYPE	O.H.V.	O.H.V.	O.H.V.	O.H.V.	O.H.V.	O.H.V.	O.H.V.	O.H.V.	O.H.V.
No. of Cylinders	1	1	2	2	2	2	2	2	2
Bore/Stroke, mm.	63×64	63×64	58.25×65.5	69×65.5	69×65.5	71×82	71×82	71×82	71×82
Bore/Stroke, ins.	2.48×2.52	2.48×2.52	2.3×2.6	2.72×2.6	2.72×2.6	2.79×3.23	2.79×3.23	2.79×3.23	2.79×3.23
Capacity, cu. cms.	199	199	348	490	490	649	649	649	649
Capacity, cu. ins.	12	12	21.23	29.8	29.8	40	40	40	40
Compression Ratio	7 : 1	7 : 1	7.5 : 1	7 : 1	9 : 1	7 : 1	8 : 1	8 : 1	8.5 : 1
B.H.P. and R.P.M.	10 @ 6,000	10 @ 6,000	18.5 @ 6,500	27 @ 6,500	32 @ 7,000	34 @ 6,300	40 @ 6,500	40 @ 6,500	46 @ 6,500
Engine sprocket teeth									
Solo	19	19	26	26	26	23	23	22	22
Sidecar	—	—	—	—	—	20	20	—	19
Clutch sprocket teeth	48	48	58	58	58	43	43	43	43
Gearbox sprocket teeth	17	17	18	20	20	18	18	18	18
Rear wheel teeth	46	54	43	43	43	43	43	43	43
R.P.M., 10 m.p.h.:									
Top Gear	980	1,075	760	670	670	597	597	608	608
						Solo S/car	Solo S/car		Solo S/car
Gear Ratios—Top	6.84	8.0	5.33	4.80	4.80	4.46 5.12	4.46 5.12	4.66	4.66 5.40
" " —Third	9.04	11.6	6.32	5.69	5.69	5.30 6.1	5.30 6.1	5.55	5.55 6.42
" " —Second	14.05	18.1	9.37	8.44	8.44	7.55 8.7	7.55 8.7	7.88	7.88 9.13
" " —First	20.30	26.3	12.96	11.66	11.66	10.9 12.5	10.9 12.5	11.38	11.38 13.2
Carburetter—Make	Zenith	Zenith	Amal	Amal	Amal	Amal	Amal	Amal	Amal-Twin
" —Type	18MXZ C17	18MXZ C18	375/32	375/35	375/35	376/246	376/244	376/40	376/233
Front Chain Size	⅜" Duplex	⅜" Duplex	⅜" Duplex	⅜" Duplex	⅜" Duplex	½"×.305"	½"×.305"	½"×.305"	½"×.305"
Rear Chain Size	½"×.205	½"×.205	⅝"×⅜"	⅝"×⅜"	⅝"×⅜"	⅝"×⅜"	⅝"×⅜"	⅝"×⅜"	⅝"×⅜"
Tyres—Dunlop:									
Front, ins.	3.25×17	3.00×19	3.25×17	3.25×17	3.25×17	3.25×18	3.25×18	3.25×19	3.25×19
Rear, ins.	3.25×17	3.50×18	3.25×17	3.50×17	3.50×17	3.50×18	3.50×18	4.00×18	3.50×19
Brake dia., ins. (cms.)	5½" (13.97)	5½" (13.97)	7" (17.78)	7" (17.78)	7" (17.78)	7" (17.78)	8" F (20.32) 7" R (17.78)	8" F (20.32) 7" R (17.78)	8" F (20.32) 7" R (17.78)
Finish	Grey/Black	Ivory/Blue	Shell Blue/ Black	Red	Black/ Ivory	Charcoal Grey	Black/ Ivory	Ivory/ Aztec Red	Grey/Blue
Seat height, ins.(cms.)	29" (73.7)	30" (76.2)	29¼" (74.5)	29¼" (74.5)	29¼" (74.5)	30" (76.2)	30" (76.2)	30½" (77.5)	30½" (77.5)
Wheelbase, ins. (cms.)	49" (125.5)	49" (125.5)	51¾" (131.4)	51¾" (131.4)	51¾" (131.4)	54½" (138.5)	54½" (138.5)	54½" (138.5)	54½" (138.5)
Length, ins. (cms.)	77" (195.5)	77" (195.5)	80" (203)	80" (203)	80" (203)	83" (211)	83" (211)	85½" (217)	85½" (217)
Width, ins. (cms.)	25" (63.5)	25" (63.5)	26" (66)	26" (66)	26" (66)	28½" (72)	28½" (72)	28½" (72)	28½" (72)
Clearance, ins. (cms.)	5" (12.7)	6" (15.2)	5" (12.7)	5" (12.7)	5" (12.7)	5" (12.7)	5" (12.7)	5" (12.7)	5" (12.7)
Weight, lbs. (kilos)	220 (99.7)	210 (95)	345 (156.3)	350 (159)	363 (165)	392 (177)	390 (176)	393 (178)	393 (178)
Petrol, galls. (litres)	3 (13.5)	2⅝ (11.9)	3½ (16)	3½ (16)	3½ (16)	4 (18)	4 (18)	3 (13.5)	4 (18)
Oil, pints (litres)	2¾ (1.55)	2¾ (1.55)	5 (2.8)	5 (2.8)	5 (2.8)	5 (2.8)	5 (2.8)	5 (2.8)	5 (2.8)

Specifications for all the 1960 models at a glance.

Initiation

TRIUMPH SERVICE EXCHANGE UNIT RETAIL PRICES			
Unit Description	Model		
ENGINE	T20	TR25W	350/500 & 650 c.c.
Engine and gearbox unit complete with Generator Reground crankshaft with new big end and main bearings	£30 0 0	£45 0 0	£60 0 0
		£4 0 0	350/500 c.c. £7 0 0
			*650 c.c. £6 4 0
Recond. big end assembly (plain bearing type)	£2 12 0	—	—
Recond. flywheel assembly (roller bearing type)	£6 0 0	—	—
Recond. flywheel assembly (plain bearing type)	£5 5 0	—	—
Rebored cylinder with new piston	£3 0 0	£3 5 0	£7 10 0
Recond. clutch plates (each)	4 0	5 0	5 0
		*N.B. 650 c.c. crankshaft, less undersize bush	
FRAME			
Recond. frame complete	£12 12 0	£12 12 0	£22 0 0 Comprising of front and rear frames
Recond. front frame	£7 10 0	—	£14 0 0
Recond. rear frame	£5 2 0	—	£8 0 0
Recond. swinging arm fork	£3 18 6	£3 12 6	350/500 c.c. £3 12 6
			650 c.c. £4 0 0
Repair and enamel petrol tank	£5 0 0	£5 10 0	£6 0 0
Repair, rechrome and enamel petrol tank	£7 10 0	—	—
Reline brake shoes 5 ins. (per pair)	12 6	—	—
Reline brake shoes 7 ins. (per pair)	—	£1 2 0	£1 2 0
Reline brake shoes 8 ins. (per pair)	—	—	£1 7 0
Front forks	£13 7 6	£21 10 0	*£21 10 0
		*N.B. T20 Sports as 350/500 and 650 c.c.	

All previous price lists cancelled from April 1st, 1968.
Prices do not include carriage charges.

Nowadays, these exchange prices for factory-reconditioned parts make you wish for a time machine.

Jimmy Brown, chief tester (third from left) with the Johnny Allen 'Streamliner' at Elmdon airport. From left to right: Alan Campbell (works driver), Eric Miller, Jimmy Brown, Norris Harrison, Stan Jinks, Peter Cooper, Sid Shilton, Charlie Wallace, and under the DC3 wing, Jack Wickes.

Triumph Production Testers' Tales – from the Meriden Factory

Top: The view as you came out of the factory and turned to go up to the top of the Hill, circa 1980 ...

Above: ...the same view from Bonneville Close in 2011, with the factory memorial on the left.

cleaning and to have the petrol and oil tanks drained before being placed in line for despatch.

The old replaced items would not be wasted altogether. Although the pistons and rings would be thrown in the scrap metal bin, the cylinder barrel would go back into the boring section in the machine shop for re-boring to +0.010in (ten thousandths of an inch), then sent up to the service repair shop for use as a reconditioned item.

The work rate of the knacker gangs was extremely high when you consider that twelve testers were throwing bikes at them throughout the day.

Most of the testers had by now picked out another bike, their first machine of the day. Whilst they were busy checking over their chosen mounts, I noticed a small, slightly built, silver-haired lady wearing a green overall, cross the main gangway carrying a wooden tray with twelve tin mugs of tea on it. She smiled at me as she placed the tray on the testers' bench, saying "The new mug is yours." At the factory I'd never had a mug of hot tea first thing in the morning, only at stipulated teabreaks, but apparently this was accepted practice for the testers, most especially appreciated on a cold morning before going out on the first bike.

After the testers made a cursory check to ensure all of the cable-operated controls were working freely, the brake and clutch cables were adjusted, as was the rear brake. Next, they would go over to the petrol bowser, a fifty-gallon square container with a rotary pump handle, flexible hose and filler nozzle. It had three small diameter, rubber-tired wheels; two fixed at the back, and a free swivelling one in the centre at the front. On the back was a 'pram handle' with which to push and steer the thing. The rotary handle was on the side, so after the nozzle had been introduced into the filler neck of the petrol tank, cranking the handle allowed the petrol to flow into the machine about to be tested. For the official test route, four pints, or half a gallon, was all that was required, and this equated to four complete revolutions of the rotary handle.

Chief Tester at this time was Jimmy Brown, a lovely, affable chap who had previously been Chief Tester at our sister company, BSA Motorcycles. Due to internal politics, Jimmy could not move directly from Small Heath to Meriden, but went from BSA to a main BSA dealership first. He had sought to move to Meriden for some time, he told me, during the conversation we had whilst he worked with me at Coventry Motor Ltd in Coventry.

I had worked at the Motor Mart, as it was called, as a trainee mechanic when Jimmy turned up as the new workshop foreman. We worked together for some six months until he left to take up the post of Chief Tester at Triumph, an appointment widely believed to have been fixed up by my old friend Alex Scobie.

It was only after the workshop fire at the Motor Mart where I was burned whilst salvaging customers' machines, and was admonished for my troubles, that I left its employ. My father called in to see the two directors, and after giving them "a good talking to," and kicking a desk up in the air, we left together. They told

Initiation

me off because they wanted to claim insurance, and by doing what I did, I messed things up. When you're young, you don't think of things like that; I just tried to do what I thought was right.

On the Saturday morning, I went for a ride over to Jimmy's house in Solihull, to help him put up a new back garden fence. The subject of me working at Meriden was mentioned. As explained in my previous book, after talking to my Dad, and turning down an opportunity to become a Police Cadet, we visited Dad's lifelong friend, Jack Wickes, who then fixed up an interview with Mr Sid Tubb, Manager of the Finishing Shop, and Jimmy Brown's immediate boss. The rest, as they say, is history.

Very sadly, whilst on holiday in Devon with wife Thelma and their family, Jim suffered a massive heart attack and died. Jimmy Brown was always a gentleman, and I can remember the good times we had working together for that short period at the Coventry Motor Mart.

The rest of the chaps played a trick on him when he came to take over the position of Chief Tester from Reggie Ballard. It was the norm when anyone joined the testing gang, it didn't matter who you were, an initiating prank was always carried out. This time it was crab legs tucked up inside the webbing of Jimmy's crash helmet.

It took some time for the smell to permeate, but every now and then, when Jimmy had his helmet on ready to go out on a run, he would ask, "Can anyone smell fish?" Of course, the chaps carried this on for as long as they could, but even when the crab legs were removed, Jimmy's helmet smelt of fish for weeks. Poor Jimmy, I don't think he even knew!

The Meriden island and entrance to the top of the Mile beyond the hoarding on the left, in 2011; plus Meriden centre in 2011.

Meriden village green with the original monument, understood to be the exact centre of England. The chevron board on the left points down the 'Mile.'

Immediately upon Jimmy's death, Dennis Peacock was promoted to the position of Chief Tester, so this obviously created a vacancy in the ranks. I knew my friend, Eddie Dent, not long out of the Royal Navy and living two doors down from me in Bedworth, wanted a job. He was an experienced motorcyclist and actually owned a brand new Norton Dominator 88 he had purchased with some of his navy gratuity. I put forward his name to Stan Trowell and Mr Tubb, and after completing the interview, the job was his for the asking.

Eddie and I used to ride into work and home at the end of the working day together. It was always a good

Triumph Production Testers' Tales – from the Meriden Factory

idea to ride in pairs, in case anything untoward should happen. Norris Harrison and Bill Letts who lived in the same area did the same, as did Charlie Wallace and Bert Watmore from Birmingham.

So, that was the scene this first morning, and all I had to do now was go into the office and let Mr Tubb know I had arrived, ready to start my new job. I had already collected and signed for my own set of trade plates, so, resplendent in my new suit, I awaited the arrival of Mr Tubb's second-in-command, Stan Trowell, who I knew from my pre-army days when I worked in the Service Department Repair Shop and the Experimental Department. Mr Tubb didn't usually arrive until nine o'clock, although for some reason he was early this particular morning. It was Stan who was going to 'run me through the job,' though, and with the time clock just on half past eight, the rubber swing doors burst open and with a roar of exhausts, Stan appeared.

Giving him time to get into the office and disrobe, I tapped on the glass door and poked my head in. He didn't wear a riding suit as we did, but had on what appeared to be a Despatch Rider's coat, exactly the same as we were issued with in the Signals. Hanging this on a coat hook, he turned, and I said, "Morning, Stan, come to report for me new job." "Come on Hughie," he replied: "I'll run you through the drill and then you can go out with someone on your first run."

Although Stan went to great pains to explain the test route, I already knew it, and nodded my head as he was talking. He made it crystal clear that, under no circumstances whatsoever, should I deviate from the route, as doing so could end up with me getting the sack!

So, as Stan told me, the route was out past the Time Office, with a quick wave (left hand) to Pop Wright and Joan as I passed to go down the inclined drive to the road, making sure nothing was approaching from the right, pulling out and proceeding toward the top of Meriden Hill.

Quickly looking down, I checked to ensure all was well, and that the engine wasn't 'peeing' out oil in copious quantities. On a big twin, a quick glance at the Oil Pressure Release Valve 'tell-tale' button reassures that it isn't in the 'in' position, which will mean a loss of oil pressure to the big-ends. If everything is satisfactory, it's a case of proceeding through the gears at normal road speed, allowing the engine to increase in revs easily without undue load.

Passing over the brow of the hill, speed increases to about sixty miles an hour down the hill towards Meriden village. Taking care not to 'load' the engine too much, proceed down the hill to the slight right-hand bend at the bottom, where the thirty miles an hour limit begins.

Generally, the village residents had a good relationship with the testers, due mainly to Arthur, the village policeman, whose house was on the corner of Leys Lane. As there was a school in the village, he was somewhat of a stickler about not speeding through his domain, and we all, without exception, treated him with the greatest respect.

Coming off the bottom of the hill at about sixty miles an hour means you hit the thirty zone way over the limit, but if you had shut off and were on the over-run with speed decreasing as you went by Arthur's police house, he understood. I don't think any tester was taken to task by Arthur in the couple of years I was riding the new bikes, an understanding was always there, unspoken and mutually respected.

After 'trickling' through the village, past the pond on the left at the junction of Berkswell Lane, on up past the green and memorial on the right, you come to a small island. It was right turn for Fillongley and Nuneaton, straight on for Birmingham and Tubby's Cafe, or the 'Thatch' as it was called for obvious reasons, or left for Hampton Lane, or, as it was more commonly called, 'The Mile.'

Along this straight length of road it was possible to open up and go virtually flat out through the gears, changing into top just as you passed Bostocks Farm on the left. After checking that everything functioned properly at full throttle, you could shut the throttle completely, which, as well as slowing the bike, had the effect of sucking oil up the bores, ensuring that the motor didn't 'nip up.'

'Trickling' down to Cornets End Lane junction, the majority of testers simply turned around here, and slowly rode back to the lay-by on the left, just before Somers Lane, approximately one third of the way back up the 'Mile.' Some turned into Somers Lane, just off the road, and waited for the bike to cool down, sitting on the fence, and – those who smoked – having a fag.

The bike can be checked visually at this point for any oil leaks. To be fair, I did not have to reject any model I rode for this reason, despite what people say. Many's the time I have been out on my 1952 Tiger 100, and been asked by the crowd that usually gathers round why there are no leaks? I remember one chap referring to his own six-fifty twin as the Torrey Canyon, then adding: "If it don't leak, mate, there can't be any oil in it."

The bike is restarted and the motor allowed to tick over, with, if required, fine adjustment of the pilot mixture and tickover speed. Then it's a slow ride back to the factory, and up the ramp into the finishing shop, where trade plates are removed, test card completed and stuck under the nearside kneepad, and the bike pushed to the Rectification section. In a queue of machines, it would take its turn for to be checked over and have any necessary adjustments.

This was the official version of events.

On the first run out with Joe 'Sooty' Price, I was 'educated' about the little amendments which were absolutely essential to allow you to visit either the Thatch on the main Meriden Road just after the island, or Fred's cafe on the Meriden to Fillongley Road. We frequented these havens of warmth each day at approximately ten thirty in the morning, and three to three thirty in the afternoon.

At both venues, it was possible to ride your bike straight around the back so it was out of sight of the main roads, and thus any factory hierarchy that may be passing. It was a delight to spend fifteen or twenty minutes in either of these two warm little places on a wet cold afternoon when you had been out in it all day. A mug of tea would warm your hands and make those last couple of hours before knocking off time more bearable.

After Stan's briefing, we walked down the lines of newly-finished machines looking for Joe. We knew he was about because his silver ACU helmet, gloves and trade plates were on a nearby Tiger Cub twin-seat. Just then, a booming Liverpudlian voice exclaimed: "You looking for me?" Joe was kneeling down beside a standard home market Cub, the rows of bikes easily obscuring him from view. Stan said: "Sooty, got young Hughie here, he's been given the low down, he's got his kit; look after him and show him the ropes." Sooty replied: "Alright, Stan," then looked at me and said: "Bloody behave yourself, no fancy army riding tricks here." All I could do was nod my head in thanks as Sooty continued: "Come on, I'll show you how to fix your plates," whereupon he took mine from me with the instruction to watch what he did. Joe had a dry sense of humour, but always exuded quiet menace. It was rumoured that he and his brother were in a spot of bother a few years before, but I never broached the subject with him.

So began my first day on Production Test, almost halfway through 1960.

The first ride out

Each tester had his own issued trade plates; in other words, the twelve sets of plates were differently numbered, so all you had to do was memorise the three digits.

My two issued plates had brackets made from black stove-enamelled strip, measuring one eighth of an inch thick by three quarters of an inch wide. The front bracket was secured horizontally across the back of the plate about midway by two quarter inch diameter nuts and bolts, with a four to five inch length bent at right angles. At the end of the cranked section was a three eighths of an inch clearance hole so that it would fit on the fork stanchion pinch bolt. Each tester carried in his riding suit pockets two spanners, together with a few more essentials, such as a pair of pliers, and a Triumph toolkit reversible screw driver – Phillips 'Posidrive' one end and flat-bladed the other. We also had a small, plastic-handled electrical screwdriver.

The two spanners were again from a toolkit, both a quarter by five sixteenths, one open-ended, the other a ring. By using the ring on the fork pinch bolt nut and the open-ended on the chromed head of the bolt, the pinch bolt nut could be undone. By sliding the hole in the right-angled front trade plate mounting bracket over the bolt, the washer and nut could be refitted, the latter tightened so that the front trade plate was held in the vertical plane facing the pavement.

The rear trade plate had a flat strip of the same dimension as the front one, bolted across the middle horizontally, with about one and a half inches of strip protruding each side. Because the nuts and bolts would cause damage to the black gloss paint on the face of the rear number plate, two lengths of one inch thick foam rubber strip were stuck horizontally, top and bottom, on the back face of the trade plate, thus keeping the ends of the two fixing bolts and nuts off the number plate itself. I seem to remember the nuts and bolts that held the strips onto the plates were the same as those used to hold the front mudguard stays to the front mudguard blade on the Bonneville and Trophy models. (It wasn't until a few years later that the Ministry of Transport deemed the front plate no longer necessary; I presume for safety reasons.)

By cutting a couple of nice, wide rubber bands from an old inner tube and knotting them together, it was possible – with the aid of your knee – to press the rear trade plate against the rear number plate, holding it in place and, at the same time, stretching the rubber bands behind the number plate and hooking each end over the protruding strip. This held the rear trade plate securely in place, but what was really needed was a 'belt-and-braces' job. Whatever happened, you didn't want the rubber band to break and your rear plate go flying off into a ditch.

A quarter inch diameter hole was drilled in one of the top corners of the rear trade plate, and a length of hairy string was passed through and knotted, leaving a couple of free lengths of ten inches to a foot. Once the trade plate was positioned, courtesy of the rubber band, the string was passed around the lifting handle portion of the rear number plate, and tied off in a double bow. It was a simple precaution to prevent the loss of a rear plate during the test run, because it was not ever missed until it was too late. With one pothole or bump in the road, it could disappear forever into the depths of any of the miles of grassy roadside ditches that lined the test route. And Heaven forbid it should come adrift on one of the 'off-route' lanes leading to our two watering holes, and found and handed in by some well-meaning person ... So it was that I tied mine on with extra diligence and an extra reef-knot, and not just a simple shoelace bow.

Joe explained the procedure, because – don't

The first ride out

forget – these bikes had not actually been fired up, simply put on rollers, which motored the engines in fourth gear. This enabled the fitters to ensure that the engine oil was circulating and returning to the oil tank, and, indeed, that all mechanical functions were performing satisfactorily.

These rollers, set in the finishing shop floor, were electronically powered and geared to run the motors at approximately thirty miles per hour with the machine in fourth gear. With oil in the oil tanks and the right amounts in the gearbox and transmission, running the bikes for a few minutes like this ensured that the oil was properly circulating prior to the motor actually being fired up. A pair of stands each side of the rollers, set into the concrete floor with hinged clamps secured by wing nuts, solidly held the bike by its rider footrests, the rear wheel on the rollers and the front wheel on the solid concrete floor. Once the bike was affixed, the rollers were started, the clutch lever was pulled in and first gear selected, and then the clutch let out so that the engine would be turning over. By de-clutching and changing up though the gears until fourth gear was engaged, the machine could be left for a few minutes, happily motoring away with oil circulating and all functions working.

When we came to put our plates on a bike, we were confident that old Fred – Fred Walson, who was in charge of this operation – had done his bit on the rollers. To see him start the rollers and 'clunk' up through the gears, running his hands over the timing and primary covers to feel for anything untoward, was strangely comforting, knowing you were going to be riding a bike he had on the rollers, and basically given his blessing to.

Thinking back, I can only remember one instance where Fred had to move quickly by pulling in the clutch and stopping the rollers to prevent damage.

Good old Fred, he was a star, really, as he appeared in a promotional black and white film called *It's a Triumph*, which showed in detail how a motorcycle was made at Meriden. Also featured in this film (which has been copied onto both VHS cassette and DVD) are the testers, walking around in their long testing coats that were so popular in the late 40s and early 50s, before the waxed cotton suits became the uniform of choice. The film shows the Finishing Shop with its rubber doors, and at the beginning, Reggie Ballard, the Chief Tester, with a pillion passenger. It was Reggie that Jimmy Brown took over from.

After checking the levels and running your eyes over the main items, such as wheel nuts, chain and brakes, the next stage was the petrol bowser.

If you were near enough, you could put the bowser pipe nozzle directly into the filler neck of the petrol tank, if not, you could use the big, one imperial gallon Shell can that had a spout. With four turns of the pump handle, you had your half a gallon of juice. If it was in the shell can, you took the big funnel, and introducing that into the machine's petrol tank filler neck, carefully poured in the fuel, taking care not to splash the lovely paintwork on top of the tank.

Next to check were the lights and electrics. Making sure you had both head and dipped beams, pilot, speedo, tail light and horn, you depressed the rear brake pedal and, if required, adjusted the stop light switch. Now to switch on the ignition. Turn on the fuel, making sure the carburettor wasn't leaking from any of its many joints, because the last thing you wanted was a leaky or flooding carburettor, more so, when it came to the big six fifties with their Lucas Magneto twin high tension pick-ups nestling directly below the big Amal Monoblocs.

On the T20 standard Tiger Cub for 1960, the carburettor was the horrible little Zenith 18 MXZ, the choke for cold-starting located on top of the mixing chamber cap. This you pulled up to its full extent, and then depressed in stages until the engine was warm. Quite a fiddly operation when wearing Barbour over-mitts. The trick, therefore, was to get the pilot running for a few minutes until you could fully depress the choke knob, then, with quick little blips of the throttle, away you go.

You had to be careful to do all this outside in the main yard, because on full choke, when the engine fired, it would start 'eight-stroking' and puffing thick black smoke out of the silencer almost immediately. It was necessary to be extra diligent about this, because the fitters on the two knacker gangs, sitting on their little wooden boxes beside the machines they were working on, were directly in the line of fire, so to speak.

Because all of the fitters spent all day sitting on these little boxes, they had customised them. Some just had openings on the front face, others had little drawers, where they kept the pens and books into which was entered details of every bike that passed through their hands. On the top of the boxes – without exception – there were comfortable little cushions made out of the Triumph twinseat sponge inserts. If the weather was really inclement, during our dinner breaks three or four testers – myself included – would draw these little boxes round to sit on and play a couple of hands of brag for money. Percy Tait, on his way back from the canteen,

Triumph Production Testers' Tales – from the Meriden Factory

always came over and sat in with us, and we always had a good laugh. It was only for pennies, then worth one, two-hundred and fortieth of a pound. It was great to see Percy's face when he thought he had a winning hand, only to find out Bert Watmore had a better one!

Once the motor was running, you could put on your helmet and gloves, and carefully ride the bike out through the rubber doors, down the ramp, and into the yard. After another quick check – and maybe slight adjustment to the tickover speed and a last glance into the oil tank to ensure the engine oil was returning – the run could begin.

It was difficult not to yell "yippee" as I rode up the main A45, and past the front of the factory, savouring the moment of my first official test ride. Even though it was on a lowly standard Tiger Cub, this didn't matter one bit.

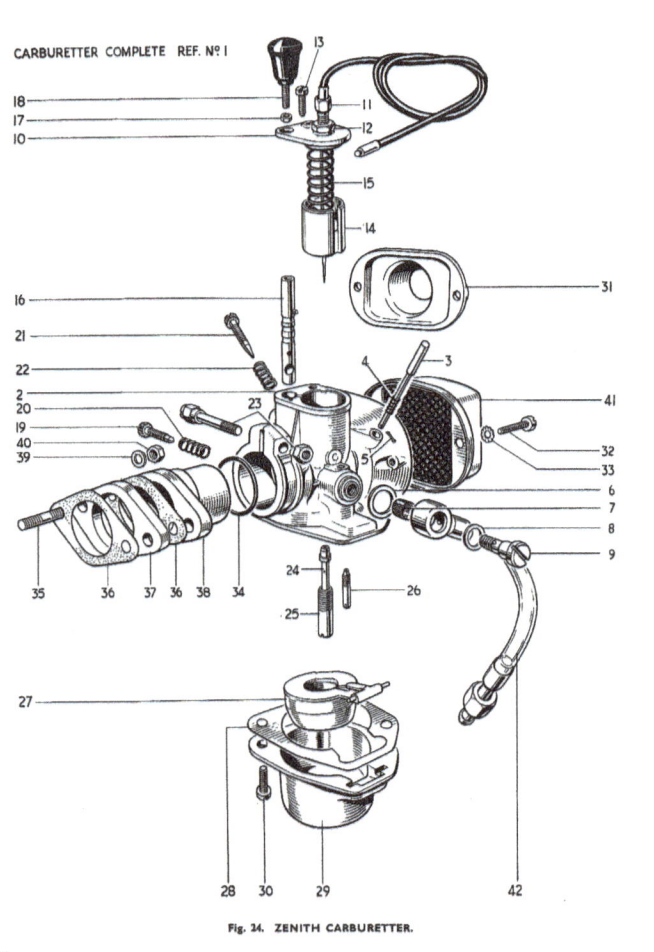

Little Zenith carb fitted to 1960 Cubs – exploded view with associated part numbers.

The Cubs

There was no denying the fact: the Cub, generally, was a little motorcycle, but with the feel of one of its bigger brothers. With its punchy, four-stroke engine, it did not seem like a tiddler when you were riding it. Okay, so it only developed a heady ten or twelve brake horse power, but the lovely muted bark from its Burgess silencer made it somehow seem more.

We were halfway through the year already, and it would only be a few more months before the 1960 models came to an end and the 1961 new models would begin coming off the lines.

With Joe leading to give me some idea of the speeds involved in testing the little Cubs, we proceeded up past Millison's Wood on the way to the top of Meriden Hill. Both Cubs – the T20 and the T20S – had the same engine and carburettor, but the sports model had bigger forks, upswept exhaust, and a higher riding position, and came with Energy-Transfer ignition which enabled it to be ridden in competition without a battery. I don't suppose the sports version was very much faster than the standard model, but it seemed to be, especially with the sports cam and stronger valve springs. The engine was also a little noisier, due to

Standard T20.

1960 T20S sports Cub still with the Zenith carburettor, which restricted its performance somewhat.

Triumph Production Testers' Tales – from the Meriden Factory

having a 9 to 1 compression piston rather than the 7 to 1 standard item.

As I followed Joe up to the top of the hill heading toward the village, I suddenly became aware of the beautiful exhaust note that Joe's machine made, coupled with that of my bike. It wasn't noticeable on the twins, so I suppose it was because they were single cylinder machines that this peculiar strobing effect came about. I remember back in the early 1950s, as a regular visitor to Oulton Park and Silverstone, hearing the big Manx Nortons pulling hard in a bunch, and giving off this very same effect. It was almost like the 'wa-wa-wa' sound of the out-of-sync engines of the Heinkel III German medium bombers when they 'visited' Coventry in 1940.

There was no doubt that, with its nacelle, pull-back handlebars, and Triumph patented twin-seat, the little bike sold like hot cakes. It was the bread-and-butter bike for Triumph, and the going-to-work-on bike for the masses. Wages in 1960 were round about fifteen pounds a week in the big car factories, so it was no surprise that, at one hundred and forty four pounds and fifteen shillings, including purchase tax, the little Cub was a bargain.

1960 T20 factory picture, right-hand view. The new crankcase centre join cannot be seen.

1960 T20 factory picture, left-hand view. New 18in wheels were tried, but the factory reverted to 17in for 1961.

The Cubs

1960 T20S factory pictures; left-hand (above) and right-hand view. Equipped with energy transfer ignition system. No battery meant direct lighting.

Triumph Production Testers' Tales – from the Meriden Factory

The factory price list for all models in 1960. This is where that time machine is again required.

Cresting the brow of the hill, Joe opened up a bit on the downward run toward the village. Passing Church Lane on the left, the place where Peter Cooper was killed, we approached the village in tight 'line astern' at about fifty miles an hour. Easing off, we slowed and trundled past Arthur the policeman's house at roughly thirty miles an hour, giving a quick glance over to the right to see if he was in. You could usually see his police spec Cub – equipped with a screen, and a radio-transceiver on the specially adapted twin-seat – parked on the drive at the side of the police house if he was in residence, but if it wasn't there, you had to be very wary as he could appear behind you at any time on the test route.

The radio equipment on Arthur's bike was made by PYE of Cambridge, and wasn't transistorised, so was about the size of a breeze block, and twice as heavy. With an aerial on the back and a special fitting on the top of the petrol tank to take the two-way handset, we reckoned that, with its rider's weight added, the police Cub would do all of thirty miles per hour downhill with the wind behind it.

Going through the village on a very light throttle ensured a pleasing 'wuffle' from the Burgess silencers, nothing that anyone could take offence at, really. The T20S sports model was noisier, probably because it had a slimmer style silencer, with a thinner-than-standard main body. You really could elicit a staccato 'bark' that did, on occasion, annoy some of the elderly residents of the village if two or three Cubs were ridden together.

Approaching the island in the village centre, with its cyclists' memorial on the green, Joe changed down into third and indicated with his left hand that we were going to dive down to our left, on the start to the 'Mile.'

The Police T20. Sometimes these little machines were fitted with screen and leg shields, depending on the particular police authority requirements.

Following suit, I heard Joe start to accelerate in third, and then change up into top.

Running easily at about fifty miles an hour, we proceeded slightly downhill along the 'Mile' in close formation, the exhaust notes mingling and 'strobing' delightfully. Depending on how you felt the motor was running, you could increase speed momentarily to sixty miles per hour to ensure all was well, but your left hand hovered over the clutch lever all the same should

Meriden village, 2011.

Triumph Production Testers' Tales – from the Meriden Factory

it require 'snatching' in the event of a tightening motor. Thinking back, I never, ever had a seizure on any model I rode, but my friend, Big Bill Letts, had untold difficulties in 1953-54 when the first Terriers came out. Bill said they were "little buggers" that would nip up anywhere; on the centre stand when you were getting ready to go out, when you pulled out of the factory, when you shut off on the over-run, they seized just about anywhere. He reckoned, given half a chance, they would even seize when the engines were being built on the Terrier/Cub track!

It was definitely something to do with combustion chamber temperature when the engine was running under its own power, because they didn't nip up on the rollers when Fred ran them. It turned out to be piston material expanding too quickly under combustion working temperatures. Bill said it was all sorted out satisfactorily, but there weren't half a lot of Terrier re-bored barrels sent up to the Service Repair Department for service exchange items!

At the bottom of the 'Mile' was the Cornets End Lane junction, and at this point we shut off and braked. Looking over our shoulders to ensure none of the Big Boys were bearing down on us at speed, we U-turned and headed back up to the lay-by, and Somers Lane rest area.

Only a couple of weeks ago, I went for a ride down the 'Mile,' and now at the bottom is a large island, but the old lay-by is still there, just as it was all those years ago. I was disappointed to see Somers lane was no longer a lane, but a fully fledged road, and an entrance to a plush golf club which has expanded to both sides of the 'Mile.' Billy and Bonneville's field is still there, but now it's occupied by horses, not the couple of splendid rams that trotted up to greet us every time they heard our engines.

The corner of Billy and Bonneville's field with the remains of the grass bank we used to sit on in the foreground.

Somers Lane, now the entrance to the golf course – widened, resurfaced, and renamed Somers Road.

The Mile, looking up towards Meriden, with the lay-by and entrance to Somers Lane on the left. This mostly remains unchanged, except the golf course has now spread to both sides of the road.

Billy and Bonneville's field is still the same except for a new fence and metal five-bar gate. The top right-hand corner was the location of their little lean-to shelter. It's now a pony paddock.

The Cubs

A 1960 UK T120, restored by the author for a Derby businessman. Equipped with rev counter and remote-float carburettors. Drive-side view.

1960 UK T120 timing-side view. Pearl grey and Meriden blue livery.

Pulling the two Cubs onto their centre stands, we immediately removed our gloves and helmets, placing them on the grass bank where we sometimes lay in the sun. Then, our trusty reversible screwdrivers in hand, we set about adjusting both tick-over speed and pilot mixtures. By having the motors at working temperature, it was easy to slow the tick-over, then gradually wind in the pilot mixture screw until the exhaust became lumpy, then out again from this point until a steady, firm exhaust note was achieved. All that was necessary then was to

Triumph Production Testers' Tales – from the Meriden Factory

reset the tick-over to the desired speed, which, on the standard Cub, was approximately six hundred revs per minute. The bikes could then be switched off and rested for a little while, whilst a roll-up was savoured and enjoyed.

By this point, two or three of the other chaps had arrived on the Meriden Blue and Pearl Grey twin carburettor Bonnevilles, amidst much noise and throttle 'blipping.' I badly needed a pee, and Joe suggested I go down the lane a few yards and behind the hedge. In his Liverpudlian accent, he said: "It's the testers' urinal, even the Jaguar boys use it." It seemed a good idea, so off I toddled, leaving my crash helmet and gloves on the ground, and key in the ignition, like a lamb to the slaughter. Halfway through my pee, I heard the Bonnevilles start up and roar off, closely followed by Joe's Cub. "Oh, well," I thought, "I'll follow in my own good time." Struggling to pull up my over-trousers, I walked back to my Cub standing forlornly alone. Suddenly, the penny dropped. I couldn't believe it: the rotten sods had buggered off, not only with my hat and gloves, but also the ignition key out of the PRS8 Lucas lighting and ignition switch on the nacelle top cover!

Laughing and cursing at the same time, I got on the Cub, pushing it forward off the centre stand. "Bugger it," I thought, "I'll not get caught like that again." (I subsequently learned that this was a mild introduction to the testing gang compared to what some of the other poor luckless sods went through.)

Luckily, I had in my Belstaff jacket pocket a small, plastic-handled electrical screwdriver. By introducing the blade of this through the slot in the rubber cap in the centre of the Lucas PRS8 lighting and ignition switch, and turning it clockwise until I heard a click, the ignition came on. Riding slowly back to the factory – rather weird without helmet, gloves or goggles – I turned into the main gate and up past the Time Office, to be met by funny looks from Pop and Joan. "Bluff it out" I thought, and gave a cheery wave. I turned right up the ramp leading to the rubber swing doors, and, with a bang, hit them with my front tyre, just as a labourer was coming the other way carrying about twenty empty tin mugs on his wooden tray, en route to the canteen. I didn't actually knock over the poor chap, but the tray and mugs went flying into the air, and the noise when they came down and hit the floor was awful. To make matters worse, in panic I stalled the Cub, caught between the rubber swing doors, where I was held fast in a vice-like grip.

These doors were half an inch thick, and made of industrial rubber sheet; they were also spring-loaded to boot, to keep them shut in windy weather, I supposed. This is why the testers hit them with such a bang on entry and exit, as being timid left you in a fix similar to the one I now found myself in.

The left-hand door edge had somehow trapped itself between the nearside rider's footrest and foot brake pedal, whilst the right-hand door was between the offside footrest and gear lever.

To make matters worse, my left leg was inside the Finishing Shop, whilst my right leg was still outside, with the right-hand door preventing me from reaching the gear lever to select neutral. I was stuck there, like some helpless fly in a spider's web, listening to the howls of laughter from the chaps watching as I struggled to free myself.

Obviously, the mugs hitting the floor had turned people's eyes in my direction, hundreds of them, and I just had to sit there, taking it and getting redder and redder.

In the Finishing Shop there were different sections, each manned by dozens of workers. For instance, there was Tom Cashmore's packing section, where the crates for the overseas bikes went to be packed prior to shipping.

There was the main production track, about sixty yards long, with workers two abreast along its length, and then there was the wiring and petrol tank sections, as well as the two rectification gangs. All-in-all, a lot of people with their eyes turned in my direction. I think it must have been the most cringe-making moment of my entire time at Meriden, as I hung there, listening to the howls of laughter whilst struggling to free myself. And all the while I was doing so, I could see my helmet, gloves, and ignition key sitting innocently on the twinseat of a yet-to-be-tested machine ...

It was no use, there was no way I could free myself, I simply had to wait for help. When – finally – a couple of chaps came over to release me, I had no choice other than suffer their ribald jokes and comments as I scurried back to the test section. I put the Cub on the centre stand at the end of the line of Cubs, and, wishing the earth would swallow me up, squatted down, mainly out of sight, to gather my senses. For the time being, all I could do was put up with the jokes, but I knew who it was that had taken my kit, and I was determined I'd get even, one way or another. I resolved not to leave my stuff lying around out of my sight again. If I had to answer a call of nature, no matter where I was, my kit and ignition key were going with me!

More cautiously this time I went through the

The Cubs

1960 6T Thunderbird in Charcoal Grey, restored for a Midlands businessman. A very underrated, comfortable touring 650. Drive-side view.

1960 Thunderbird timing-side view, showing clean, uncluttered lines. The Americans didn't really like it, preferring the previous year's model.

Triumph Production Testers' Tales – from the Meriden Factory

The 1960 Thunderbird, with its new rear enclosure, in the sales catalogue.

procedures for the next test ride, and ventured out on my own, sticking religiously to the speeds Joe and I had travelled at on my first disastrous run. I was in no doubt that, with all the miles I had covered riding to and from North Yorkshire for the two years I was in the army, and also the distance covered whilst in the White Helmets on the TRWs, I'd be able to apply good sense and judgement to whichever bike I was riding.

Going through the village toward the island, and the start of the 'Mile,' two testers passed me going the other way on Charcoal Grey 6T police machines, and they actually waved. Well, it wasn't so much a wave as a quick lift of the left hand about six inches off the handlebar and back again, but it was an acknowledgement and that's what counted.

The bulk of police 6T Thunderbirds – somewhere in the region of two hundred and fifty, I seem to recall – were for the metropolitan police. This version was identical to the standard machine in appearance, except for a specially adapted hinged twinseat that had a mounting on the pillion seat to take the radio equipment. I didn't know it then, but I would encounter these very machines again at a later date in the Service Repair Department.

It was during this period that one of the police authorities decided to have its machines finished in a new brilliant white for high visibility, which was immediately christened Motorway White by our publicity wizard, Ivor Davies. The colour did not really catch on, though, until about 1965, when the unit construction police model named 'The Saint' came along.

The Cubs

The special paint job Police 6T, seen here on the HIII being ridden by (from left to right): Jimmy Brown; Bill Letts; Morris Harrison (obscured); Jock Copland; Joe 'Sooty' Price, and following with his white 'nappy' around his neck, Charlie Wallace.

By then the M6 motorway was in need of fast patrol bikes, and the Lancashire force was one of the bigger users of 'The Saint.'

I'm not entirely sure if it's true, but it was rumoured that Sid Shilton, our Police Sales Head, came up with the name, claiming that the bike was not named for the popular Roger Moore television series, but because this super fast machine could "stop anything in no time."

The little Cubs were beautiful to ride, and I could see why they sold well when the majority of the other lightweights were powered by stinky two-stroke engines.

Even the feisty little T20SL Sports Cub, capable of giving a three fifty twin a run for its money, was only £164.1s including purchase tax, on the road. Value for money Triumphs were a good buy in the early 1960s, with wages creeping up and petrol only around three or four shillings a gallon – and these little Cubs did nigh on a hundred miles to the gallon if ridden sensibly. Factory reconditioned engine units were available from the Service Repair Department for the princely sum of thirty pounds if you handed in your old unit. And they came with a three month warranty. Super value for money, and no mistake.

When I was too young to ride on the road legally, I enrolled in the RAC/ACU riding scheme, which was operated by a couple of big motorcycle dealerships in the Coventry area, and the Triumph Engineering Company Limited. It was held on a Sunday morning on the big service roads that ran through the main Dunlop factory in Holbrook Lane, and adjoining Burnaby Road. It was free, and young chaps could go along, listen to the instructors, and get to ride the machines supplied on the private roads. No licence or insurance was required back in those days. Coincidentally, one of the instructors on that scheme was someone who would play a big part in my Triumph life later on, a certain Alex Scobie ...

But what I'm getting at in a roundabout way is that, out of the three machines available – a Bantam 125cc DI, a Francis Barnett Falcon, and a lovely little Amaranth Red Triumph Terrier 150cc, it was always the Triumph that had the biggest queue of lads waiting to ride it. Says it all, really.

Triumph Production Testers' Tales – from the Meriden Factory

With summer really upon us, the Belstaff suits were getting too hot. Even if you took off the over-trousers and used the jacket only, it was necessary to take these off, too, when not outside. Some of us were wearing only a singlet underneath, but that didn't soak up the perspiration like a shirt did, so the tartan lining used to get wet and smelly. To try and counteract this, the best thing to do as soon as you got home was to hang the jacket outside on the washing line in the fresh air to dry out.

Triumph management, in its infinite wisdom, decided to equip us with lightweight Belstaff jackets and trousers, made of material akin to black PVC. The jacket was double-breasted, and was styled on the jacket that Marlon Brando wore in the film *The Wild Ones*. The only thing was, as the material couldn't 'breathe,' wearers still got a bit hot and sweaty.

Some of the chaps mixed and matched, depending on the type of day it was, and some days we dispensed with the trousers altogether, although company policy would not, under any circumstances, allow us to go out on to public roads without a jacket and gloves. This was for safety reasons, of course, as sliding along the tarmac in only shirt sleeves and without gloves could result in horrible injuries.

This was a sublime period to be a motorcycle tester as you were the envy of all who stood at a machine, workbench or production track. Once out on a bike, you were, to all intents and purposes, your own boss, and, as long as you did your quota of twelve bikes a day, didn't go too far off route, speed, or, Heaven forbid, spend too long in either of the cafes, you got along fine.

The little standard Cub in 1959 had sixteen inch wheels, which made it look chubby, so that's what it was called at the factory, the 'Chubby Cub.'

It was suggested that the wheel sizes on the standard model would be changed from sixteen inch to eighteen inch, and be fitted with Dunlop universal

The 1960 standard T20 Tiger Cub forks assembly exploded view, with associated part numbers. Rather spindly forks, but they worked well enough on the little Cub.

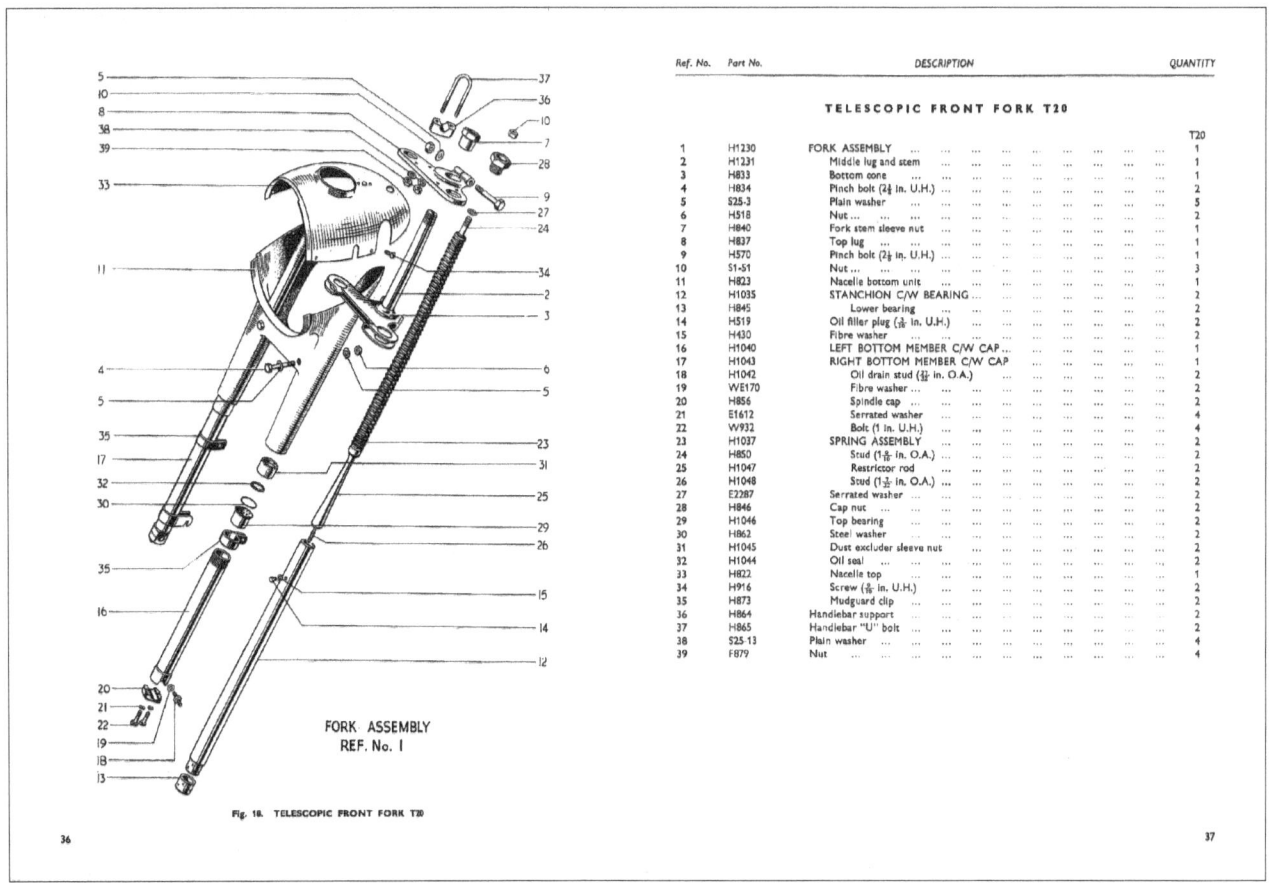

The Cubs

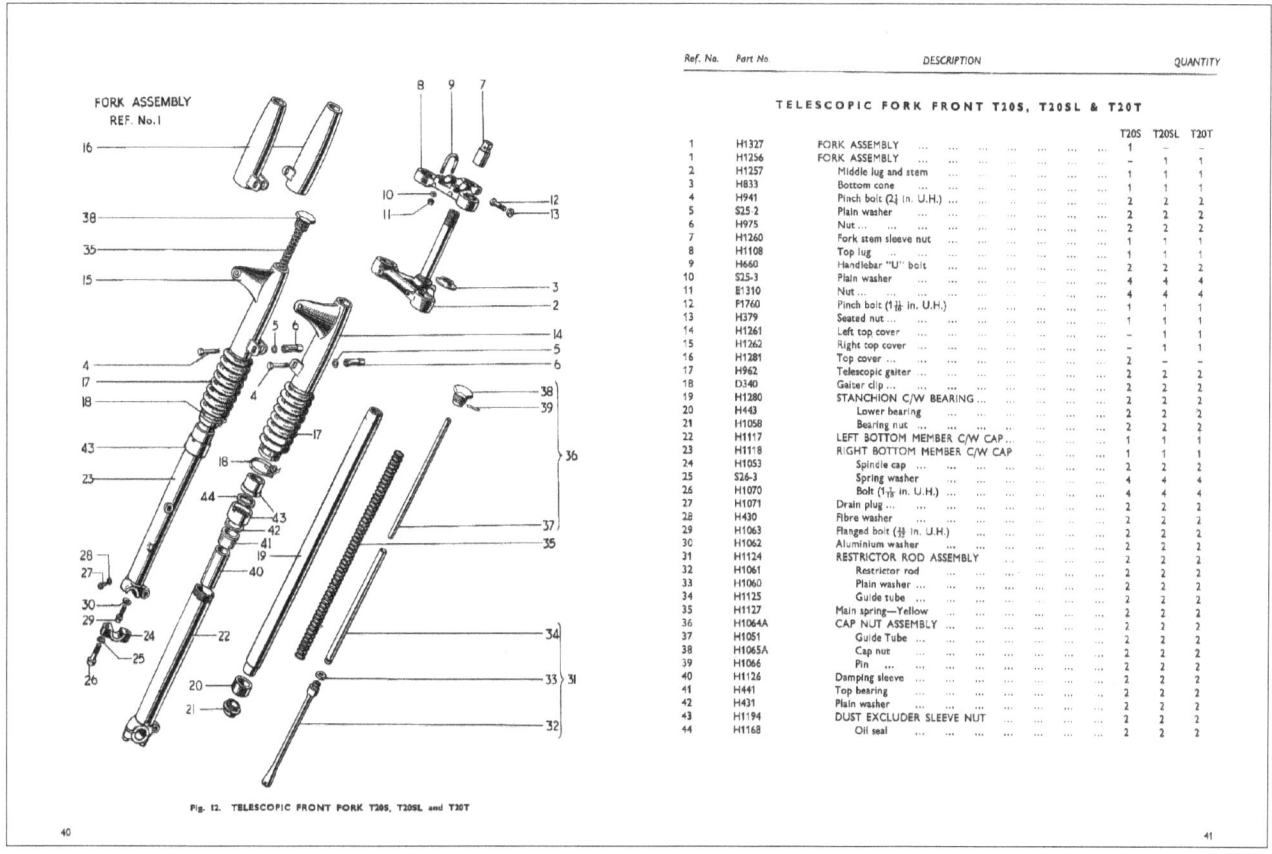

The 1960 sports Cubs front forks were almost identical to the larger models. They were more robust for competition work.

two-seven-five section (2.75in) tyres, but this idea was dropped in favour of the seventeen inch wheels fitted with three-two-five (3.25in) section tyres. This size then stayed with the standard Cub until it was finally phased out.

The standard model had the nacelle forks incorporated in the nacelle top, Lucas PRS8 lighting and ignition switch, speedometer, and headlamp, which, although a little flimsy, worked well enough. The sports models had the larger machine type forks with headlamp mounting 'ears' on the top fork covers, and concertina-type gaiters in black PVC to protect the bare portion of the stanchions.

The T20S for America had a high level exhaust, high-rise bars, energy transfer ignition, and an Amal carburettor. It was a flamboyant red and silver in colour: very nice.

The internals of these bigger forks were the same as those used on the TR6 Trophy and T120 Bonneville, with an hydraulic damping system in order to handle rough terrain when used in competition. A much better proposition altogether.

I always chose to ride home on an American Sports Cub, as it seemed bigger and faster than the ordinary home market model, which I guess made me feel as if I was progressing to bigger things. Little Bill Hemmings, Joe Price, Alan Armitt and myself were the four Cub testers; the first three because they liked them, and me because I was not yet allowed on anything bigger. Little Bill did go home on a big bike on the odd occasion, but, being on the short side, he had to make sure that, when passing through Leamington Spa, down the main street with at least four sets of traffic lights, he could pull up next to the kerb should the lights change to red!

The Cubs all had the same four-speed gearbox, although the internal ratios were different between the standard and sports models. Depending on the build requirement, the competition models may have had the widely spaced 'wide-ratio' cluster. The clutches were all the same, with neo-langite lined plates, and a three-

Triumph Production Testers' Tales – from the Meriden Factory

eighths duplex primary drive. As the sports models had high performance cam shafts, they required stronger-than-standard valve springs, and these complemented the little unit. With the Amal Monobloc carburettor, a staggering sixteen brake horse power could be obtained. When you consider that the 3TA three-fifty twin developed only eighteen-and-a-half brake horse power at 6500 revs per minute, you can appreciate why the lighter sports Cub, at two hundred and twenty pounds as opposed to the three fifty's three hundred and forty five pounds, could be faster.

One of the tricks that the Cub boys liked to play was to see who had prepared a bike for test, then, as he went to get his helmet, gloves and plates, quickly, without him seeing, slacken off the distributor clamp screw by three or four turns with the Triumph toolkit reversible blade screwdriver.

The engines still used the Lucas 15 DI distributor, which was mounted vertically rearward, and slightly to

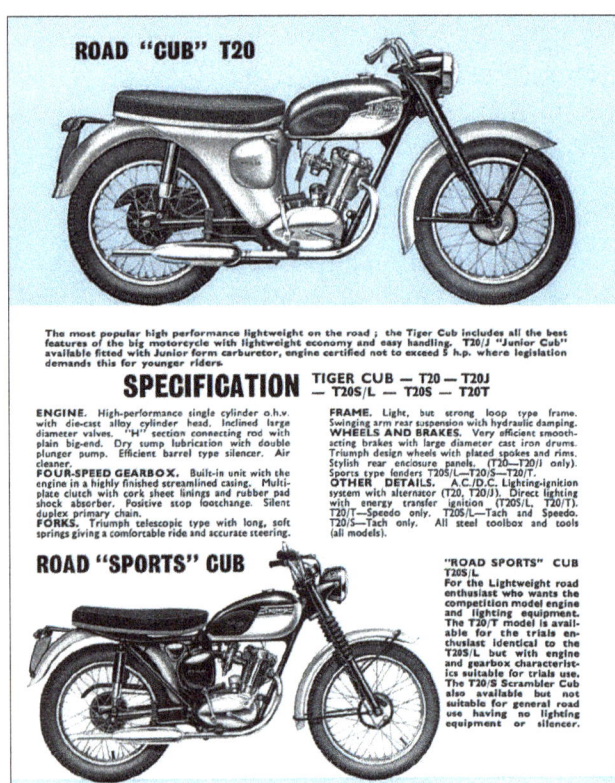

The technical specifications for Jomo machines going to the West Coast of America.

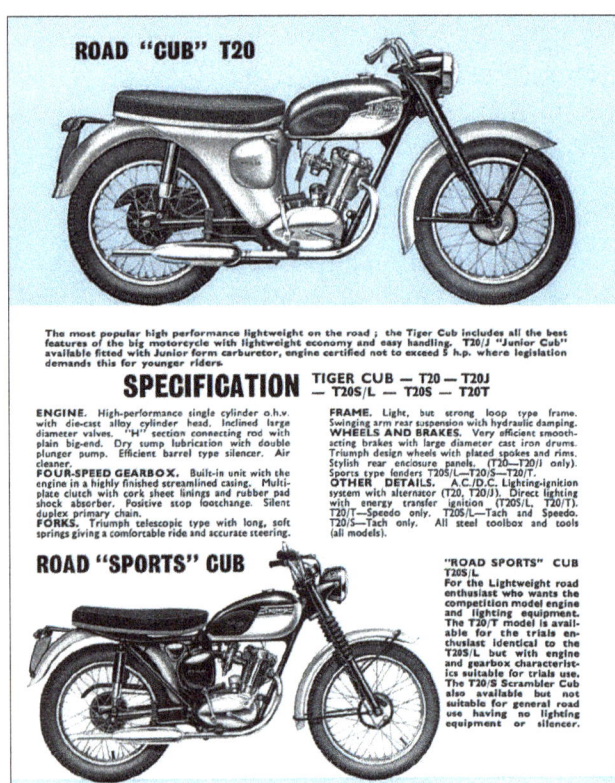

The 1960 Johnson Motors (West Coast distributor) standard T20 Cub with high-rise bars and no front numberplate. America deemed them dangerous and called them 'pedestrian slicers.' Also shown: the T20SL with big Amal carburettors and direct lights.

the right of the cylinder barrel, secured into its crankcase housing by a hidden clamp. This clamp was actually inside the engine, but the Phillips-headed clamping screw was accessible from the outer face of the timing cover, so that, should the ignition timing need altering, it was a simple case of undoing the screw a couple turns to allow the distributor to be rotated one way or the other, thus advancing or retarding the ignition.

The ignition timing was set very accurately when the engine was still on the assembly line, awaiting fitment of the cylinder head. This enabled an exact piston position before top dead centre (TDC) to be ascertained using a calibrated depth gauge placed on top of the barrel face. The engine could then be wound over until the piston could be brought up to contact the depth gauge on the compression stroke. At this exact piston position before top dead centre, the distributor could be set and the clamp tightened, a job that took an experienced fitter no more than thirty or forty seconds, before the cylinder head, push rods, and tube were bolted into place, the tappets set, and the engine slung into its frame.

The thing was, if you left the clamp screw undone, not quite enough for the distributor to turn of its own accord and alter the timing, but enough for the torsional force of the driving 'skew' gear to nudge the distributor

The 1960 Black and Ivory Experimental mileage T100A that the author used to collect his new Belstaff suit on. Drive-side view.

This particular machine was still on Energy Transfer Ignition System, but rectified lighting. Timing-side view.

upward in its housing, the spade drive would disengage and, bingo! the bike would coast to a standstill accompanied by a cacophony of bangs and pops from the exhaust.

Because of this, I always grasped the distributor and tried to turn it prior to going out (by which I mean I sat on the bike with the engine running and my crash helmet on when I did, so no-one could get at it when my

Triumph Production Testers' Tales – from the Meriden Factory

back was turned!). You really did have to be prepared for anything and everything, and have eyes in your backside if you were a relatively new chap. Never mind, I was ex-Repair Shop, ex-Royal Signals and ex-Les Williams ace joker, so I was up to a lot of tricks myself. And I was still biding my time and keeping my eyes and ears open to see if I could pick up in the general banter and jokey conversation, who had gone off with my helmet, gloves, and ignition key.

Riding the Cubs had begun to get a little boring, and I cast envious eyes at the other chaps riding the bigger models. I didn't mind not being allowed on the six fifties; the five hundreds would do very nicely, thank you. Letting me go to Staffordshire on a mileage T100A to collect my new riding suit, then being told I could only ride Cubs was a little frustrating, to say the least. It reminded me of my army experience of being made to wear L-plates and ride a girder forked BSA M20 side valve machine all week at thirty miles per hour, then jumping onto my one hundred mile an hour Triumph twin and blasting home to Coventry each weekend.

The standard Cubs had rear quarter panels with 'windows' in each side: one for the oil tank and one for the battery box. The sports models had no panels at all: they had an oil tank but no battery box on the nearside because a battery was not required on Energy-Transfer sparked ignition systems.

The high tension spark was created via a special Energy-Transfer coil, in conjunction with the alternator rotor in the primary chain case being timed and fixed to the drive-side crankshaft in a critically exact position.

The Lucas distributor, although outwardly identical to the standard item, had only a ten degree range on its automatic advance and retard mechanism as opposed to the usual twelve degree range on standard machines. This restriction was to prevent the spark occurring outside its useable range, and thus preventing the engine from starting and running properly. Indeed, later on, after these models had been sold to customers and had covered a few thousand miles, they began to experience running and starting difficulties due to slight wear on the advance and retard bob weight mechanism.

These weights would 'fling' outward against light spring tension with the centrifugal force of the distributor spinning, and advance the ignition by the supposed number of degrees in doing so. However, after a time, due to wear on the pivot points, the weights would travel beyond the acceptable range, thereby sparking the plug in the wrong place. When this happened, the bike was impossible to start. If the timing was altered by slackening off the distributor clamp and turning the distributor until the bike could be started on the kick-start, when you tried to rev the engine, it would simply misfire and refuse to pick up on the throttle. If the distributor was altered again so that the motor would pick up and rev, there was no chance of restarting it, should it stall or cut out.

It was something of a catch-22 situation until Uncle Joe Lucas came up with a swift remedy. A minute steel sleeve, with a wall thickness of 0.005in (five thousandths of an inch) was made to slip over the automatic advance and retard mechanism stop peg, thus reducing the range of the Auto unit and preventing the problem occurring.

One of the Cubs that we all tried to avoid was the T20J Junior model, aimed at learner riders in America, and Bermuda, which had a blanket thirty mile an hour speed limit. These little things were detuned with restricted inlets and smaller carburettors, and struggled to top forty miles per hour. The engines were restricted to such a degree that they developed just five brake horse power (5bhp) and, as such, the model was a little terror to ride. You simply did not want to go out on one because you knew, you just knew, that one of the chaps was going to buzz you at a high rate of knots somewhere along the test route.

The sports Cub that appeared later on in 1960 was being turned out in very snazzy livery of Meriden blue and ivory. The top half of the petrol tank was blue, with the lower half in ivory. Both mudguards were ivory, but with a three-quarters of an inch wide centre blue stripe, edged in one eighth of an inch gold pinstriping each side. Everything else was in gloss black and chrome. Very nice.

The standard model was still in Crystal Grey for 1960, but 1961 models had a new livery of black and silver-sheen, with the sports models in ruby red and silver-sheen. The T20 still had the side panels, but now the tank was black on the top and silver on the lower half. With silver-sheen oil tank, battery box, side panels, and mudguards, the bike looked bigger. Maybe it was the more sparkly silver-sheen instead of the darker grey that gave this illusion. The mudguards had central raised ribs, and these were black with a gold pinstripe each side. The standard T20 and the T20T had the same low compression engine with the standard camshaft and small Zenith carburettor.

The T20S and T20SL models finished in ruby red and silver-sheen had a higher compression rate of

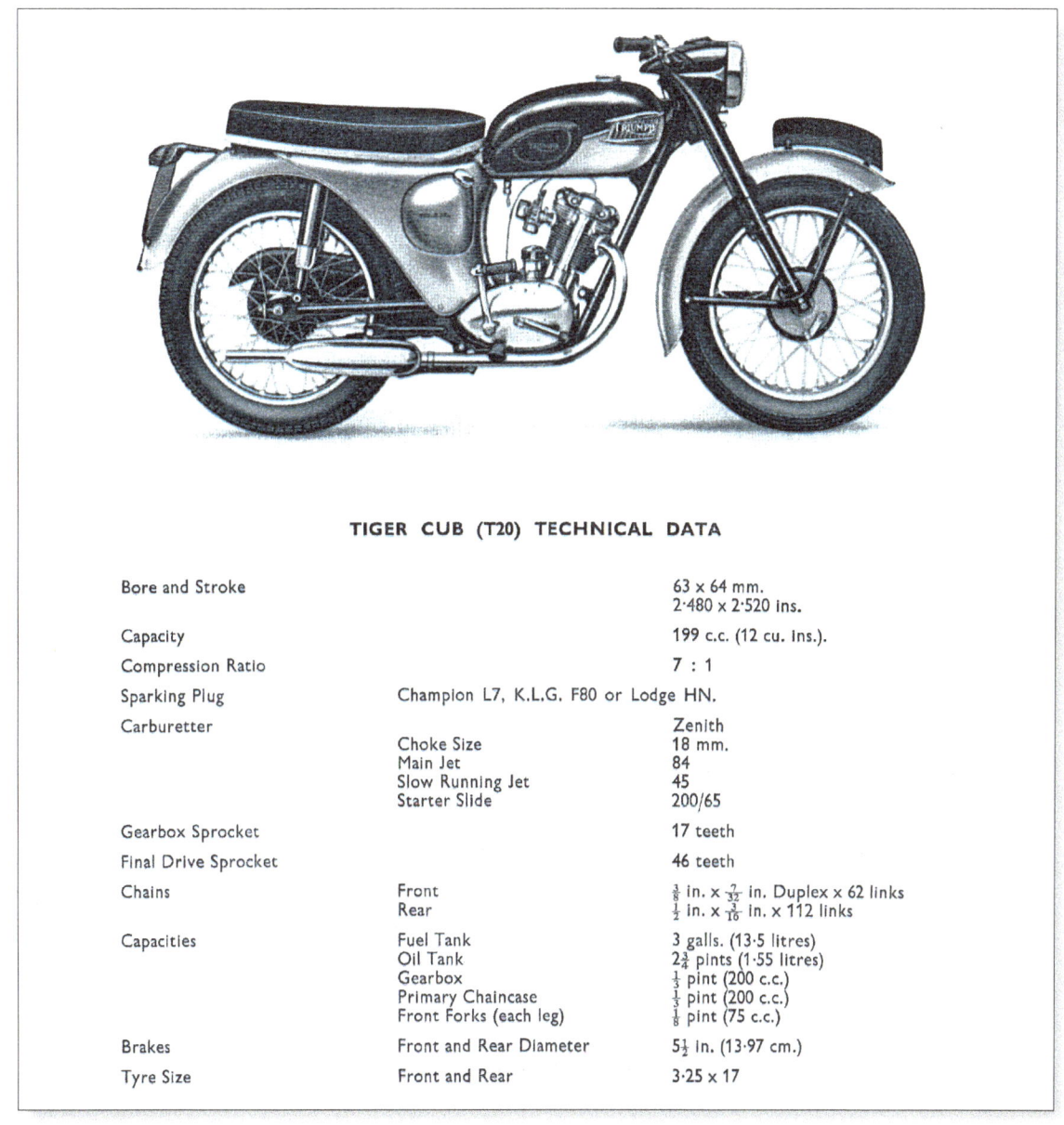

TIGER CUB (T20) TECHNICAL DATA

Bore and Stroke		63 × 64 mm. 2·480 × 2·520 ins.
Capacity		199 c.c. (12 cu. ins.).
Compression Ratio		7 : 1
Sparking Plug		Champion L7, K.L.G. F80 or Lodge HN.
Carburetter		Zenith
	Choke Size	18 mm.
	Main Jet	84
	Slow Running Jet	45
	Starter Slide	200/65
Gearbox Sprocket		17 teeth
Final Drive Sprocket		46 teeth
Chains	Front	$\frac{3}{8}$ in. × $\frac{7}{32}$ in. Duplex × 62 links
	Rear	$\frac{1}{2}$ in. × $\frac{3}{16}$ in. × 112 links
Capacities	Fuel Tank	3 galls. (13·5 litres)
	Oil Tank	$2\frac{3}{4}$ pints (1·55 litres)
	Gearbox	$\frac{1}{3}$ pint (200 c.c.)
	Primary Chaincase	$\frac{1}{3}$ pint (200 c.c.)
	Front Forks (each leg)	$\frac{1}{8}$ pint (75 c.c.)
Brakes	Front and Rear Diameter	$5\frac{1}{2}$ in. (13·97 cm.)
Tyre Size	Front and Rear	3·25 × 17

Standard T20 with general spec data.

nine to one (9:1 CR), a sports camshaft, and the bigger Amal Monobloc, 376-272 carburettor. Petrol tanks and mudguards on both models were ruby red top half and silver-sheen bottom half.

The sports mudguards were in silver-sheen, with the three quarters of an inch wide stripe in ruby red, pinstriping in gold. The T20S and T20SL were on Energy-Transfer ignition, which meant no battery and direct lighting.

There really was no competition as far as lightweights were concerned, especially after the works riders notched up a series of wins in the trialling world, namely the Scottish Six Days of 1959.

Percy Tait rode a Cub with Earles leading link forks at Mallory in 1959, and Johnny Giles, Scott Ellis, and my old friend Roy Peplow all rode them in either scrambles or the British Experts Trial. Many of the machines were prepared by Henry Vale and Vic Fiddler in the Competition Shop situated at the bottom of the Service Repair Shop.

Triumph Production Testers' Tales – from the Meriden Factory

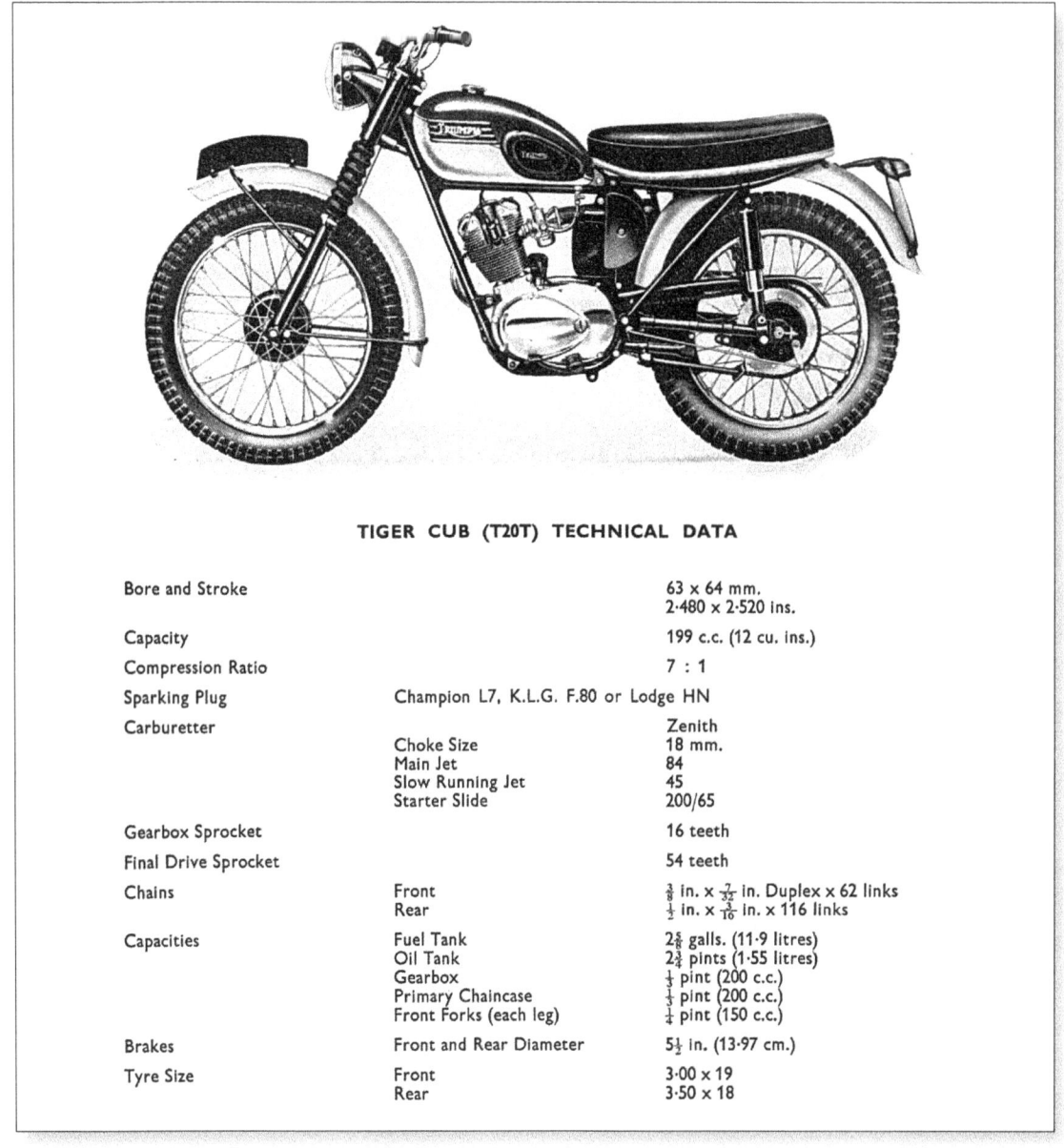

T20 Cub with general spec data.

It was a testament to the sturdiness of these little bikes that, back in 1956, journalist and friend Anthony Smith, whilst in Cape Town, on impulse walked into a Triumph dealership in Waterkant Street, where he saw a little Shell Blue, sheen-coloured Cub at the back of the showroom. It was second-hand with plunger rear suspension, but otherwise in good nick. Equipped with stout English tweed jacket, cap, goggles, and gloves, Anthony set out to ride it all the way home to England, from which journey came a bestselling book entitled *High Street Africa*. On his return to England, we, in the Repair Shop, totally restored his Cub free of charge, and he then took it back to his London home and put it in his basement.

Many years later, when I had started my on restoration business, Anthony looked me up for a particular reason. You've guessed it, he wanted to do the journey again on the Cub, but this time the other way, and with his nineteen-year-old son, Adam, on another Cub. The only thing was, he wanted me to find and

The Cubs

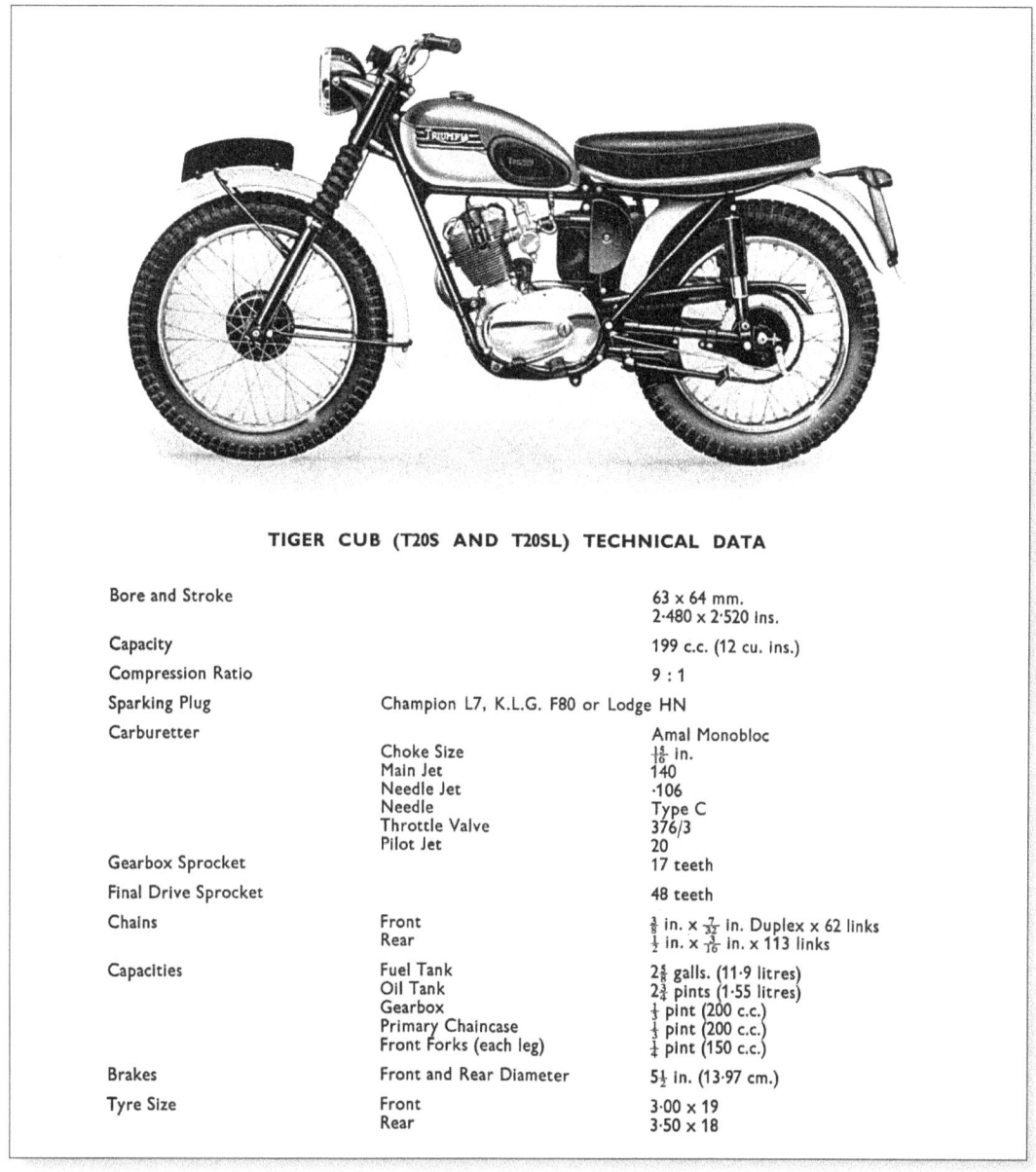

TIGER CUB (T20S AND T20SL) TECHNICAL DATA

Bore and Stroke		63 × 64 mm.
		2·480 × 2·520 ins.
Capacity		199 c.c. (12 cu. ins.)
Compression Ratio		9 : 1
Sparking Plug		Champion L7, K.L.G. F80 or Lodge HN
Carburetter		Amal Monobloc
	Choke Size	$\tfrac{13}{16}$ in.
	Main Jet	140
	Needle Jet	·106
	Needle	Type C
	Throttle Valve	376/3
	Pilot Jet	20
Gearbox Sprocket		17 teeth
Final Drive Sprocket		48 teeth
Chains	Front	$\tfrac{3}{8}$ in. × $\tfrac{7}{32}$ in. Duplex × 62 links
	Rear	$\tfrac{1}{2}$ in. × $\tfrac{5}{16}$ in. × 113 links
Capacities	Fuel Tank	2$\tfrac{5}{8}$ galls. (11·9 litres)
	Oil Tank	2$\tfrac{3}{4}$ pints (1·55 litres)
	Gearbox	$\tfrac{1}{3}$ pint (200 c.c.)
	Primary Chaincase	$\tfrac{1}{3}$ pint (200 c.c.)
	Front Forks (each leg)	$\tfrac{1}{4}$ pint (150 c.c.)
Brakes	Front and Rear Diameter	5$\tfrac{1}{2}$ in. (13·97 cm.)
Tyre Size	Front	3·00 × 19
	Rear	3·50 × 18

T20S and T20SL with general spec data.

obtain a Cub for Adam, then prepare the two bikes for the journey. This I did, and they went off on their epic journey; essentially, two non-motorcyclists heading off to the great continent of Africa. Where angels fear to tread is a phrase that springs to mind, but they made it on the little bikes. What an adventure!

Thinking back to when I worked at the Coventry Motor Mart, I remember we sold many makes of motorcycle as well as being main agent for BSA and Sunbeam. The other big bikes we sold new were AJS, Matchless, and Ariel, and there was a plethora of lightweights, all powered by two-stroke Villiers engines: Francis Barnett, DOT Excelsior, Norman James, and Sun. Having two-stroke engines of the 1950s era meant that, on the underside of the petrol filler cap, the portion that goes inside the tank, was a measure, into which was poured a level amount of oil that was then tipped into the tank with a gallon of petrol. Imagine the fun and games you would have had with that on a trip through the Sahara desert ...

One out, one in

Getting into the job, and with more riding time, my confidence increased as the weeks progressed. I and the other Cub stalwarts – Joe 'Sooty' Price, Alan 'Streak' Armitt, and little Bill Hemmings (affectionately known as 'Binder') – pressed on with the test runs. When a shortage of Cubs occurred, I at last swapped to the 3TA three fifty twin model.

This was a typically smooth – though a little lacklustre – low powered, small capacity twin; the sort of machine that you got on and rode by remote control, because everything was so laidback about it. The larger capacity Speed Twin was a better bet as far as performance went; after all, the only difference between the two models was the engine. Effectively, the 3TA three

West Coast 3TA, exactly the same as the UK model except for no front number plate, high-rise bars, and grab-strap over the seat.

One out, one in

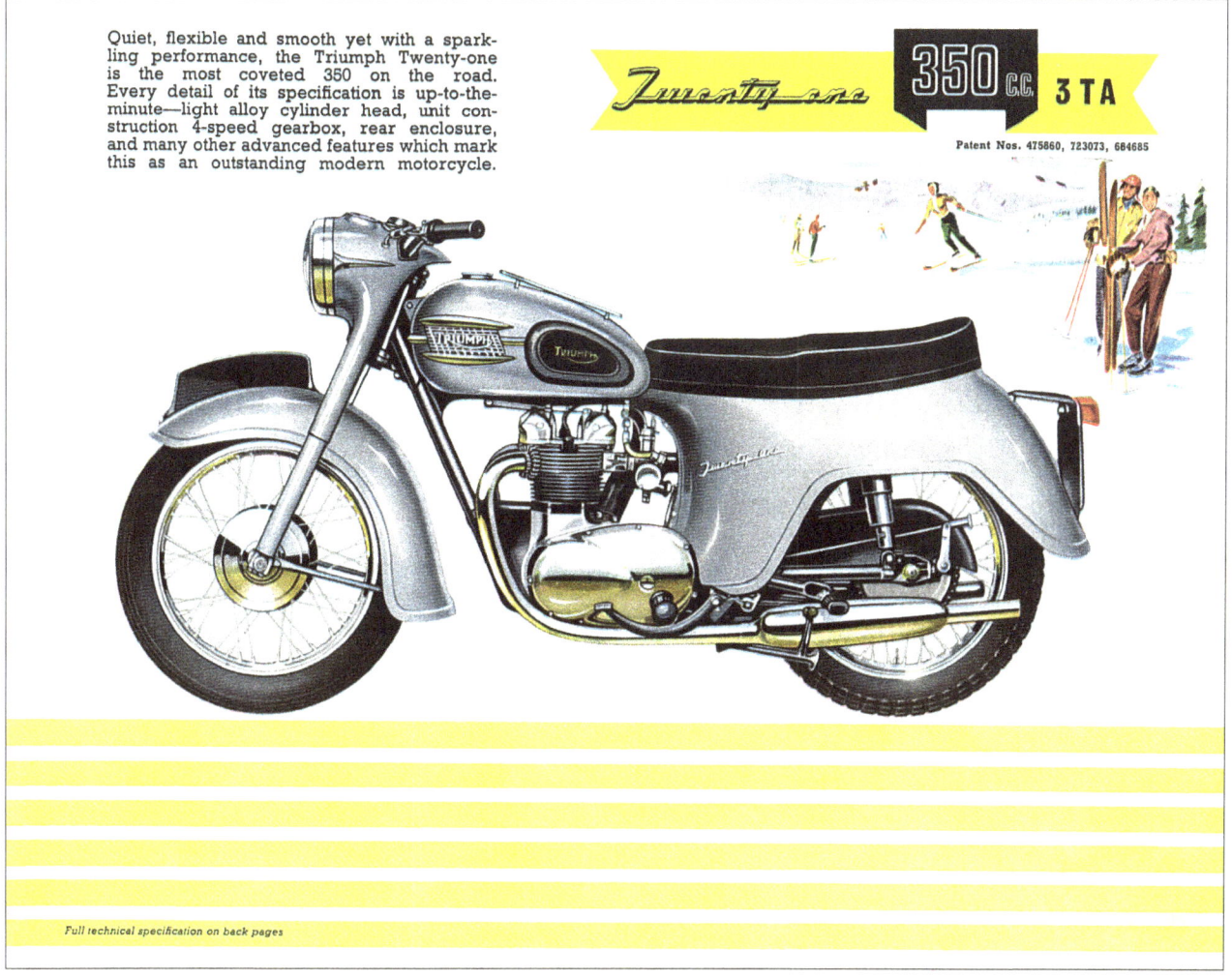

The little twin that suffered with '3T-itis,' cutting out unexpectedly when you were about to move off. 1961 home-market model in Shell Blue sheen.

fifty was pulling the 5TA Speed Twin rolling chassis; therefore, it was understandably under stressed. This did not stop me from riding the 3TA, however, as it was a twin cylinder machine, and, as such, a step nearer the big models.

Terrible news from Devon arrived during the summer holidays. Jimmy Brown had suffered a heart attack, collapsed, and died whilst on the beach with his family. Obviously, everyone was speechless and really there were no words that would convey our feelings at that time. Gentleman Jim was a good man, father, and husband to Thelma. Bill Letts and myself were detailed to go to his funeral at the Robin Hood cemetery in Solihull, together with a couple of other representatives from both management and the union. We travelled there in the Transport and General Workers Union Convenor's car, and duly stopped at the Engine pub in Hampton-in-Arden on the way back for a quick pint and to toast Jim. I didn't know whether this would be frowned upon, but, at that moment, I don't think we cared.

Within the week, Dennis Peacock was made up to Chief Tester, which, as previously mentioned, created a vacancy in our ranks. The long-established testers didn't seem to mind the sudden change in rank; Dennis was liked by all, and he quickly became something of a father figure, much as old Jim was.

I went home each night on a new 3TA twin, parking it in my motorcycle shed in the back garden, next to JRW 405, and each night a chap called Eddie, who lived a couple of houses up the road, would call round to ogle

Triumph Production Testers' Tales – from the Meriden Factory

the new machines. We had known each other since he came out of the Royal Navy some months previously. He served on HMS Broadsword, the old one, not the latest, and coming from Ipswich, decided to come and live with his elderly aunt and try for a job in the engineering centre of England. "Well," I thought to myself, "Triumph Engineering Company Limited, that's the engineering bit taken care of, and centre of England equals Meriden. Got to be a sign there somewhere."

Eddie had already been well-schooled in the art of motorcycling, owning several in his native Suffolk prior to his navy service, and now he was the owner of a splendid, new Norton Dominator 88. He had decided to treat himself using some of his navy gratuity, and now owned a really beautiful bike, in metallic grey livery, hump-backed petrol tank, 'feather bed' frame, and short 'Road holder' forks. With polished alloy, chrome plate, and red pinstriping, it really was eye-catching, and I wondered why he was looking at 3TA three fifty twins when he owned something like this.

A couple of nights later, I mentioned the vacancy to Eddie. His eyes lit up and he began to chortle, as if he was laughing to himself under his breath. In his broad Suffolk accent, peppered with lots of 'my boy' in his sentences, he agreed to come to the factory for an interview, so the following morning, after I had parked my going home bike and completed the test card, finally pushing the bike up to the knacker gang, I wandered down to get my mug of tea from Evvy.

This was a ritual that began back in 1949 or 1950, carried out no matter who came or who went on the testing gang. Evelyn, or 'Evvy,' was like a mother hen looking after her chicks, we each had our own mugs, and every morning, dead on eight o'clock, a wooden tray loaded with everyone's mugs full of Evvy's tea would be waiting for us as we roared into the Finishing Shop, ready to start another day. There would also be a mug for Stan Trowell when he arrived at about half past eight, and he, like us, really appreciated it.

When Stan arrived and I had got my first bike of the day ready, I popped my head round the office door. "Stan, have you got someone for the job yet? If you haven't, I've got someone, a motorcyclist, just out of the navy – any good?" Stan told me to get Eddie in for ten o'clock sharp the next day, and I was to go and tell 'Pop' Wright that someone would be arriving on a Norton! He was then to take Eddie into the canteen, where Stan would interview him.

It was all straightforward, so when I got home that evening, I went round to see Eddie, gave him the low down, and told him that he must be at the Time Office for exactly ten o'clock as Pop was a stickler for punctuality. The following morning, getting to work as usual, I got my first bike ready while I drank my tea, and went out on my first run, hoping to be back for when Eddie arrived.

Getting back a little earlier than anticipated, I managed to make myself inconspicuous for half an hour or so, then wandered outside, but there was no sign of Eddie. Oh well, I thought, I'll go and get my next bike ready, then bring it out in the yard where I can keep my eyes open. This I did, and while setting the pilot mixture and tickover on my next 3TA test bike, in he swept, it was five minutes to ten.

He parked his Norton outside the front of the Time Office and tapped on the door before stepping inside. The Time Office had windows on three sides; on the front of the factory drive up toward the Experimental side, looking forward down the sloped drive to the main road, and on the yard side which had the sliding window, through which Pop poked his head each night to say "Off you go lads." I had an excellent view of Pop and Eddie, but because I was crouched down behind the 3TA on its centre stand, I wasn't in plain view, so Eddie had not yet spotted me. I swear Eddie was only in the office for two minutes before he had both Pop and Joan rolling with laughter. What he said I don't know, and I never did find out, but he certainly hit it off with both of them straight away. That's the sort of person Eddie was. After the other testers got to know him, they reckoned he could have charmed Adolf Hitler.

Pop came out of his office with Eddie, and as they walked past me on the way up the yard to the front doors of the canteen, Eddie looked over and gave me an enormous wink. "It's in the hands of providence now" I thought, as I put the plates on the 3TA and buggered off out of it for a while.

That night Eddie came round to let me know how he'd got on with Stan at the interview, and by all accounts, it was very favourable. Within the week, Triumph Engineering Company Limited, Meriden Works, had acquired a new production tester. Somehow, I really don't think the factory was ready for Eddie Dent; some of the pranks that came about later as he settled into the job are now legendary, and, I must admit, as good as the ones pulled by the arch joker himself, Les Williams. Upon reflection, I think they were as good as each other, it was too close to call.

I finally found out who had taken my hat and gloves; none other than Peter West, 'Westy' for short. He was, and still is, big mates with Alistair 'Jock' Copland,

One out, one in

The testers' 'do' at Fillongley. Left to right: Dennis Peacock; Pete West; Eric (surname unknown); Colin Smith; Jock Copeland; the author; Eddie Dent; Jim Lee; Fred Swift; Ken Cornish and Eric Miller.

one of my old army, ex-White Helmets pals. I began thinking of a way to get my own back. It had to be subtle, not traceable to me, and had to confound and perplex at the same time. Something that would happen out on the road, almost by remote control, and ideally when I was nowhere around.

Jock was demobbed from the army a year before me, but, like Les Williams, had been in another job before being called up. Both of them were in the Display Team, and on visits back to the factory with the Team bikes, secured jobs for after their demob. I, on the other hand, was at Meriden prior to call-up, so knew most people there.

Westy was somewhat of a comedian in his own right, and, being ex-Royal Navy too, was almost bound to get on well with Eddie. Pete was a very hard man, though, what they called in the navy, a 'hard hat diver' during his time on the briny. I finally settled on my strategy for Westy, after thinking back to when I was corporal in charge of maintenance of the factory-supplied TRW machines.

As well as being tasked with keeping the Team bikes in trim, I also took part in the complete programme of tricks for each show we did. I was in the opening, middle, and closing ride, as well as the jump ride, backward threes, taxi, six-bike fan, or six-bike pyramid as it is also known. It was between shows that the bikes were checked over, adjustments made, and any little jobs that were required attended to by me, whilst the riders to whom the bikes were charged out did the polishing and cleaning.

On more than one occasion, a machine would splutter and misfire, before fading out and rolling to a standstill. It was only after a while that I discovered that the over-zealous use of wax polish had bunged up the breather hole in the centre of the petrol filler cap. This had the effect of causing a partial vacuum inside the petrol tank after a few miles, and of course, also prevented the fuel from flowing to the carburettor float chamber, thus causing the engine to first of all struggle, then misfire before finally stopping altogether. The thing was, although you knew you had not run out of petrol, you still took off the filler cap and peered into the tank. Of course, this simple action released the vacuum, the fuel flowed and the bike started and ran perfectly until the vacuum formed again. And so it went on ...

This was perfect, I thought, as I scrounged a new filler cap and cork washer from the petrol tank section girls.

The breather hole is visible on the top chromed surface of the cap, so it would have to be blocked off

Triumph Production Testers' Tales – from the Meriden Factory

on the underside where it would not be obvious. In my dinner hour, I went for a walk up to the Service Repair Department to see my old mates, and, borrowing a soldering iron, some flux in a tin, and a spot of solder, I blocked the breather in the cadmium-plated body on the underside of the cap.

Now, I knew Westy was a good tester, but I banked on him not knowing about this particular dodge. He wasn't on test when I went into the army, so in all probability had only been in the job two or three years.

The other dodge that confounded people was the graphite pencil line from the terminal on top of the plug, down the porcelain to the main metal body. This, in effect, caused the high tension spark to 'track' down the graphite pencil line and earth out, meaning that there was no spark inside the combustion chamber. However, this ruse meant putting the pencil line on the sparkplug whilst the bike was in the Finishing Shop, so if Westy started the bike when he was carrying out his checking procedure, and it only ran on one cylinder, he would reject it to the knacker gang straight away. It had to be something that occurred out on the test route, which meant the petrol cap blocked breather hole.

During his time in the navy, Westy trained as a full suit, hard hat diver, which meant he was kitted out in the full rubber suit, with lead-weighted belt and boots, and fed air via an umbilical which also carried the communications two ways. He was one of the chaps who worked for hours on the bottom on salvage or similar. These divers were a special breed of men, and very well respected, even amongst their own. My father was in the navy during the war on motor torpedo boats, operating out of Felixstowe, and he told me of the 'iron in the divers' who went down, even to look for mines, laid overnight by the Germans. I know Peter was a diver in peacetime, but nevertheless, in such a claustrophobic environment, you had to admire them.

I waited until Pete had got his bike ready, then, when his back was turned, I saw my chance and quickly swapped the filler caps. After he had gone out, I killed a bit of time in the outside yard, and then took a slow ride out to see what was going on.

Sure enough, at the bottom of the Mile, there was Westy sitting astride his bike, with the petrol cap off, peering into the tank. Pulling up, I yelled, 'What's up, Pete?" "Dunno" he says, putting the cap back on. Of course, he'd now released the vacuum and the petrol had been able to flow again to the carburettor. He didn't know what was wrong, and after struggling back to the factory, pushing his bike up to the knacker gang section,

he remained in earnest conversation with little Eric Miller for some time, obviously explaining the symptoms. When neither of them was looking a little while later, I quickly swapped the petrol tank filler caps, putting the joker in my riding suit pocket and fitting the original with a quick push down and twist.

When, after exhaustive checking, little Eric couldn't find anything wrong with the bike and no reason for the problems that Westy had detailed on the test card, he called Pete over. By now, I was beside myself with mirth, listening to the increasingly heated exchange between them, peppered with cries of "Are you trying to waste my time?" To this day, I've not mentioned the episode, although I nearly did at the 50th Bonneville celebration.

Westy came to the anniversary celebration with his wife, and I, of course, was with my wife, Gloria, so the conversation was about other things as we had not seen each other for so long. Maybe he or another of the testers will read this book, and he will remember the incident, or be reminded of it by someone else. I hope he laughs about it, or I had better put my running shoes on!

When Eddie started work on the following Monday morning, Stan Trowell shouted for me. I had ridden in with Eddie that morning, me on a new Triumph, and Eddie on his Norton, which was in the car park. As I walked down the Finishing Shop, along the long lines of bikes toward Stan's and Mr Tubbs' office, I could see Eddie in his new Belstaff suit, holding his silver helmet in the crook of his left arm, standing to attention next to Stan with a big dopey grin across his face.

I had no idea at that time of the chaos that this amicable Ipswichian was going to inflict on our testing group. As an example of his zany, comedic behaviour, a celebration of the Triumph Motorcycle Marque was organised by Coventry City Council, starting out at Meriden, and terminating at the Coventry Canal Basin Heritage Centre, which isn't a million miles away from the site of the old factory prior to its bombing in the Second World War.

It was a glorious day, and naturally I went on JRW 405, my beloved Tiger 100. We congregated at Meriden, where Eddie duly turned up on his Kawasaki, and a good laugh was had by all. Why, I don't know, because there are far more deserving riders than me, but I was asked to lead the parade to Coventry. I was greatly honoured, of course, and we started off.

What we didn't know at this point, even though Eddie was all teeth and smiles, was that he had been diagnosed with terminal cancer, which he kept from us right to the very end. It was remarkable, really; even in

One out, one in

Top left: Eddie turned up at a Triumph gathering on his Kawasaki and thought it great fun. Just like Eddie.

Middle left: Eddie and Jim Lee at the Heart of England gathering, sharing a joke. Eddie chortling as usual.

Bottom left: Eddie and Jim Lee at the Coventry gathering of Triumph owners. A fine day was had by all – especially Eddie.

the hospice he was joking with the nurses, and when the duty vicar came visiting, Eddie said to him, "I'll be meeting your boss soon, got any messages for him?" What a really splendid chap he was.

On the run, one of my Triumph friends, Colin Smith, who, incidentally, was to take my place in the Royal Signals Display Team, and who rode back to camp at Ripon on the pillion of JRW 405 on many a cold foggy Sunday night, was in the parade riding his 'trick' Trials Tiger Cub. We had known each other since 1954, and on the parade ride into the city, Colin came up on my nearside, looked at me, then put his right arm around my shoulder and I put my left arm around his, and we rode along, a couple of ex-Triumph, ex-Signals Display Team blokes at peace with the world. Friendship is a wonderful thing when it lasts this length of time.

Stan Trowell shouted to me, "You got him the job you show him the ropes." So the friendship that Eddie and I shared began right from his first ride out on a Cub.

The author's long-time friend Colin Smith, who worked at Meriden and became the display team fitter after the author's demob.

The C range

Work quotas were met, and with Eddie getting into the swing of things riding with me, as I did with Joe, I found I was riding the three fifty, and now also the five hundreds, more than the Cubs. Joe and Bill Hemmings, together with Alan Armitt, seemed to stick to riding the tiddlers, and I can only ever remember seeing little Bill Hemmings using a big six fifty model to go home on. I guess Joe and Alan felt happy on the Cubs, so why do something different?

There was a policy that if another department, either the Experimental or Repair Departments, required the services of a tester, they were loaned out. So it was with Bert 'Whistle' Watmore when he came up to Experimental for the frame breaking stint at the Motor Industries Research Association proving ground, on the Belgium pavé. But now Bert was back, whistling and being his usual cheerful self. He was such a good-looking chap, with his shock of blonde hair, that the Publicity Department borrowed him for any shots it needed. He had some pictures taken on the works Tiger with one of the office girls, then some more with him on a Cub, and I remember one on a Tiger 100S, looking at a

The 1960 TR6R, showing clearly the early single crossbar frame.

Bert Watmore got the girl again. 1960 T110 publicity photo with one of the office girls.

lovely house in Showell Lane, at the top of Meriden Hill. Without a doubt, Bert was really photogenic.

As already mentioned, Edward Turner was a great one for keeping down unit costs, and this was demonstrated again in the C Range nacelle models sporting the rear enclosures. Everything, with the exception of the engine units and colours, was identical on the 3TA, 5TA, and T100A models, to facilitate universal cycle parts finished in primer and undercoat only. With the three fifty 3TA finish of Shell Blue Sheen, the five hundred 5TA of Ruby Red, and the T100A models in Black and Silver for 1961, it was relatively easy, once production requirements were known, to pass on instructions to the paint shop to finish a certain number of items in the colour required, with perhaps an extra ten in case of accidental damage at assembly.

Any spare items left over were sent up to the Service Department to use as either new or service exchange items. If there happened to be a specific item in a specific colour, they would go to the Spares Stores to be packed and sent out to various destinations. Sometimes, if there was a shortage of Ruby Red tanks, then either some Shell Blue, or black and silver items would be put through the paint shop again. This also explains the many enquiries I had over my twenty five years of restoring Triumphs from people saying they have found another colour under the top colour that had now worn or polished through. I've even had claims of patches of maroon being found under the black top coat on the frame.

Of the three models, the most similar were the 3TA three fifty and the 5TA Speed Twin, both on 6 volt AC lighting and ignition systems, with the Lucas PRS8 lighting and ignition switch housed in the nacelle top, along with the speedometer and two-inch diameter Lucas ammeter. The wiring looms were identical, as were all other ancillaries. Even the crankcase assembly, crankshaft and flywheel, camshafts and main bearings

Triumph Production Testers' Tales – from the Meriden Factory

RETAIL PRICES FOR GREAT BRITAIN & NORTHERN IRELAND

MODEL		BASIC RETAIL	PURCHASE TAX	TOTAL RETAIL
T20	TIGER CUB 200 c.c. O.H.V.	£123 0 0	£25 7 5	£148 7 5
T20T	TIGER CUB 200 c.c. O.H.V.	£134 0 0	£27 12 9	£161 12 9
T20SL	TIGER CUB 200 c.c. O.H.V.	£136 0 0	£28 1 0	£164 1 0
3TA	TWENTY-ONE 350 c.c. O.H.V. Twin	£194 0 0	£40 0 3	£234 0 3
5TA	SPEED TWIN 500 c.c. O.H.V. Twin	£202 0 0	£41 13 3	£243 13 3
T100A	TIGER 100 500 c.c. O.H.V. Twin	£208 0 0	£42 18 0	£250 18 0
6T	THUNDERBIRD 650 c.c. O.H.V. Twin	£212 0 0	£43 14 6	£255 14 6
T110	TIGER 110 650 c.c. O.H.V. Twin	£226 0 0	£46 12 3	£272 12 3
T120R	BONNEVILLE 120 650 c.c. O.H.V. Twin	£239 0 0	£49 5 11	£288 5 11
EXTRAS (When supplied with machine)				
Q.D. REAR WHEEL (All Twins)		£3 3 0	13 0	£3 16 0
PROP STAND (All Models) (Std. on T20T & T20S/L)		16 6	3 5	19 11
PILLION FOOTRESTS (All Models)		16 6	3 5	19 11
STEERING LOCK (except 3TA, 5TA & T100A)		11 0	2 3	13 3

All retail sales are subject to the Guarantee published in the Company's current catalogue and the prices quoted on this list are for Delivery Free of Charge at Dealer's premises. The prices quoted here operate on and after 1st September, 1960, and all previous lists are cancelled. The Company reserves the right to revise prices without prior notice and Purchase Tax also is subject to revision.

1st September, 1960

TRIUMPH ENGINEERING CO. LTD., Meriden Works, Allesley, COVENTRY
Ref. 600/60

The price list for the 1961 models, including purchase tax levied at about 21 per cent.

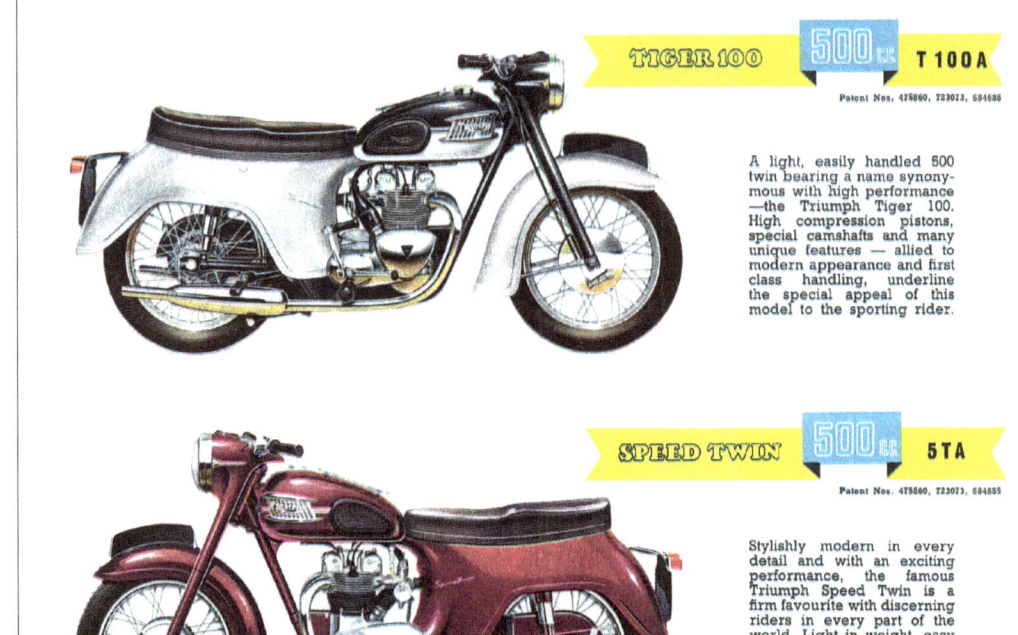

The 500 twins, sport and touring for 1961. The T100A in Black and Silver sheen, and the 5TA speed twin in Ruby Red.

remained identical, the only difference being the con-rods. On the three fifty they were cast iron, and because of the smaller pistons, the gudgeon pin diameter was identical to that of the Tiger Cub models. On the five hundred, however, the con-rods were H section RR56 alloy, a lot beefier and with gudgeon pins the same diameter as the six fifties. Both the cast iron and alloy rods used the same size 1.437in big-ends, and consequently the same E3706 big-end shells. Obviously, cylinder barrels were different as they had different-sized bores: 58.25mm for the three fifty, and 69mm for both five hundred models. This, of course, affected the cylinder heads and carburettors, with the three fifties having smaller combustion chambers and valves than the five hundreds.

The Amal Monobloc carburettors differed in choke size, also; the three fifty having something like a $^{25}/_{32}$in bore and the five hundreds nearer to one inch. The only remaining differences were the number of teeth on the gearbox or output sprocket, and the number of drive and driven plates in the clutch chain wheel. To cope with the extra power and torque, more plates in the clutch and stronger clutch springs were required.

That really just about covers the differences between the two 6 volt AC models. I knew 3TA three fifty owners who changed the required bits, ending up with what, to all intents and purposes, was a super-fast 3TA, three fifty, in brackets, five hundred twin. It was, of course, illegal in those days as the road tax paid was based on engine capacity, so, the bigger the engine, the more you paid. But nobody bothered, and because they could not be visually distinguished, their owners were not unduly worried. I remember going home one night on the A45, and a Shell Blue Sheen 3TA three fifty twin passed me doing about ninety. The bike absolutely flew by me, so I had no doubt that it had been converted.

The T100A was a different kettle of fish altogether to the two previously mentioned models, as it was more of a sports bike, harsher, and with E3134 form camshafts, 9:1 CR, nine to one compression ratio pistons, and, of course, the dreaded Energy-Transfer ignition system. To be fair, though, it wasn't until these models had done a fair few thousand miles that the problems with starting

The service bulletin 219, which enabled the conversion from energy transfer electrics to coil ignition on troublesome T100A models.

– similar to those that affected the T20 and T20SL models of Tiger Cub – occurred. We adopted a different approach on the Energy-Transfer T100A however, as simply fitting sleeves over the automatic advance and retard mechanism bob weight stop posts did not cure the misfiring.

It was four to six months later that the complaints began coming in from customers with T100A ET models, so the Service Department decided to do something to resolve the problem, once and for all. Don't get me wrong, some T100A models ran trouble-free on the Energy-Transfer system for years, but others were nothing but trouble from the word go, and it was these that were referred to the Service Repair Department by the Triumph dealerships for rework.

The only satisfactory solution was – from engine

Triumph Production Testers' Tales – from the Meriden Factory

number H22430 – to change the electrical system from Energy-Transfer to the same 6 volt AC system used on the 3TA and 5TA machines. The bikes would come back to the Repair Shop, where the Energy-Transfer parts were removed, including the entire alternator, comprising the rotor and stator, distributor, coil, nacelle switch, and wiring harness. Although many of the biggest problems were due to the type of system, the job was not done completely free-of-charge. An allowance was made on the replaced parts against the new items, and customers generally accepted this. Ultimately, the problem was rectified, and the T100A was suddenly a real little belter. It gave the best of both worlds: reliability, and a little five hundred that went like the clappers. Best of all, it started first kick! Incidentally, the time allowed to swop the wiring loom and parts was forty to sixty minutes.

All in all, the T100A became a very quick, small, sporty twin, which would easily top ninety miles per hour, the 5TA Speed Twin would do eighty plus miles per hour, and the 3TA three fifty seventy plus miles per hour. Altogether, a nice little collection, especially when prices were £234 for the 3TA, £243 for the 5TA, and £250 for the T100A, just a £16 difference overall.

There was still one problem, however. When out riding the little three fifty twin on a nice sunny day, pootling down the Mile with your brain in neutral, you were fair game for Percy Tait. He was still out and about on Bonnevilles, testing something or other, so it

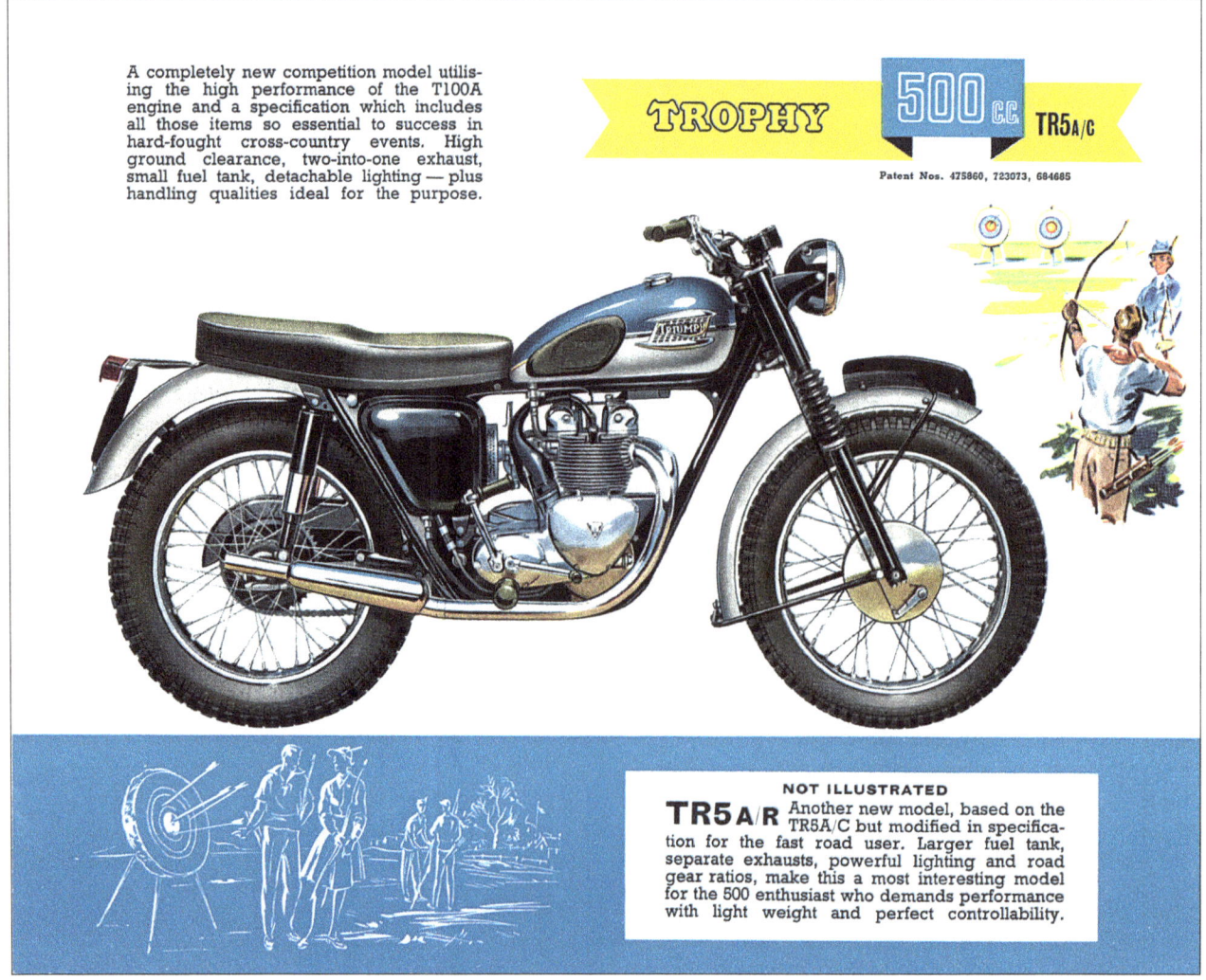

The 'Cubby' 1960 5TAC, commonly called the US Trophy. No battery, direct lighting, and energy transfer ignition. Mainly used for 'cow-tracking' in the desert.

The C range

The later TR5AC with sports engine had a high turn of speed. Its two-into-one exhaust made a beautiful noise.

wasn't uncommon for him to come from behind, out of the sun at a high rate of knots, and buzz you, really, really close. It was enough to give you heart failure. He probably could have touched you he was that close; very scary.

Sometimes he would call at Tubby's cafe, just the other side of the Meriden island from the village centre, and wait for his arch rivals, usually led by the sidecar racer, Chris Vincent. They were just about as bad as one another: Chris, a high speed mileage BSA tester, and Percy, a high speed mileage Triumph tester, both racers and both utterly barmy. It just wasn't safe for the rest of us to be out there when they were about.

The two models announced for 1961 were the TR5AR and the TR5AC, both primarily for the American market. They were the forerunners of the naked T100SS, due to replace the little T100A for 1962.

A TR5AC had been running around on a works number for some time, acquiring mileage, and although I hadn't seen it, the Publicity Department had taken some photographs of it.

The other TR5 model was the AR, which was essentially a road-going model of the AC. If I remember correctly, only the TR5AC made it to production. The AR was for use on the road but, as the Tiger 100SC was just around the corner for 1962, I don't suppose it seemed worth it for one season. I know that I never saw or rode one during my time on test.

The Americans did not want the nacelle models anymore, they were more interested in the separate headlamp, gaitered fork legs, no bathtubs, and sports mudguards: to all intents and purposes, a mini T120 or TR6 Trophy.

I still adore the nacelle in its 1950 form. I think when Jack Wickes drew it he had a touch of genius, and it was included in the 1949 line-up to coincide with the introduction of the 6T Thunderbird launch. It was again a cost-saving exercise, because the chromium-plated

Triumph Production Testers' Tales – from the Meriden Factory

The 1959 alloy-engined Tiger 100 was probably the prettiest of the last single down-tube models.

Finished in Black and Ivory to match its bigger brother, the 1959 Tiger 110.

The C range

The 1959 Tiger 110, identical in every way to the smaller-engined Tiger 100 except for the 650 capacity.

Drive-side view of 1959 Black and Ivory Tiger 110.

Speed Twin and Tiger 100 – and 3T, for that matter – petrol tanks, with the instrument panel carrying the inspection light, light switch, ammeter, and oil gauge were actually going rusty before the machines were even sold.

The switch, speedo, and ammeter needed to be

Triumph Production Testers' Tales – from the Meriden Factory

The Daddy – a 1959 T120 Bonneville with remote-float carburettor setup and finished in Tangerine and Pearl Grey.

Timing-side view of the 1959 T120 Bonneville.

grouped together neatly in some sort of housing on top of the forks, but had be stylish. There was now a visual tell-tale button on the pressure release valve at the bottom of the timing cover, which activated under engine oil pressure when the motor was started, so money was saved on the 0-100psi oil gauge.

In its slightly later form from the end of 1951 for the 1952 season, a nice little Lucas underslung parking light was included, which complemented the whole job. Originally, in 1949, the headlamp was the smaller, 6.5in diameter with separate reflector, glass, and bulb holders. After 1951, the aperture for the headlamp was increased slightly to 7in to take the new Lucas 700 pre-focus light unit which had better lighting properties.

The C range

The beautiful lines of the nacelle and chrome petrol tank on a 1949 Tiger 100, with the original iron motor and internal rocker-drains from the cylinder head.

Jack Wickes at the Fillongley Triumph gathering. Note the original Triumph logo tie.

Jack's touch of magic, the flowing lines of the 1955 Speed Twin nacelle and petrol tank styling bands. Note the Lucas PR58 switch and underslung pilot light.

Many times other companies have attempted to emulate the Triumph nacelle, but no one has come even close to the beautiful Wickes lines. The nacelle continued from its introduction for the 1949 season to 1962 in pre-unit form, then a slightly modified version on both 3TA and 5TA up to 1966, the same as the unit 6T Thunderbird when it finally phased out.

Jack Wickes was probably the most gifted man I ever came into contact with. His ties with my family go right back to the early 1930s, when he and my father, as young men, lived next door to each other on the Holbrook Lane, opposite the White and Poppe World War 1 munitions factory. The name of the semi-detached property was Park Villas, because on the other side of the road was a big public park. My father, his elder sister, mother and father, lived in the right-hand property, whilst Jack, his sister Ethel, mother and father, who worked at the Triumph factory in Coventry, lived in the left-hand side of the property.

Jack's Dad was a Manager at Triumph, and young Jack, working there as a Draughtsman, got to come home each night on a works bike. My Dad had a five hundred hand-change Triumph already, and one night Jack mentioned that some works competition machines

Triumph Production Testers' Tales – from the Meriden Factory

A 1951 all-alloy Tiger 100, the first year for this die-cast alloy top end.

were being overhauled and sold off afterwards. Did my Dad want him to put his name down for one?

It was 1935, and the sports machines were the 5/4 and 5/5, both five hundred singles but with the new positive stop foot change gearbox. Dad jumped at the chance: being in full employment as a carpenter and joiner, working on a row of semi-detached houses, putting in the complete woodwork would take him months, and he required reliable transport.

The machine Dad ended up with was ridden by Alan Jeffries of Shipley, one of Triumph's top dealers, and coincidentally, the father of Tony Jeffries who worked for a short while in the Repair Shop as an apprentice in 1965, just before I moved on to the staff in the Service Office.

Top view of the 1952 6T Thunderbird Blackbird and the MC2 SU carburettor, which gave credence to Edward Turner's '70mpg at 70mph' statement.

The C range

Jack and Dad lost touch when they both married, but I always remember Dad talking to me about Jack's wonderful oil paintings and his talent as a pianist. They hadn't seen each other for twenty years until the night I went to Jack's house on the Baginton Road to see about my job at Meriden in 1954.

One of the things I do remember Jack telling me was how, on the night of the big Coventry raid by German bombers in November 1940, he could see the city burning, so jumped on his motorcycle and sidecar, sped off to the factory, and saved all the drawings from the Drawing Office in the main factory building before it received several direct hits. He went out of the city and parked up on the Tamworth Road, a high vantage point above an area known as Corley Rocks, where he could see the entire city burning. He sat up there all night until the all-clear sounded, having saved a lot of important technical stuff.

This came up in conversation one night when I went over to his home in Kenilworth in 1996. Sadly, Jack's wife, Meg, had passed away, so he was living on his own, and as it was the annual Triumph 'do' at Fillongley, I went over to pick him up. We came from his house in Kenilworth to Coventry, and then out of the city on the Tamworth Road, passing the exact spot where he had sat all those years ago.

Again in 1996 was the anniversary of Johnny Allen breaking the speed record (unofficially 1956). I couldn't believe it was forty years ago that the streamliner stood in the factory on show, whilst Johnny, his wife and Jack Wilson, the tuner from Texas, were looked after and feted by the factory bosses.

It was so long ago, but the National Motorcycle Museum at Bickenhill put on a super show, and although Johnny Allen was no longer with us, his wife and Jack Wilson attended. It was a very special event, attended by Triumph owners and enthusiasts from all over the world with extended celebrations carrying on into the evening.

Ex-Meriden men and wives at the Johnny Allen celebration in 1996 at the National Motorcycle Museum. Left to right: Dennis Peacock, ex-chief tester; June Nelson; John Nelson; Fred Swift; 'Skip' Peacock; Percy Tait; Jock Copland (obscured); Dave Green; the author and Jack Wickes (seated).

Triumph Production Testers' Tales – from the Meriden Factory

The 1960 West Coast TR7B US model with high-rise bars and twin upswept exhausts. This has the remote-float carburettors and the early single crossbar frame.

The TR7B, drive-side view. The quickly detachable headlamp plug can clearly be seen.

This was held at Stoneleigh at the NAC showground in one of its big hospitality suites.

We had a questions and answers forum for a couple of hours with Percy, Norman Hyde, John Nelson and myself fielding all manner of technical questions from the stage. It was a bit like being back in the Service

The C range

Timing-side view of the US East Coast T120 competition, called the US TR7B. Note the silver-painted cylinder barrel. Remote-float carburettors were the spec.

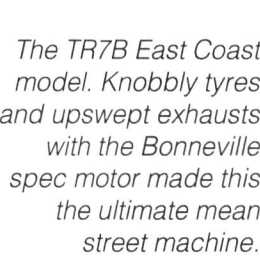

The TR7B East Coast model. Knobbly tyres and upswept exhausts with the Bonneville spec motor made this the ultimate mean street machine.

Triumph Production Testers' Tales – from the Meriden Factory

Tailpipe showing mute and pop-rivet fixing, loaded and ready for firing out.

Department, really, and a damn good weekend was had by all.

The TR5AR and A/C models were essentially naked versions of the T100A without rear enclosures, and had the sports gaitered forks with separate headlight. The A/C Enduro had downswept two-into-one exhausts on the timing side into a single Cub-sized silencer. Both models had the high-rise bars for the American markets (the road model with standard ratio gear cluster and road tyres), whilst the competition model had wide ratio gear clusters and knobbly tyres. There was no battery as it ran on Energy-Transfer ignition, and had direct lighting.

The unusual thing about these models was that no prices were announced, nor any spares lists or service books printed. As far as I am aware, they all went to America's east and west coasts. If they went to the east, the distributor was the Triumph Corporation, Baltimore, and in the west it was Johnson Motors, Pasadena, California. Both of these big concerns had their own aftermarket kits that were fitted to standard machines, thus making the standard, straight-from-the-factory US- version into something a little more exotic.

Some time ago, during a conversation I had whilst judging the concours at the 50th Anniversary celebration of the Bonneville at Gaydon, I was asked if I had ever heard of a TR7. The only TR7 model I knew of was the seven fifty capacity twin of the early 1970s, so I replied "Yes, it was the oil in frame model." "No," said the chap "this is a 1960 Bonneville TR7, which has a leaping Tiger painted on the front number plate with flames coming out of its backside." He told me it was genuine, and just as it had come from the factory in 1960. I told him that there wasn't a cat in hell's chance that ET would allow something like that to come out of Meriden; besides, I was on test then and I'm sure I would have remembered a front number plate that had a picture of a tiger with its arse on fire!

After a little research on the American models, it transpires that this was an aftermarket gimmick by the American distributor. There was also a model nomenclature I knew nothing of, and that was the 1960 TR7! It was called the West Coast competition Bonneville US TR7B, so even I learnt something new. It transpired that for the 1960 season, the T120R and T120C models were re-designated TR7A and TR7B by both the Triumph Corporation and Johnson Motors. It only lasted for a year, though, and went back to the well-known T120R and T120C for 1961. Upon reflection, I suppose the chap was half-right, and I was half-wrong.

My old friend Bill Letts, one of the most senior testers, reminded me some years ago of a particular problem with the C range 350 and 500 twins, although I never did experience it. Due to a rather acute steering head angle, the front forks were very upright compared with the earlier pre-unit framed models up to 1959. This caused a very disconcerting problem to occur with the steering, especially if, for some reason, you had only one hand on the bars and were travelling over a rippled road surface at the same time. The bike's head would begin to shake violently, in other words, the handlebars would oscillate very rapidly from side to side, so quickly you could barely hold on with one hand, and too fast to allow you to get your other hand on to at least try and control the shaking. Bill said it happened to him twice, on both occasions on the same stretch of tarmac, and roughly at the same speed.

It was brought to the notice of the powers-that-be, and a slight alteration to the frame head angle stopped the problem altogether. Needless to say, Bill never took his hand off the bars again on that particular stretch of road to, as he put it, "scratch my nose or bugger-all else."

Jokes still abounded around the section, and on the odd occasion, there would be an ear-splitting bang that echoed around the Finishing Shop, eliciting a chorus of yells from the various sections allied to the main production track. The bang was usually followed by a choice oath, then silence. The cause of this was usually Westy or Eddie, who would watch to see if a tester had prepared a coil ignition twin for test, and, when his back was turned, quickly swap the plug leads from one side to the other. This would put the ignition timing out by some 180 degrees, which meant that the spark ignited the petrol-air mixture on the wrong cylinder when the exhaust valve was wide open. They chose to do this on the coil ignition fired twins such as the 3TA, 5TA or 6T Thunderbird, because the intensity of the spark, generated by battery, contact breaker and ignition coil, is just as strong at kick-start speed as when the engine is running. Thus, an explosion through the silencer is assured.

This also caused another problem for the unfortunate person who had got his bike ready to go out, because for 1961, exhaust mutes were used to lessen the exuberant bark that came from the beautiful Burgess silencers. The mute was a conical, fluted device, secured in the silencer tail pipe end by a pop rivet, and had the effect of diffusing the exhaust pulses, making the exhaust note more 'splashy.' Whether it was an Experimental recommendation to also aid running, I don't know, or possibly it was something to do with noise pollution back in the early 1960s.

Anyway, all models, including the inoffensive standard Cub, had them. They were awful little things, about eight inches long, tapered, and closed at one end, but with a split along their length. The fluting provided a certain amount of springiness, and, being slightly larger diameter outside than the inside dimension of the silencer tail pipe they were to fit into, a sharp tap with a rubber mallet drove them in, pointed end first, until they were flush with the end of the tail pipe. They were fitted on the exhaust section, via a hole through the bottom of the tail pipe, made by a 1/8in twist drill, about half an inch from the end, through which a 1/8in alloy pop rivet was fixed to secure the mute in the silencer.

The mute, of course, was the first thing to go when a crossed lead explosion took place. They would skitter across the Finishing Shop floor, invariably ending up in some awkward place that couldn't be reached. With a resigned shrug, the unlucky tester would set about removing his plates ready to fit the next bike for test, and would then have to write on the test card 'Machine not tested, refit exhaust mute.' Needless to say, while all this was going on, the perpetrator would be well out of the way, somewhere on the test route. The trick was, as I had learnt to my cost, not to leave your bike unattended once you had prepared it to go out.

Another situation to be wary of was if riding behind someone on a 3TA or 5TA. Knowing you were there, several yards behind, and travelling at about 50 miles an hour, the rider would switch off the ignition and then

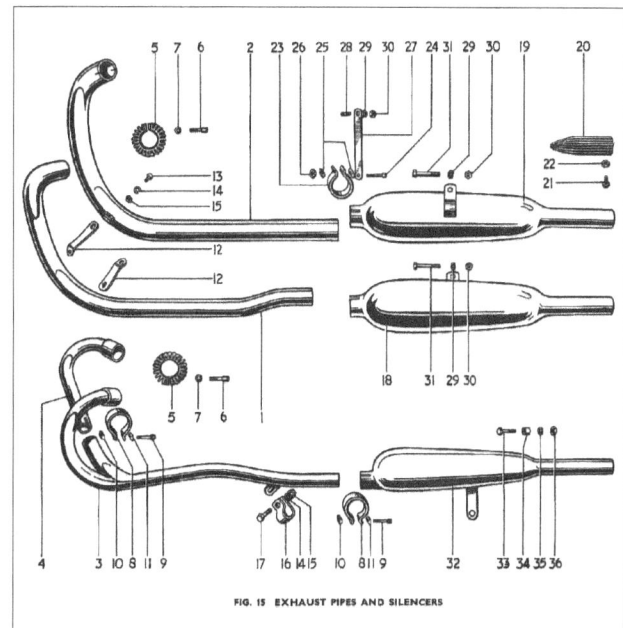

The exhaust system for the UK, showing the dreaded 'mute' – item number 20.

quickly switch it back on with the throttle held open. This caused the same big explosion, and the mutes shot out, straight at you. It was dangerous but, back then, a fairly typical prank.

Bill's story

One of the testers, Bill Letts, or 'Lettsy,' as he was known, was a close friend that I owed a lot to. He died some five or so years ago, but was also big chums with Norris Harrison.

Bill came from a small village called Cubbington on the outskirts of Leamington Spa, whilst Norris came from Leamington itself. From Leamington, through Stoneleigh and on to the A45, then towards Birmingham brought BOTH to Meriden and the factory. All-in-all, a journey of approximately ten or eleven miles.

Norris was a big man, some six feet three or four inches tall, but Bill, although slightly shorter, was half as broad again. His father was the village policeman in Cubbington, and he was big, too. Bill showed me a photograph of his father in uniform, standing with one hand holding his pushbike. He had his police cape slung over one shoulder, and the bicycle was the tallest I'd ever seen; you'd need a step ladder to get on it.

Bill left Meriden in 1971, and moved to a little place called Wrentham, near Wangford in Suffolk. By 1971, he said the writing was on the wall, and he couldn't see things lasting much longer, with the advent of the oil in the frame models, and all the problems they brought with them. So he and his wife, Beryl, upped sticks and went to live in a lovely spot by the Suffolk coast town of Southwold. Bill had his pension, but being into making wrought iron gates and welding, he managed to earn money repairing gear on the fishing boats at Lowestoft, just a couple of minutes down the road.

As a matter of fact, he made a pair of lovely gates for the entrance to Covehithe church, which Gloria and I stood admiring some years ago on a visit to Southwold for a few days' holiday.

Bill and I kept in touch, and many times have I travelled down the A14 and A11, then on to his lovely little cottage, but none so sad as the last journey I made to his funeral. The memories came flooding back during that drive, of our time together, both on Production Test, and later in the Service Repair Shop when little Stan Whitcomb came in from the cold and Bill came up to take his place.

When we had our tea and lunch breaks, because I had moved back onto the fitting bench in the Repair Shop at the end of 1962, just in time for the new unit six fifties to begin coming in under warranty, Bill and I used to sit and talk about archery, Bill's sport.

I remember one day, when we were still both on test, Bill arrived one morning with what we, the other testers, thought was a set of fishing rods slung across his back. He burst through the rubber doors on his going home bike, and, after he had clocked in, removed the item from its cloth bag to show us a beautiful five foot, five inch long bow. During the course of the morning, he told us it was one of his wife's bows, a Yeoman Lion that he had to make a slight alteration to concerning the knocking point (the point at which the arrow fits onto the bow string). It was for her to use that coming weekend, and I was amazed to learn that Beryl was, in fact, the National Ladies Field Archery Champion.

To say I was impressed is an understatement because he also told us she went to her accountancy job on her Ariel 500 Huntmaster twin. Phew!

Field archery differs from target archery greatly. It's a more instinctive style of shooting rather than employing the exactness of a micro-adjustable sight to shoot at a target at a known distance. Usually, target archery tournaments are so many dozen arrows at, say, one hundred yards, so many dozen at eighty, so many dozen at sixty, finally ending at so many dozen at forty. The target is divided up from the Bulls Eye or Gold, through red, blue, and white. There isn't much that looks more impressive on a summer's day than a line of archers facing a line of targets a hundred yards away, on full draw, ready to loose. Agincourt springs to mind, but field archery is a different ballgame altogether.

Firstly, there's no sunlit flat field, shooting with sights over known distances, checking after each shot with a pair of powerful binoculars to see where your arrow has landed. Field archery takes place in a wood or a forest, shooting around bushes and under the low branches of trees, over unknown distances with a bare bow, and no sights.

The targets are usually straw bales, with small animal silhouettes pinned to them. Whoever lays out the field course must be experienced, as arrow flight paths must not cross each other so that there is no danger of accidental injury. It's all very complicated but immense fun, and is where, with Bill and Beryl, I learnt the ancient art of handling a bow.

Anyway, come lunchtime, we all crowded round whilst eating our sandwiches as Bill, with such deceptive ease, bent the bow against one leg, and slid the looped end of the bowstring into its groove at the tip of the limb. After one or two test pulls, we watched in silence as he pointed out the main features of the bow, and told us of its power and performance.

On the other side of the main gangway which ran down from the main offices through the Finishing Shop and on down to the rubber doors, through which we exit onto the drive, was the Packing Department. Up in the far corner, about forty yards away, stood huge rolls of corrugated cardboard, about four or five feet in diameter, stacked right up to the girders of the factory roof.

Bill picked up one of his own arrows, and, in one smooth movement, drew back the bow until the string touched his right cheek just beneath his eye, then let fly. In swift succession, he drew back five more times, and five arrows flew across the Finishing Shop into the top roll of cardboard. You could have covered the space they landed with a pocket handkerchief. It was amazing, and

The sports Bonneville T120R. Early frame, no twin seat strap, remote-float carburettors, tachometer and road tyres. Very desirable.

Triumph Production Testers' Tales – from the Meriden Factory

TR6C scrambler. The one we all liked, even on knobbly tyres.

The West Coast TR6C, a rorty twin, or desert sledge. Note the scrambler rear tyre for fast off-road use. Also note the silver cylinder barrel, coded 'V' in spare parts catalogues.

Bill's story

The West Coast TR6R. Achingly beautiful and such a favourite with all the testers.

we had never seen anything like it. I was hooked, as you might say.

So it was that Bill sparked my interest in serious archery; unfortunately, Bill's exhibition did not go unnoticed by Tom Cashmore, the Packing Department Foreman, who nearly had a fit when he saw the six arrows protruding from the roll of cardboard. Nothing came of it, however, and the incident provided endless opportunity for discussion each morning as those six little holes looked down on us during our tea breaks.

Bill used to like the American TR6R, or the TR6C with high-rise West Coast bars and twin upswept exhausts. They made a lovely noise – no mutes in these models, thank you very much. They were a very nice little bike, and some say that if you got a good one, they were equal to the Bonneville for performance, but with less bother. Apart from the high-rise handlebars, revolution counter, straight through silencers, and over the seat strap, they were the same as the UK and general export models.

One day, Bill, Norris, Charlie, and Jock, my old army pal, were returning to the factory from a spell of rest and recuperation down the Mile. I was out on a standard Cub – why, I don't know. As I started to climb Meriden Hill at a heady forty miles per hour, past the Queen's Head pub on my left, I heard a noise, almost like a low-flying, old aircraft. "Maybe an old Douglas Dakota DC3," I thought to myself, low on its approach to Elmdon (now Birmingham International Airport). But, no, it wasn't. The four returning testers came past me at about seventy

Triumph Production Testers' Tales – from the Meriden Factory

miles an hour, all on TR6R models, and all close together, with the straight throughs bellowing, what a noise!

The Bonneville T120C, with its high-rise bars, twin separate upswept pipes, silencers and knobbly tyres was another very moreish model, by which I mean the more you wound it on and heard the glorious noise, the more you wanted to.

With Bonnevilles figuring largely in my last thirty years of restoration work, putting people's dream back on the road, the problem was always with carburation. It was a devil to get right, especially if the mixing chamber bodies were worn. It was no good to opt for new slides, they still rattled around in the bores of the mixing chambers, allowing unmetered air past them.

When I began restoring in 1980, the Monobloc carburettors were not being re-manufactured, so it meant that to rectify any wear in the bodies, they had to be bored out, and oversize throttle valves fitted. This was not always a success as sometimes the process of boring left ridges in the actual bore, and the induction suck against the throttle slide made it stick to the bore. Most unnerving when you came to shut off and continued motoring instead.

The main pleasure of the new machines at Meriden was the ease with which you could set up and balance the twin carburettors, something sadly lacking for a good few years. Now, of course, with the new re-manufactured carburettors that are available, that ease of setting up has returned, and indeed, a good pair of carburettors can make a Bonneville. If the carburettors are rubbish in a superb rebuild, the bike will run like rubbish.

On test, we didn't have any special tools, we just depended on hand-eye coordination. The easiest way to set up twin carburettors is to slacken off all cable adjusters, then start the machine. Set the tickover so that there's an even exhaust note from each silencer, and, if required, wind in each pilot mixture screw until the tickover becomes lumpy and rich, then wind out again until tickover becomes even and smooth. Reset the tickover speed on the throttle stop screws so that the exhaust beat from each silencer is equal.

Stop the motor and adjust the individual adjusters so that the slides lift off the throttle stops in unison. To do this, lean over the bike from the timing side, right hand on the twist grip, middle finger of the left hand on the timing side carburettor slide face at the same time, peering into the driveside carburettor at its slide. Now, by gently opening the throttle and co-ordinating hand-eye, adjust the individual cable adjusters so the slides lift in unison. Nip up the adjuster lock nuts, then take up any excess cable slack on the main cable adjuster that comes from the twist grip. Job done.

All very easy after you've done a few hundred, but not so easy with rain running down your neck because the factory workers in the Finishing Shop did not appreciate being gassed by the prolonged running of engines in their working environment. The rectification chaps had flexible exhaust extractor pipes which they had pushed over the end of the silencers, and this got rid of the exhaust gasses through vents in the factory roof.

It was Percy who originally showed me how to set twin carburettors the easy way. I'd not had much experience of them, as they weren't around before I went into the army in 1957, and it was only when I came out and went into Experimental, working on the prototype Bonneville, that I came into contact with them on a regular basis. This was one of the checks we carried out on the Monster when Percy arrived back for lunch from his morning run down to Apex corner at the bottom of the newly-opened M1 motorway. Percy had a few years' experience of twin carburettors due to racing Triumph twins with, of course, the twin carburettor cylinder heads, or in the case of the earlier motors, the twin carburettor inlet manifolds.

The single downtube frame models from 1956 to 1958 were offered with an optional high performance kit, listed in the back of the appropriate year and model spare parts catalogue. With the introduction of the Delta splayed port cylinder head, firstly for the close pitched fin engine of the pre-unit Tiger 100, then for the six fifty Tiger 110 for clubman racing, we thought it looked quite ugly, especially as the Tiger 100 engine was so beautiful.

Bill continued to talk to me during breaks, down the Mile in our favourite rest area in Somers Lane, in the cafe, and during our lunch hour. In the nice weather, we sat out on the front lawn eating our sandwiches, small pieces of which we fed to our tame crow, George. One day, Bill began to recount a tale so vividly that it has lived in my memory ever since. He split the telling of it into instalments, which continued over a week or more, and this, I suppose, made it all the more exciting. It was the real story of the English archers at Agincourt, and Bill's prowess at storytelling, with arms waving and the depth of passion that he imparted, meant that we couldn't get enough of it.

It's a story that's been told and retold in word and on film over the years, but Bill's account has always been the one I've tended to hope is the most accurate. It went like this. King Henry's archers numbered some five thousand men, who had been on the march for two

The author's 1952 Tiger 100 die-cast alloy engine. A thing of beauty. Drive-side view.

The author's engine, fitted with original twin carburettor and remote-float, mounted on the front of a one gallon oil tank.

The timing-side view of the 1952 Tiger 100 alloy engine. Not much in the way of motorcycle engines look better than this.

Close-up of author's 1952 alloy engine and twin carburettor setup.

weeks or more in October. They were wet, hungry, and exhausted when they arrived at the road to Calais.

For the last four days, the army had eaten only what it could forage from the land. The archers had to get to Calais or starve, but the problem was that the whole of the French army now stood in their way, and they were not about to step aside and let Henry and his men depart.

The French were only one and a half miles away, and the Englishmen could see them; the glittering array of armour was enough to chill the blood. Even the humblest archer knew they were at least fifty thousand men short of being able to give the French a good scrap.

The rain made everything sodden, and with only woollen blankets to wrap themselves in, and woollen tunics and trousers, the wet and cold had seeped through to their bones, sapping strength and, more importantly, hope after the long march to the coast. A large number of men were suffering badly with stomach upsets, and they found it better to leave off their woollen trousers, going naked from the waist down. Despair and despondency could be read in their eyes as their Captains walked amongst them, cajoling, bullying and threatening the men, trying to lift their spirits for the confrontation they knew was about to take place.

The Captains handed out to each archer two sheaves of 'war arrows', each containing two dozen shafts. The archers, now with purpose, examined each shaft closely, and, placing their woollen cloaks on the sodden, muddy grass, laid out the arrows in methodical

Triumph Production Testers' Tales – from the Meriden Factory

order. The shafts were made by an army contractor, and although good in the main, required a final inspection as each archer knew his life depended on them.

As well as the contractor's arrows, every archer had two dozen of his own, very carefully made shafts, against which the contractor's shafts were assessed. Usually, the war arrows would be too thick, too heavy, or too stiff, which meant they would fly out of the bow differently, so the purpose of this assessment was to group the shafts. The first thick shaft would be released in order to note its flight and where it landed, and correctional sighting employed to ensure they landed more-or-less in the same place.

Usually, an archer sorted his arrows into three piles. The first pile consisted of light arrows with shaved feathers; these were the long-range boys. They had bodkin points, and could penetrate plate armour at eight to ten score paces, or one hundred and eighty to two hundred yards.

The second pile of arrows were standard shafts, of planed pine some twenty seven to twenty eight inches long and the diameter of a modern-day pencil. Their heart-shaped heads would not penetrate armour, except at close range.

The third pile consisted of rejects, not to be used except in dire emergency, and these were either warped because of the exceptional wet conditions, or their fletchings (feathers) were not properly fixed to the shaft, so the arrows would not go where they were aimed.

The bows themselves were transported or carried in waxed cloth bags, which provided weatherproofing to a degree. Some were made of English yew, and some of Spanish yew, but all were six feet, six inches long and one and three quarters of an inch thick through the handle and mid-section.

Archers knew that shorter bows could cast the arrows faster, but longer bows tended not to break in the heat of battle. The English yew long bow was more reliable than shorter bows, and the last thing you wanted was for your bow to break in the midst of a French charge.

Archers had pouches slung from their belts, in which they carried a lump of beeswax mixed with tallow, which they used to wax the bow limbs and string, then burnished these very carefully with the palm of the hand. All the while that this preparation was going on, the English could hear the French, laughing and making merry, as they were just four bow shots away.

I was always amazed at Bill's storytelling prowess, be it the tale I am recounting now, or Walt Disney's cartoons, when he would laugh and wildly fling his arms about when describing Wile-e-Coyote chasing the Roadrunner, using his Acme rocket-powered roller skates.

And it wasn't just me who listened intently as he spoke about Agincourt, so did Norris, Charlie, and Jock, munching away on our sandwiches, all ears as he told his story. Obviously, there were many questions that the non-archers amongst us wanted answers to, which I knew but dare not interject as Bill patiently explained to their satisfaction the queries they raised.

Bill would then resume, picking up the strand of the storyline with "Now, where was I? Ah, I know." I am recounting this episode from memory, trying not to miss out any of his tale, but it *has* been fifty years, so bear with me.

The French knew how much Henry's army had suffered on its long, wet march to the channel, and in their minds had already defeated their English cousins. The French battle plan was very simple; they just had to walk, encased in their fine armour, into the midst of the English mob, and hack them to bits. In this respect, Bill thought that the French either had a mental block, or had deliberately chosen to attribute the terrible lesson the English archers had inflicted on them at Crecy to a fluke.

Popular rumours circulated many years later that the captured English archers had had their middle and index fingers chopped off so that they could never again draw a long bow. This may or may not be true, but from it developed the old two-fingered salute, which basically says, I've still got mine, up yours.

Most of the French were noblemen from the highest born families of the land, who refused even to consider that the dirty English rabble were their equal.

Henry's army lined up, a thousand yards long and six men deep, one thousand knights and men-at-arms, and five thousand archers. The line stretched across the valley, with woods on each side, and ploughed fields, slippery and sodden after days of rain, in-between the two armies. The trouserless English soldiers were walking ankle-deep in clinging mud, so knew that the French foot soldiers would find it impossible, in their armour, to move at any sort of steady pace.

Watching Bill speak, I could just imagine him standing there with his bow. Although just a smidgen over six feet tall, he was immensely broad of shoulder, with a barrel chest. I actually saw him in later years, when we were both in the Repair Shop, lift a bike onto a workshop bench for a laugh. He was a proper countryman and proud of being so; a typical archer in Henry's army, or so I like to imagine.

Bill's story

In the 1940s film *Henry V*, starring Sir Lawrence Olivier, the French charged on horseback over sweeping green fields to the music of Walton. Not so. The later Kenneth Branagh version was more accurate, showing the hand-to-hand fighting in the mud in all its brutality.

When the French advanced, it looked as if a great metal wave was crashing toward the English. Then it was realised that only a very few of the French knights were on horseback; most were on foot, and there wasn't a man-at-arms or a company of archers among them. All the knights from all of the great noble families of France, were walking, in armour, through the thick, sticky mud. It just didn't make sense.

The Captains were now running up and down the lines of English archers, yelling instructions. Bill reckoned that many of the French foot soldiers must have died from a heart attack, given the effort of walking in full armour across the ploughed field.

The Englishmen waited and waited until the French reached the four score pace distance, then, on the command of their Captains, five thousand bows loosed five thousand arrows toward the struggling Frenchmen. With awful efficiency, the archers knocked, drew and loosed arrow after arrow. The noise of the bows, the noise of the arrows flying, the screams of dying men, and the terrible sound of arrow heads striking plate armour, Bill brought it all alive. The sky between the opposing sides was suddenly black with arrows, and as each one struck square, it penetrated the French armour. And even if it didn't, it still struck with enough force to fell the target as if the soldier had received a huge blow from a sledgehammer.

A visit to Warwick Castle during my school years bore testament to the power of the English longbow. I remember standing in front of a thick wooden door, splintered by arrows fired from these fearsome weapons that reigned supreme until the advent of the firearm. When you consider that the draw weight of my modern magnesium and carbon fibre bow is only forty pounds at twenty eight inches, the longbow draw weight, at the same length of arrow, was eighty to ninety pounds. The average English archer must have been built like Bill, and not like me.

The archers' fight at Agincourt lasted about twenty minutes, and five thousand archers shot as fast and as accurately as they could. Nearly a million arrows had hit a French target over an area a thousand yards long and ten yards deep; a hundred arrows landing in every square yard. The English had to administer the coup de grâce to stricken men in armour, usually by inserting a dagger through a handy eye slit in the helmet, or cracking the skull with a maul. The French were dealt a stinging blow to their aristocracy, every noble family in the land losing fathers and sons. Bill reckoned that the French have never forgiven us to this day, and, in his words, would "kick us in the nuts if given half a chance."

I remember Bill with great fondness, and will always be indebted to him for introducing me to the wonderful world of bows and arrows, especially through his stories.

We continued to test throughout the autumn, and as the weather got colder and wetter, Management decided, in its wisdom, that more suitable riding gear was required to contend with the approaching winter.

The waxed cotton suits were okay, but, after a time, when the newness had worn off, water would seep through the stitched seams, especially around the crotch area. Although we all treated our suits with the proofing wax supplied, nothing seemed to work. If it was a rainy morning, you would have ridden to work in the wet, and then been out half a dozen times in the morning. This usually meant that you went through the afternoon and the ride home with soggy knickers. Not very comfortable, I can tell you.

Belstaff came to our rescue with a jacket and over-trouser set made of thick PVC, with electrically welded seams and a thick, quilted lining. One morning it was so cold that it made the PVC stiff, so stiff I couldn't bend down or even kneel next to a bike. We called them Mr Michelin Men suits. They certainly did keep you warm and dry, though sometimes it was all you could do to bend your knees enough to get your feet on the footrests. The only other problem was the heavy trousers, we had to have special braces just to keep them up. These trousers were so stiff, you could take them off, and, if you balanced them just right, they would stand up on their own. They were made to sit in all day on a bike and keep you warm and dry, which they certainly did. When indoors, however, even with the jacket undone, you soon began to overheat. Never mind, they did what they were meant to, all day long.

A lot of us with young families used the old white towelling nappy around our necks to soak up any water that may have got past the riding suit collar. These we would take off at lunchtime and spread out on a nearby radiator to dry out ready for the afternoon stint. It was nice to go out on your first bike after lunch with a warm, dry nappy around your neck.

The six fifties

The six fifty cubic capacity twins were split into four models, the 6T Thunderbird, the Tiger 110 (although this was about to come to an end when the new 1962 models began coming down the line), the TR6 Trophy and, of course, the T120 Bonneville.

With the first 1959 Bonnevilles looking exactly the same as the 6T, T100 and T100 of that year (except the new model sported the snazzy pastel colours now desired in the US), the Americans were nevertheless a little reticent about buying it. It certainly was the quickest thing to come out of Meriden, but its appearance did not convey to them the rugged sportiness they craved. Beautiful as it was, it looked old hat, with its deep valanced mudguards and nacelle. It simply did not look sporty. Strangely, all these years later, it's the 1959 Bonneville models that are the most sought-after and command the highest prices.

At the Gaydon Bonneville 50th Anniversary, there were, of course, the majority of the surviving Meriden men, as well as the children and families of Edward Turner and Jack Wickes. John Nelson, my old Service Department boss, and I were conscripted to carry out the thankless task of concours judging. When I finally got there on the Saturday morning, I'd never seen so many Bonnevilles all in one place, even in the Finishing Shop at Meriden. What struck me immediately, though, was that there were so very few 1959 models. Duplex framed pre-units from 1960 to 1962, and loads of unit jobs, but only half a dozen or so of the nacelle models.

So, the new-look 1960 models were going to be as the Americans wanted; more sporty-looking, more aggressive. The TR6 Trophy and the T120 were identical apart from the number of carburettors and colour. We even heard a whisper through the grapevine that the new 1960 models would go on sale fitted with some sort of rear enclosure. Wouldn't that have been a disaster?

The author (left) and his old boss in the service department, John Nelson, judging the concours at the Bonneville Celebration, Gaydon, 2009.

They didn't, thankfully, and the specification remained unchanged, apart from the modifications for 1960, 1961 and 1962 for both home and American markets.

Due to riding conditions in the States, the bikes needed to have a more butch image, definitely not the French or Italian 1960s scooter look suggested by the rear panels of the 6T and T100.

The Gaydon gathering brought three of my long-time friends together, Jim Lee, ex-Production Development tester, Tony Healey, a Coventry chap, who literally eats, sleeps and breathes Triumphs, and an old ex-army friend, Mike Wallis, owner of a 1961 Bonneville. Tony Healey actually built the lovely Tangerine and Pearl Grey machine, used on all the 50th Anniversary literature

The six fifties

The four pals, coincidentally outside the beer tent. Left to right: the author; Mike Wallis; Jim Lee, and Tony Healey, builder of the poster Bonneville.

The actual poster Bonneville, as built by Tony Healey at the Gaydon 50th anniversary celebration for the Bonneville, parked in front of itself on a poster.

Triumph Production Testers' Tales – from the Meriden Factory

and posters. Mike had me do an engine job on his machine some years ago, and we've stayed in touch. Needless to say, in the photograph, we are next to the beer tent!

Some years ago, my son, Simon, although a motorcyclist from a young age, decided he wanted to swap his 1967 Tiger 100S for a larger model. Still wanting a Triumph, he opted for a 1961 T120 Bonneville that we purchased from an old pal of mine, who used to be the manager of the Triumph dealership in Coventry.

The initial outlay for the bike was very reasonable, so we set to and totally restored it to how it would have come off the end of the line in 1961. I think back now and wish I had kept a pocket notebook in which to jot down the date and engine number of every model I tested. Who knows, maybe I tested my son's bike?

Simon wanted one or two things on his bike as per the 1962 model, so it wasn't exactly as it should have been, but it was his bike and, if that's what he wanted, then that's what he could have. To start with, he decided on the four hundred by eighteen (4.00 x 18in) rear wheel and tyre, the oil tank and toolbox to be finished in gloss black instead of silver, and a grey-topped twin seat. Later on came a rev counter timing cover and tachometer, together with the one hundred and forty miles per hour speedo head instead of the one hundred and twenty 1961 item. So now he had the model he wanted, but we were not prepared for the aggravation from its original owner, who was less than pleased to see it transformed into a 1962 model. He confronted us at a Founders Day Vintage Motorcycle Club gathering at Stamford Hall near Rugby, making several aggressive remarks to which I replied, "So what? It's my son's bike, it's how he wanted it."

The bike has appeared in several magazines, and John Surtees rode it in the early nineties for a video called *The Power and the Glory*. I knew John's father, Jack, when he used to come to the factory, and we sometimes speak on the phone when John has a project on. Simon still has, 969 MFC, I don't suppose he will ever sell it.

Later on in the day at the Gaydon do, talking about the prototype on which I worked with Alan Gillingham, who should turn up but Percy. Stories bounced all over the place, and one, which Percy related himself, stuck with me because I was there in Experimental when it happened.

The author's son's T120 parked outside the workshop. There were problems with running until new monoblocs and balance pipes on inlet manifolds were fitted. Timing-side view.

The six fifties

Simon Hancox's T120 UK Bonneville: a handsome tool.

The Hancox junior Bonneville out on a run. Note the Dunlop elastic bands wrapped around the twist-grip rubber – an old DR trick passed on by the author to facilitate easier gripping.

Triumph Production Testers' Tales – from the Meriden Factory

Alan and I looked after the Tiger 110, which had been modified to twin carburettor specification, along with the other high performance parts listed in the back of the 1958 B range parts catalogue. It was, in fact, the first of the Bonnevilles, although our name for it was the Monster.

We carried out a quick maintenance procedure each day, which enabled Percy to ride from the factory, down the A45, onto the M1, all the way to Apex Corner, and then back again. Twice a day.

Every morning, by the time Percy had clocked in, drunk his mug of tea, and been to the toilet, the bike was ready and he was off. Toward lunchtime, he could be heard approaching the factory at high speed along the A45 main Birmingham Road, shortly after bursting into the Experimental Shop, dropping the bike onto its side stand, and dashing off to the toilets for a wash and freshen up before going into the canteen for his lunch, ordered the day before.

In the meantime, Alan and I would put the Monster up on the trestle and, with him on one side and me on the other, we would check all the nuts, bolts, screws, oils, chains, controls, etc, finally wiping over the bike and topping up the tank with fuel.

Dropping the trestle down, the bike was placed on its centre stand, facing the double doors which led out onto the drive along the front of the factory, given a final wipe over, spinning the rear wheel and wiping away any oil on the rim or back of the bike that may have been blown there by Percy's morning 100mph blast. This was the usual run of events; what follows is a slightly different version, however ...

Alan, myself, Dennis Austin, and Pop Tilley were sitting on our chairs in a circle in the middle of the shop floor, eating our lunchtime sandwiches and enjoying our mugs of tea, when we heard the unmistakable sound of the Monster approaching at a very high rate of knots. With it being a nice day, both the doors were open out onto the front drive, and we could look down over the front lawns to the main A45.

The first canteen sitting was just about to start, and Percy was usually in time for this. The works canteen was quite small, so two sittings were necessary. Percy liked to be on the first one, or else his afternoon timetable was thrown out of whack, in which case he would moan and moan.

There was no doubt about it, the Monster was on full song and Percy approacheth. Swift changes down and seconds later he was straight in through the open doors, just missing us, screeching to a halt. Dropping the bike on its side stand, he ran across to the corner of the workshop where the steps down to the cellar were. Percy almost dived down the steps, and we sat there stunned, looking at each other open-mouthed until, that is, a huge shape appeared in the open doorway: a traffic policeman, no less. Looking past him, I could just see the front of the Sunbeam Talbot 90 parked outside on the drive, with its chromium-plated bell just above the front bumper, and the blue illuminated 'Police' sign in the middle of the radiator grille.

The copper was big, at least six feet three or four, in his flat cap, belted tunic jacket, jodhpurs and highly polished black boots with calf length gaiters. He stood there, feet apart, clenched fists on his hips. He looked at us, then at the Monster, and asked "Has a chap just come in here riding a bike?" We all looked blank, shaking our heads as one, sandwiches halfway to our mouths in one hand, mugs of tea in the other, and replied "No, Officer." He stared hard at us, then again at the Monster on its side stand, by now cooling, and gently cracking and tinging. "Well," he said, "you tell the bloke who hasn't just come in here, sooner or later we'll catch him." And with that he turned on his heel and got back into the Sunbeam, reversing down the drive.

I think it was Alan who shouted, "Okay, Sam," (Percy's nickname), "he's gone, you can come out now." Percy went off for his lunch while Alan and I went through our routine. They did get him a few days later, the same copper. I bet he grinned with satisfaction when he finally got Percy. Later on, I came into contact with that very policeman when I came off Production Test and went back to the Repair Shop. He was from Little Park Street Central Police Station, and his name was Reg Voss. A very nice chap when you got to know him.

The six fifties, as with the C range models, all used the same frame except for one or two differences with regards to small brackets on the 6T Thunderbird and Tiger 110 models with rear panels, rather than the TR6 Trophy and T120 Bonneville variants.

As well as the nacelle forks for the two panelled machines, the wheel sizes were one inch smaller at eighteen inches diameter front and rear, with the sports models on nineteens. The rear wheel on the sports models went down an inch for 1962 from nineteen, fitted with the three fifty by nineteen tyre, to an eighteen inch fitted with a four hundred by eighteen larger section tyre. As the rolling radius remained the same, no alteration was required to the speedo drive or gearing, although the speedometer dial was altered from one hundred and twenty to one hundred and forty miles per hour.

The six fifties

The Tiger 110 out on test, minus the front numberplate, which was away being sign-written.

A perfect T120? Owned by one of the author's friends, Len Boland of Solihull. As near as can be to original factory specification.

A 1961 T120 Bonneville restored by the author, out on extended road test, equipped with the one trade plate required by law.

75

Triumph Production Testers' Tales – from the Meriden Factory

T120 UK model rear end, with standard wheel.

The single carburettor engine of the Tiger 110 and TR6 Trophy.

The T120 UK model front forks, wheel and 8in single-leading shoe brake. Not rated as very good.

All the B range (six fifties) had seven inch rear brakes and eight inch fronts, with the exception of the 6T Thunderbird which retained the seven inch stopper on the front.

In outward appearance, the T110 and TR6 engines were identical except for a competition Lucas Magneto fitted to the TR6 Trophy, and its cylinder barrel was enamelled silver, available in the spare parts catalogues under number E3332V, as opposed to E3332 for the black item.

I always thought that this was to give the appearance of an alloy barrel, mainly because the model sported the name Trophy. I must say, with the alloy head and polished rocker cases, it did look rather smart.

The sports twins had smaller engine sprockets to drop the gearing overall, and this allowed them, equipped with sports camshafts, to rev more freely, giving better all-round performance. The 6T Thunderbird was slightly longer-legged, having a twenty four tooth sprocket as opposed to the sports model's twenty two teeth engine sprocket.

I must say that when I was on test, the 6T Thunderbird always seemed drab in comparison with the two-tone pastel shades of the sports models. 1960 saw the 6T in Charcoal Grey, a metallic dark grey which, as I got older, grew on me, and now I seem to like it. In 1960, the Tiger 110 was in black and ivory, the same colour scheme as its smaller brother, the Tiger 100A. The pastel colours demanded by our biggest customer, North America, were very eye-catching. The TR6 Trophy was in ivory and Aztec Red, but only the tank and mudguards, mind; the remainder was gloss black and chrome. It looked superb. The tank was Aztec Red on top, ivory below, whilst mudguards were ivory, with Aztec Red centre stripes, edged in gold pinstriping. All very splendid and a splash of colour amongst the sea of Charcoal Grey Thunderbirds.

Coincidentally, in 1959, the last of the single downtube frame model Thunderbirds was also in Charcoal Grey, and the TR6 Trophys were in Aztec Red

The six fifties

and ivory, but with the ivory on top of the tank and the Aztec Red below. With their two-into-one upswept exhausts, they were a really good-looking bike.

Depending on where the Trophys were going, they had either Dunlop Trials Universal competition knobbly tyres, two-into-one upswept exhausts passing over the top of the primary chain case on the nearside, into one of those little Tiger Cub-sized silencers, or they could have separate twin upswept pipes, each into one of those little silencers. The upswepts had nicely contoured, chromium-plated leg protectors where the rider's legs could come into contact with the pipes when riding. This would cause a nasty burn, or, at the very least, ruin a good pair of riding over-trousers.

All the American models had high-rise bars, though those for the East Coast differed from the West by being a little flatter and wide. Why the difference, I never really found out.

The TR6 Trophy was the bike chosen by nearly all of the testers as their going home bike, mainly due to its eye-catching colours, which, in the early sixties, meant it stood out in a crowd. Besides, the smaller Cub-sized silencers made a beautiful rasping noise under hard acceleration, especially when two of the same model were being ridden in close harmony. They were easier to check over before firing up than the Bonneville, with its twin carburettors and one-into-two throttle cable layout incorporating three separate adjusters. The TR6 Trophy was a dream, considered by many to be the ultimate twin.

One night, Eddie and I chose identical TR6 models to go home on. With Eddie living only a few yards away from me, naturally, we came in and went home together.

The 1961 T120 Bonneville for the home market.

Triumph Production Testers' Tales – from the Meriden Factory

The 1959 UK TR6 Trophy finished in Aztec Red and Ivory, with two-into-one exhaust. Drive-side view.

1959 TR6 Trophy with QD headlamp plug, air-scoop front brake, and flat bars.

The six fifties

The 1961 East Coast TR6C scrambler, timing-side view.

1961 East Coast TR6C, drive-side view.

Triumph Production Testers' Tales – from the Meriden Factory

The route through the back lanes took us down Oak Lane opposite the factory, left onto Wall Hill Road, then a quick dive right into Pikers Lane (where Charlie fell off the footbridge into the brook), then a quick right and left into Hollyfast Lane, at the end of which is the main Tamworth Road. We exited Hollyfast Lane in exactly the same spot where Jack Wickes sat on the night of the Coventry blitz, overlooking the burning city, side car laden with works drawings.

In three hundred yards, a dive right off the Tamworth Road down Rock Lane took us through a local beauty spot called Corley Rocks, and it was here that we could get the Trophys airborne. Halfway down the lane was a very nice dip in the road. Going home, if you hit it at about sixty miles an hour, you could aviate the entire bike; going to work, hit it at the same speed and ride on the back wheel for forty to fifty yards. Splendid fun and the sound of the two bikes was stunning.

The Tiger 110 and TR6 Trophy were on the alloy single carburettor Delta Head, and although the 6T Thunderbird was on an Iron Head for 1960, in 1961 it also went to alloy. Due to a peculiar valve angle, when the motor was hot a funny noise emanated from the cylinder head or rocker box area, almost like a muffled squeak. After a spot of head scratching, it was found that if you took off the two exhaust tappet inspection caps, and gave the rocker arms and valve springs four or five squirts of oil out of a Wesco oil can, the noise would stop.

Apparently, the downward force of the tappet adjuster pin on the end of the valve stem not only pushed the valve open against the valve spring tension, but because of the geometry, it also forced the valve stem sideways in the valve guide bore. This was made worse by the exhaust gas heat in the exhaust rocker cavity area of the cylinder head, especially as it was mainly on the two exhaust valves.

What little oil that did find its way down between the stem and bore was only on one side of the stem, the top side. On the underneath of the stem, because of the sideways thrust, no oil was getting down to lubricate the valve in the guide, thus, it was running dry. We found, upon dismantling the head and removing the exhaust valves, that there were deep steps at the bottom of the stems where the guides had worn away the hardened stem. The answer was found in the guide valve material, which was changed from chilled cast iron to phosphor bronze. Due to a certain amount of porosity, this retained some of the lubricant within its pores.

Whenever I have occasion to re-work a Delta eight stud head from the early sixties, I always fit the T140 phosphor bronze 71-3294 and 71-3295 guides. Then, before I start and run the motor, each side of the rocker box receives half a dozen good squirts from my trusty Wesco oil can. What a lot of people do not realise, is that after a complete rebuild of a bike, as the rocker feed pipe comes off a twig on the return side of the oil system and is not under pressure as is the feed side, it takes a good twenty miles of riding before any oil finds its way to the rocker spindles and arms, let alone drops down in the valve cavity to lubricate the valves and guides.

A good tip, after starting the motor and making sure that the oil from the engine is returning to the oil tank, is to block the return hole just inside the oil tank filler neck with your finger, which will encourage oil to the rockers quicker than it would normally get there. The noise we heard was christened valve scuff.

In 1961, all of the gearboxes had a new shortened lay shaft, which allowed Torrington needle roller bearings to be fitted in place of the old top hat-shaped bushes used since 1951. For America and the home market, the sports models had no slick shift mechanism in the gearbox outer cover. This was a clutch disengaging mechanism which came into play when the gear lever was lifted or depressed to change gear. It was supposed to obviate the need for a clutch lever on the left-hand side of the handlebar, but unless it was adjusted perfectly, the bike would jump forward alarmingly when first gear was selected from standstill, and on the move, a gear change was always accompanied by loads of clutch slip.

One of the big problems we had was burnt-out clutches, mainly due to riders wearing big waders or over-boots. Because the wet weather footwear was so cumbersome, they would unknowingly ride for miles with their right foot resting on the gear change pedal, thus causing the clutch to slip or the ends of the clutch push rod to overheat and soften, causing more problems.

Although it was originally thought an excellent idea, the slick shift mechanism was discontinued in a very short space of time. The Americans wouldn't have it at any price.

Eddie and I rode home together every night. He usually led, with me keeping station about a wheel width behind and slightly to his right. This is how we used to ride in the White Helmets when on the road going from show to show.

After I was demobbed, the team came off the road and the bikes were transported in a purpose-built,

The six fifties

A 1961 TR6 UK model restored by the author for a friend and businessman in Surrey. Timing-side view.

Drive-side view of 1961 TR6 UK model finished in Ruby Red and Silver Sheen.

Triumph Production Testers' Tales – from the Meriden Factory

covered, articulated lorry with all the show equipment, whilst the men took it easy in a luxury, fifty-two seater coach. No more riding in the rain from Leicester to Perth in Scotland as we used to, the bikes so filthy it would take us an entire day to get them clean and show-ready.

Eddie set the pace as we rode the lanes home, and I can honestly say it was beyond any pleasure to be had from riding nowadays, it was a delight. He was fast, smooth and safe. We changed gear at the same time, turned into bends together, and I suppose thought together. It really was a great feeling.

The ordinary home market TR6 Trophy was a nice bike, too, with standard flat bars, ordinary road tyres, and normal exhaust system. A manual ignition control on the left-hand handlebar made it a good, serious riding bike.

The first of the Bonnevilles had the dreaded chopped Monobloc Amal carburettors with the remote float chamber fixed via a flexi-mount to the saddle downtube. The 1960 T120s still had the same carburettors, but now the remote float chamber was suspended on a threaded rod, hanging from a Metalastic bush mount on the rear engine steady plate. The critical float level was set very exactly on assembly when the bike came down the assembly line. All we had to do was go through the setting and adjustment procedure. As the remote float setup was originally intended for high performance work or racing, it was a difficult machine to pootle around on.

The Service Repair Department was inundated with customer complaints that their new Bonnevilles would not run properly, which soon prompted a production change; at engine number D7727, Monobloc carburettors with incorporated float chambers were fitted. The chopped Monobloc setups were relegated to the high performance optional extra list for racing, as it was found that the Metalastic bush mounted float chamber was insulated from vibration, and therefore did not suffer from frothing (a result of high revs).

That brings me to another problem with the remote float twin carburettor Bonnevilles, but one that has only manifested itself over the last few years.

A friend rang me the other week asking if I could help him with a problem he has with his 1959 Tangerine and Pearl Grey Bonneville, purchased a couple of years ago. It ran beautifully when he first acquired it, but over the summer months, using it around his Surrey home and on the M25, it was now giving cause for concern.

The problem occurs on slow running, he told me, and when he stops at traffic lights or a junction. Try as he might, with endless fiddling of the settings, he had only succeeded in making things worse than they already were. Whenever he came to a stop, the engine would race, even on a closed throttle. If he backed off the throttle stop screws on the remote float Amal chopped Monoblocs so that it would tick over, the next time he came to a junction and shut the throttle, the engine would simply cut out. Most disconcerting, especially if you are at the head of a traffic queue, and have to paddle the thing to the side of the road to get out of the way. The final insult was when some chap dropped the nearside window of his car and yelled, "Buy a Honda, mate!"

He was desperate, hence his call pleading for help. He didn't really want to sell the bike, but it was becoming an evermore likely possibility.

I remember some years ago when my son wanted to upgrade from his T100S, him saying how much he wanted a duplex Bonneville. As luck would have it, we dropped on a good one just right for restoration, and within six months, we had a beauty, a show-stopper. It did not, however, run as good as it looked.

The problem was carburation, a tickover that had a mind of its own, and, to make matters worse, the Amal Monoblocs were not at that time being remanufactured. We could only bore out the bodies and fit oversize slides, but this did not cure the problem. We fiddled and messed about with them for ages, and then, heaven save us, the new Monoblocs came along. I always assumed that the fast tickover was due to wear in the bores, allowing unmetered air to leak past and cause a weakening of the mixture.

As you will probably already be aware, if you set a relatively slow tickover on a correct pilot mixture setting, then slowly weaken that setting, the tickover speed will increase. This, we assumed, was the root of the problem. After all, on the new bikes back on test, we didn't get a problem. With the introduction of the larger model Monobloc 389, and then the new Concentric, came a modification that benefited both of these instruments and, coincidentally, the earlier, troublesome remote float models.

Why, exactly, Experimental introduced the inlet manifold balance pipe, I don't know, but what we do know all these years later, is if the modification is carried out on a duplex framed Bonneville, slow running and, more importantly, the tickover problem is eliminated.

The high-performance parts bulletin, issued to those who wished to make their 650s go quicker.

SERVICE BULLETIN

NO. 221 (REVISED)

<u>HIGH SPEED EQUIPMENT FOR BONNEVILLE 120 1960-62 MODELS.</u>

Part No.	Description	Price	Remarks.
E3134	Exhaust camshaft	£1. 10. 0d.	) Not advisable
E3059R	Cam follower	7. 6d.	) for road use.
T1228	Gearchange lever	11. 0d.	
T1647	Kickstarter lever	£1. 1. 0d.	
F5002	Right footrest assembly	£1. 10. 0d.	
F 33	Bolt	4. 0d.	)
S25-6	Spring washer	1d.	) For footrest
DS 48	Nut	6d.	)
F5003	Footrest and brake lever	£2. 5. 0d.	
SCZ 45	Spring washer	1d.	)
DS 48	Nut	6d.	) As standard
CP 95	Close ratio gear set	£9. 16. 0d.	For 1960 machines.
CP 193	Close ratio gear set	£10. 8. 6d.	For 1961-2 machines.
-	Carburetters with remote float chamber.	£15. 12. 5d.	All parts listed and illustrated in No. 16 Spares List.
L 24	Magneto K2FR	£30. 16. 0d.	Lucas supply.
E4174	Left silencer	£3. 7. 6d.	Straight-through.
E4175	Right silencer	£3. 7. 6d.	Straight-through.
CP 181	Tachometer kit.	£12. 2. 6d.	
Z50235	Speedometer head	-	Smiths supply. For use with close ratio G/box and standard drive.

Items are made in small batches and may be temporarily out of stock. Definite orders placed through Triumph dealers will be filled as soon as possible.

FEBRUARY 1962.

TRIUMPH MOTORCYCLES

Triumph Production Testers' Tales – from the Meriden Factory

For this benefit to be appreciated, the carburettors, of course, have to be faultless.

We had already invested in a pair of new Monobloc carburettors for my son's bike, so after we had modified the manifolds, lo and behold, it ran like a dream. To this day, we have never had any more problems in that area.

On my friend's 1959 model, however, he has a manually-controlled magneto. Many years ago, when us young chaps at Meriden with our Tiger 100s and their manually-controlled magnetos got fed up moving the lever to slow the engine on tickover, then advance the ignition again when we pulled away, decided to fit automatic advance and retard units.

This you do by removing the magneto fixed driving pinion, putting the manual lever in the fully advanced position, then wedging open the auto unit in the full advanced position before fitting it in place of the fixed pinion. Put the engine on thirty seven degrees before top dead centre with the magneto points just breaking, refit the auto unit and tighten. You can remove the wedge holding the unit open, and flick it open and closed to check that it works.

With this and the inlet manifold modification, the bike, my friend's Bonneville, has been running perfectly, and he no longer has to play with the ignition lever; it's all done by the auto unit. Magic.

The remote float setups suggested for the high performance bulletin did not have to take into account slow running or tickover, two things that didn't matter when you were racing.

The Service Bulletin 221 (revised) dated February 1962, details parts required to make the T120 or TR6 go even faster. Getting right down to it, I suppose it was for the chap who wanted to race at Thruxton or Silverstone, and who hadn't got a fortune to spend on parts. The total for everything I am about to list is £93. Another E3134 camshaft was required for the exhaust side of the engine, together with two E3059R racing cam followers.

A shortened gear lever was turned backward so that the gear selection was now one up for first, then down, down, down for second, third, and fourth. A new rear set right-hand footrest with its fixing bolts and nuts, and by turning the drive side footrest around through one hundred and eighty degrees, you now had a pair of rear set footrests. Included in the package was a shorter replacement rear brake pedal and rod.

Now comes the good stuff.

A complete close ratio racing gear cluster. There were two different setups that converted the old gearbox to achieve closer internal ratios and no drop in revs when accelerating up through the gears. The first (CP95) used lay shaft bushes, and the second, newer setup (part number CP193) had a shorter lay shaft and Torrington needle-rollers. Also included was the infamous remote float chopped monoblocs and all associated parts, and a genuine Lucas K2FR racing magneto. Finally, a pair of straight through silencers under part numbers E4174 and E4175, a complete rev counter kit, and a specially calibrated speedo head, too, for use with the close ratio gears under part number Z50235. And all for £93!

When we went to the floated monoblocs, it made a world of difference and we all got on a lot better. In fact, the testers became the kiddies on setting and balancing twin carburettors! This knowledge has stood me in good stead in all the years I have had my own business restoring Triumphs.

So, the Bonneville reigned supreme in its different guises; we had the road-going home market version for England and the Continent, and the rest were either US east or west coast models. With over ninety per cent going to North America, this meant there was a huge majority of the more exotic variants – with the small three gallon tanks, upswept pipes, and knobbly tyres – ready for testing.

Even the 6T Thunderbird and Tiger 110 were now in the much favoured pastel colours with high-rise bars and grab-straps over the seats. Really, they didn't look too bad at all: we even started going home on them.

The silencers on the American models were not fitted with mutes, but had a spoon baffle inside the silencer at the inlet end, which had the effect of deflecting the exhaust pulse sideways, through the perforated centre tube and into the sound absorbent material packed around the inside of the main body. With the twin carburettors, small bore pipes, and beautiful cigar-shaped silencers, they made the most wonderful noise on acceleration. If only Burgess still made them ...

The T120C was even hairier with the same specification except for twin upswept pipes and Dunlop Trials Universal tyres front and back. It was a beast on ordinary road surfaces, especially if you wound the power on when you were cranked over on a bend; the knobbles on the edge of the tyres tended to walk sideways. This

West Coast T120C or US TR7B, with modified front frame. Remote-float carburettors and centre stand only.

The six fifties

B3364   1960 US(W) T120C (US-TR7B)

B3363   1960 US(W) T120C

Triumph Production Testers' Tales – from the Meriden Factory

was alarming at first, but you soon got used to it, and could use it to your advantage on occasion.

Eddie and I were proceeding up the hill out of Meriden village at a steady rate of knots on a pair of Bonnevilles, when we were passed by Jock and Whistle Watmore going hell for leather. Bert was one of the testers who, with me, Percy Tait, and Stan Jinks was involved in the Duplex frame-breaking exercise at the Motor Industries Research Association proving ground. Jock was, of course, in the Royal Signals Display Team with me, actually sleeping opposite in the same barrack room, and when he left the army in 1958, got a job on the test at Meriden. He had a few miles under his belt and, in fact, raced a Gold Star in the Clubmans TT on the Isle of Man, so he knew his way round a corner pretty well – much to Bert's cost.

Whether they were racing, or Jock had simply passed Bert coming up the hill, I don't know, but there was now some sort of race going on. At the top of the hill, there is a small roundabout where you either turn left into Showell Lane, or go around the roundabout and straight on for the factory, some quarter of a mile down on the right. Just after the roundabout on the left-hand side is a bus stop, complete with lovely little wooden shelter, backed by an elder and blackthorn hedge.

Jock was a racer, like Percy, so by taking a racing line through the roundabout, he wound it on and was away before disaster struck. Poor Bert must have been on the wrong line because, knowing he wasn't going to make it, got the T120C upright and started to anchor up as hard as he could. Eddie and I, following, saw the cloud of dust as Bert went straight over the little roundabout, narrowly missing the 'Keep Left' sign, and then up the opposite kerb before disappearing behind the bus shelter. As we caught up, Bert appeared out of the bushes at the other end of the shelter. His goggles were down over his nose and mouth, and the bike had the biggest flats on the wheel rims you had ever seen.

We stopped and Bert pulled up, adjusting himself, all the while a cheeky grin on his face. Eddie asked him if he was alright, but all we got was, "Bloody hell, that was hairy!" We escorted him back to the factory on awfully dented wheel rims; surprisingly, the tyres retained their pressures, so at least he could ride, albeit slowly.

After a mug of Evvy's tea Bert made out his test card. I think he played it down a bit and wrote "check steering and wheels." A bit tongue-in-cheek, I know, but he left it at that and we all had a laugh later on, especially Jock.

Little Evelyn, or Evvy as everyone called her, was the lovely lady who always had the testers' mugs of tea ready in the morning on arrival, mid-morning break, lunchtime, and mid-afternoon break. We paid her two shillings and sixpence a week, never enough, I always thought, but on her birthday and at Christmas, she always had something extra as a sign of our appreciation. She looked after us, and, on the odd occasion, even told us off if we had misbehaved, as Eddie usually did, with the office girls ... and the dead spider on the cotton.

For those of you not familiar with the story, it goes like this. At lunchtime, the girls from the front office would walk in a bunch from the offices, past the end of the Cub track, and turn left onto the main gangway that led down to the double rubber doors, out into the main yard and on to the canteen. It also took them past the hundreds of new bikes lined up – and Eddie. Not yet married or romantically attached, he always managed to be working on a bike adjacent to the main gangway so that he could comment to the girls, who would giggle at his remarks, and with their arms invariably folded across their bosom, click clack in their high heels down to the rubber doors. Eddie, grinning and chortling, winked at me and said, "Wait til tomorrow, my boy, I've got a surprise for 'em."

It transpired that he had found the most enormous spider, quite the biggest we had ever seen – dead, luckily – under the testers' bench. Bill said, "I knew something had been getting at my grub, he's bloody big enough to pinch my pickled onions." Including the length of his legs, it must have been two inches across. Eddie obviously had something in mind for the girls, but not knowing what, I and several of the other chaps watched and waited, for it was going to happen tomorrow lunchtime.

We were beside ourselves with anticipation at the thought of what Eddie could get up to with this. He found an old match box and carefully put the dead spider in it with, "There you go, my beauty, I'll see you tomorrow," and then got on with some work.

The following day, as we were having our early mug of tea before starting, Eddie produced a bobbin of black cotton and a 2BA nut in black enamel, from a front number plate blade fixing, I think. We watched as he gently fixed the nut to the spider's body, drinking our tea in silence, and growing more curious all the while. He explained that the nut was for added weight, and, being black, wouldn't show up against the spider's body. I think he must have done something like this in a past life, because he set about his task knowing precisely what to do.

After tying the end of the black cotton around the spider's body, Eddie draped it over a bike's handlebars, and tested the up and down movement, pulling the spider up, then releasing it so that it dropped down. After several test tries, he decided the spider wasn't quite heavy enough, as he wanted it to drop quicker when he released the cotton. The spider's body would just about hide a slightly larger nut, so, with this in place, the job was done.

Eddie and I went about our usual business that morning, and were back in about fifteen minutes before the lunchtime bell went. By now, Eddie was chortling to himself, and we all sat with our mugs of tea on the testers' bench facing the gangway, in the best seats for the upcoming show. Evvy came over to us and wanted to know what was going on. With great difficulty keeping straight faces, we said we didn't know, which, strictly speaking, was the truth.

With a deft swing, Eddie tossed the weighted spider over a girder crossing the main gangway. It was a bracing strut of two by two angle iron, directly over the main gangway. He let out the cotton, and the spider dropped down to about eye level. Tying off the cotton on the twist grip of a nearby bike, Eddie simply pulled the spider back up to the girder, and, sitting side-saddle in his customary place where the girls saw him each day, waited.

We were all now giggling like schoolboys in anticipation of the forthcoming prank. Bill, Norris, Westy, Jock, myself, and Charlie were all eating our lunch when the girls' laughter and click clack of high heels preceded them coming around the corner. They were nattering, and giggling at us testers lined up on the testing bench, as they usually did. With about five paces to go, Eddie released the cotton. Down came the spider, stopping at just about eye level to the girls. Ear piercing squeals broke out, and, before we knew it, there was pandemonium. Some rushed past, others turned and ran back, and all of us were in stitches, Norris guffawing so much, he tipped his tea all over himself, and Bill's eyes were bulging, laughing but without any sound. Eddie was laughing so much, he fell backward off the bike and was now wedged between two Bonnevilles. A couple of us helped him extricate himself, and, quickly releasing the tied cotton, he pulled it and the spider back over the girder, winding it around two fingers and putting it in his riding suit pocket.

Of course, there was hell to pay. The Office Supervisor came down, and taking just one look at us, knew it was some sort of nonsense that we'd engineered. Mr Tubb, the Finishing Shop Manager, came and spoke to us all very sternly with the Office Supervisor present, though I reckon I saw a little twinkle in his eye as he did.

When the damaged machine that Bert had taken his little excursion behind the bus shelter on reached the knacker gang, Roger Bryant called him over. There was absolutely no way anything could be done with the wheels, they and the tyres and tubes had to be replaced, and Bert was given a severe warning, and that was that. Two new wheels came off the wheel section complete with tyres and tubes, and the old items were sent up to the Repair Shop to have the rims chopped off. The hubs would then go back to the wheel section to have new rims fitted, and, after truing, would go back to the Repair Shop and be used as service exchange items. The tyres were chopped through to prevent anyone taking them to use, as the tyre walls would be damaged and unsafe.

I often thought about Bert years later, no one seemed to know where he'd got to. Usually, the grapevine keeps us all informed about old mates, where they are, and what they're up to. But for Bert, nothing.

Then, when the Bonneville record-breaking run by Johnny Allen reached its 40th Anniversary, with celebrations at the National Motor Cycle Museum, who should turn up but good old Bert Watmore. A lot older, as we all were, and horror of horrors, thin on top. We all remembered him with his lovely blonde hair, but he was still the same smiling, good-natured Bert. He had been in America for some years, which is why we'd lost touch. I expected him to be at Gaydon for the 50th Bonneville do, but he didn't show up. I do hope he's still alright.

We pressed on with the bikes, but now the weather was deteriorating and every bike we went out on came back filthy. The inside workers who had gazed enviously at us in the summer as we rode out into the sunshine now threw us pitying looks as we banged in through the rubber doors, to stand in an ever-growing pool of water as the rain drained off us and the bike.

With the development of the full-face helmet many years later, the harshness of riding in bad weather lessened a little, as at least your head and face are protected from the elements. The old pudding basin type, with its leather sides and back, goggles for eye protection, and white towelling nappy wrapped around your neck, meant you soon got cold and wet.

I don't know who it was that came up with the idea, but I had, and still have to this day together with my old Barbour mitts, a face mask cut from an old

Triumph Production Testers' Tales – from the Meriden Factory

Triumph twin-seat cover in black vinyl. It was a largish rectangle, longer than it was wide, with a semi-circular notch cut out of the top edge to enable it to sit on your cheeks with your nose in the cut-out. In each top corner, we punched two holes, passing through a couple of knotted rubber bands cut from an old inner tube. When you had got your helmet on, the face mask could be positioned, and the rubber bands around the back of your helmet kept it in place. With your goggles down and just slightly overlapping the top edge of the mask, you were now a lot better protected from stinging rain and sleet. You weren't able to cover your nose as this would mean that your goggles misted, so that just got cold. My mask is in my desk drawer, and every time I look at it, I remember the most excellent days I spent with a great bunch of blokes.

You may wonder how the bikes were cleaned after test. At the bottom corner of the Finishing Shop, next to Fred and his rollers, were two chaps who performed this marvellous feat, day after day. The two who did this for as long as I can remember were little Jock and Billy. Obviously, the bikes had to be immaculate before going to the Packing Department, so it was up to the chaps to do their stuff.

With a high pressure air line lance which had a water feed adaptor, they could blast off all the dirt and grime before going to work with their leathers and a de-watering oil fine spray. You wondered after you had come back on a bike all mucked up to the eyebrows, how they could get it looking new again, but they did. Every one.

The snow was really bad the winter of 1961, so much so that higher management decided the testers would not go out on the main roads to test the bikes, but instead use the three hundred yard long main yard and top playing field at the back of the factory. This resulted in a lot of fun and games, I can tell you.

Riding bikes within the factory confines meant we didn't have to fit trade plates, so could actually test the bikes more quickly. Consequently, we got more than the usual number done in a day. and Little Jock and Billy were hard-pressed to keep up with us, meaning that a stack of uncleaned bikes caused a bit of a traffic jam down at the bottom end of the Finishing Shop. They enlisted the help of Big Fred, whose job involved the use of a rather large, brass-bodied syringe with a long flexible pipe on the opposite end to the pump handle. As the bikes finished testing, and before they were cleaned and sent for packing, their oil tanks had to be emptied. By far the easiest way to do this was to use the syringe to suck

The actual face mask made from an old Twinseat cover and worn in 1961-62 by the author on Production Test.

out the oil. If the plunger was full depressed, the flexible pipe inserted into the oil tank, and then the plunger pulled out to its fullest extent, the syringe would fill with engine oil. This was then siphoned into a five gallon plastic container three or four times, and a big model oil tank was empty. The oil in the gearbox and primary chain case was left. This had to be done as machines could not be transported with either fuel or oil in their tanks.

When the plastic container was full of oil, Fred would pour it into a huge square container next to the back wall of the Finishing Shop. This had a sight glass on it, and when he could see it was almost full, a tanker lorry would call and connect a pipe outside in the yard to the tank outlet sticking through the wall. The gate valve was opened and the tanker sucked the tank dry. I think the oil went for reprocessing to a company in Birmingham.

Eddie was fascinated with the big syringe: I felt a shiver of foreboding ...

Eddie and I decided to go home on Cubs during the snowy weather as they were more manageable, and, in this matter, I thought discretion was the better part of valour. I reasoned that I had a good chance of sliding off somewhere in the twelve miles we covered going home, so if I did finish up in the ditch with the bike on top of me, it was light enough for Eddie to lift it off.

By now the new next year's bikes were about to start coming down the track. We usually had sight of them about September time, so there was a stockpile for when the Earls Court or Olympia show closed, and they could be released to dealers and distributors.

With the TR6 and T120 American scramblers coming off the line equipped with Dunlop Trials Universal tyres, some of the testers took them up to the top playing field, a large grassy area at the top of the factory, backing onto fields all the way to Eastern Green. The field was about the size of a couple of full-sized football pitches, and where I, in the Royal Signals Display Team, performed at the annual Gala Day in front of my wife, mum, dad, and all my workmates. Imagine this snow-covered area, about to be invaded by a load of madmen.

Everything went well at first, with an orderly procession of riders circulating in an anti-clockwise direction, but getting alarmingly faster with each lap. I should have known, they were going the same way round that speedway riders do. Soon, it was a full-blown race with broadsides at each end of the pitch and muck flying in all directions. I wasn't tempted for one minute to join in, I just sat there watching the antics, expecting any minute someone would come off and everyone following would pile into them.

As I sat there watching, the great plumes of snow and mud being shot out by the four inch section competition tyres, my mind drifted back to when I was in the Team riding on a waterlogged pitch. We were contracted to perform at a show on the Ross Fisheries Group showground in Grimsby. When we got there, wouldn't you just know it, it was pouring with rain, and had been for two full days. Needless to say, when the time came for us to perform, the pitch was under water, and we actually had bow waves coming off our front tyres. Although these were Trials Universals, it didn't help, and in the main rides where all the bikes were used, and also in the six-bike fan (pyramid), there was simply not enough traction to achieve the necessary speed for the crossover cuts.

Consequently, the chaps had to wind it on around the ends of the arena in an effort to be on time and in the right position for the cuts or crossovers in the middle of the pitch. What chaos! Huge plumes of mud shot out from the rear tyre of the bike you were following, plastering you in the stuff and blinding you at the same time. I knew how things would go up on the top football pitch and, sure enough, that's what happened. Not only were the bikes and blokes plastered in snowy mud, but now one prat – guess who? – had decided it would be more fun to turn around and go the other way. There were bikes and riders all over the place, but luckily, coming off on the football pitch did absolutely no damage at all to the bikes. It just meant that the central drain in Little Jock and Billy's washing area would be blocked with mud from the testers' suits as well as the bikes. Afterwards, Stan Trowell came down with the instructions: no more testing on the football pitch, stay in the yard.

I found that if you rode up to the top of the yard, turned right, and rode along the back of the factory, still on a concrete drive, go right to the end, then right again, it brought you down past the back of the Service Repair Shop. You only had to turn right again, and you were on the drive along the front of the factory, past Experimental, the main entrance, and Reception, and down to Pop Wright's Time Office. A full lap of the factory seemed a better idea to me than riding up and down in the main yard where you had a good chance of being mopped up by a forklift truck.

The new models

As already mentioned, new model year bikes traditionally came off the lines after work resumed in late summer the year before. About October time, the bikes would be stockpiled in the Finishing Shop, then released for sale after the Motorcycle Show the same month. A selection of new machines would be taken up to Billy Warner's corner, a small partitioned area in the Finishing Shop, where Billy, Stan Truslove, and Dougie Cashmore would prepare them for the show stand, and ensure that everything about the models was perfect. During the show, where the bikes were on display, sales personnel would be taking orders from dealers and distributors. Immediately after the show, the sales chaps would hot-foot it back to the factory, and getting invoices and paperwork for the ordered machines sorted, arrange for despatch of same to the various buyers.

Consequently, new model year bikes could actually be registered in November or December of the previous year, and I'm often asked by owners of, for example, a 1962 model how it can be registered by this or that authority in late 1961.

I should mention the Coventry Holiday Fortnight, the two main holiday weeks when Coventry seemed to stop completely because of all the big factories that closed over that period. At Triumph it was, with ample notice, possible to take your holiday outside of this time frame, and, as a matter of fact, some of the Triumph managers were desperate to get a few people in over these two weeks to carry out annual cleaning and maintenance. If you were one of these, you didn't do your usual job, but put on a pair of blue overalls and usually worked on and around your work area, under the direction of the Works Engineer, Fred Gauge, who was responsible for the cleanliness, safety, and general appearance of the factory. I'm sure he was also responsible for a host of other things, but he was our boss for the fortnight we were on maintenance duties.

As I had not been on this dodge before, I was initially quite fastidious in my approach, but, after watching the others, Jock, Roger and Westy, I learnt not to go too fast with what I was doing. They left us testers to work around the Finishing Shop area, and the first job was sweeping. The factory floor was concrete, but very smooth; I think it was called a machine floor. In order to sweep the floor it was necessary to move the new bikes, so I suppose it made sense to use someone who was used to handling bikes, like us.

We swept and cleaned the whole area, including removing slippery patches of oil from the floor. This we did with a bucket, half full of petrol, and a cardboard box full of used, dirty wipers. These were a coarsely woven, red, duster-sized wiper, issued clean each week to everyone in the factory, from machinists to fitters in the Repair and Experimental departments. When I was in the Repair Shop, pre-army days, Arthur Ashley, the labourer, would come along each Monday morning and collect all your dirty wipers from the previous week, then take them down to Cal Gilbert in the Tool Stores and bring back the equivalent number of clean ones, dumping a bundle on each fitter's bench. It was the dirty returned wipers we now used for the floor cleaning session, and the best way to do this was to wind half a dozen or so around a brush head, dunk it in the bucket of petrol, and then scrub the affected area. The petrol evaporated, so no one smoked on this job!

After floor cleaning, the second week was taken up with painting, indiscriminate painting of anything and everything in Triumph Gloss Blue. If some poor sod had gone off for two weeks' holiday and forgotten to put away his tin tea mug, he came back to find it was now blue. The same applied to work boots, resting innocently

The new models

atop lockers; these ended up with toe caps. If someone hadn't secured his locker, his overalls would have a blue stripe up the outside of each leg and arm. One chap left his toolbox open and ended up with all blue Britool spanners. Nothing was safe.

We were supposed to freshen up the cast iron legs of workbenches, vices, and doors leading into both ladies and gents toilets, as well as their frames. I remember one chap we called Black Jack because he was always complaining about the testers, getting the inside of his locker done as well as his knife, fork and spoon. Oh, happy days!

After the summer break, things settled down again, Production clearing backorders of the year's models with short runs of twenty of this model or fifteen of that one. In the event that we ran out of some parts – especially those bought in from an outside supplier – the model might be supplied, say, with next year's seat.

The new Tiger Cub models coming in from engine and frame number 81890 had changed colour, with the sports models in a polychromatic burgundy and silver, but the standard T20 retaining its black and silver livery. Most importantly, the standard T20 dropped the Zenith carburettor and went to the nearly identical in appearance Amal 32/1 instrument. This single change made so much difference to the standard model; suddenly, it seemed to have arrived, and I didn't mind riding Cubs again.

With a black top half and silver sheen lower half petrol tank, silver oil tank, tool and battery box, rear panels, mudguards, and front brake plate, with the remainder in black, it really looked super. The raised centre ribs on the mudguards were black, and where the two colours met on the wall of the rib was a covering gold pinstripe. The finishing touches of primarily black twin-seat with grey top and side bands, alloy motor and chrome fittings made it a great little bike with a big presence.

The sports models were the T20S/S and T20SH, and the T20T and T20S/L were dropped. The home market T20S/S was the model that was used on the road, but could be readily adapted for most forms of competition, having the sports camshaft, 9-1 compression ration, and big $^{15}/_{16}$in choke Amal monobloc carburettor, finished in burgundy and silver sheen, and available with either upswept or flat roadster handlebars. It was quick at a shade over eighty miles per hour if you crouched down. Its Energy-Transfer ignition and direct lighting (it had no battery or battery box) made it sometimes difficult to start. You had to be firm with the little bugger, because sometimes, with the 9-1 compression ratio and Energy-Transfer ignition, if you gave a half-hearted kick, it would 'bite your leg,' as we would say.

The front and rear guards on this and the T20S/H model were in silver with a burgundy centre stripe, and again, a gold pinstripe each side.

The T20S/H was essentially a road-going sports Cub, and now it was fitted with the normal six volt coil ignition system, with an emergency start position on the 88SA Lucas switch housed in a special little bracket under the offside nose of the twin-seat, and the matching 88SA lighting switch housed on the nearside. Still with sports camshaft, 9-1 compression ratio, and big Amal monobloc carburettor, this little model seemed altogether improved in its running, probably due to the change from the Energy-Transfer to the same system as the standard model.

Having the sports camshaft, high compression piston, and big carburettor, both models went like stink, but a problem soon emerged on the T20S/S, with a lot of complaints of failed stop and tail light bulbs. Both the T20S/S and the earlier model T20S/L, having direct lighting, relied on the collective value of the bulbs not to blow any of them. Take one out of the system, and it could result in no lights at all. We discovered that the dipper switch, housed in the top of the headlamp shell, did not have overlapping contacts on the tumbler, so when the headlight was on and main beam was required, or the reverse of this, when the switch was activated there was an instant when the headlight bulb went out completely, not only leaving the bike with no light at the front, but sending the full jolt of juice to the tail light also, which promptly blew the bulb. We had quite a few chaps complaining under the warranty system, so Joseph Lucas modified the dipper switch so that when depressed to change beam, they both came on for a split second, at worst, causing the tail light to only dim for an instant. These little things were sent to try us ...

The American Cubs were almost identical except for high-rise bar straps over the twin-seats for the west coast. The standard Cub livery of black and silver for the home market was livened up for America, and we saw flamboyant red and silver paint jobs, which looked very nice (the same colours were used on the T20S/C and T20S/R). All were fitted with high-rise bars, but the standard Cub and SR models had road tyres, whilst the S/C had the Dunlop Trials Universals, upswept exhaust system, and, if ordered, a wide ratio cluster in the gearbox.

There was also a run of the Ministry of Defence five hundred side-valve twin in 1962, on a numbering

Triumph Production Testers' Tales – from the Meriden Factory

TIGER CUB (T20) TECHNICAL DATA

Bore and Stroke		63 x 64 mm. 2·480 x 2·520 ins.
Capacity		199 c.c. (12 cu. ins.).
Compression Ratio		7 : 1
Sparking Plug		Champion L7, K.L.G. F80 or Lodge HN
Carburetter		Amal Type 32
	Choke Size	11/16 in.
	Main Jet	85
	Throttle Valve	32/4
	Needle Position	2
	Needle Jet	0·103
	Pilot Jet	15
Gearbox Sprocket		17 teeth
Final Drive Sprocket		46 teeth
Chains	Front	3/8 in. x 7/32 in. Duplex x 62 links
	Rear	1/2 in. x 5/16 in. x 112 links
Capacities	Fuel Tank	3 galls. (13·5 litres)
	Oil Tank	2¾ pints (1·55 litres)
	Gearbox	⅓ pint (200 c.c.)
	Primary Chaincase	⅓ pint (200 c.c.)
	Front Forks (each leg)	⅛ pint (75 c.c.)
Brakes	Front and Rear Diameter	5½ in. (13·97 cm.)
Tyre Size	Front and Rear	3·25 x 17

1961 standard T20 Cub technical data.

Sports T20SS for 1961. Big Amal monobloc carburettor and energy-transfer ignition with direct lighting. A sports camshaft and high compression made it a quick little bike.

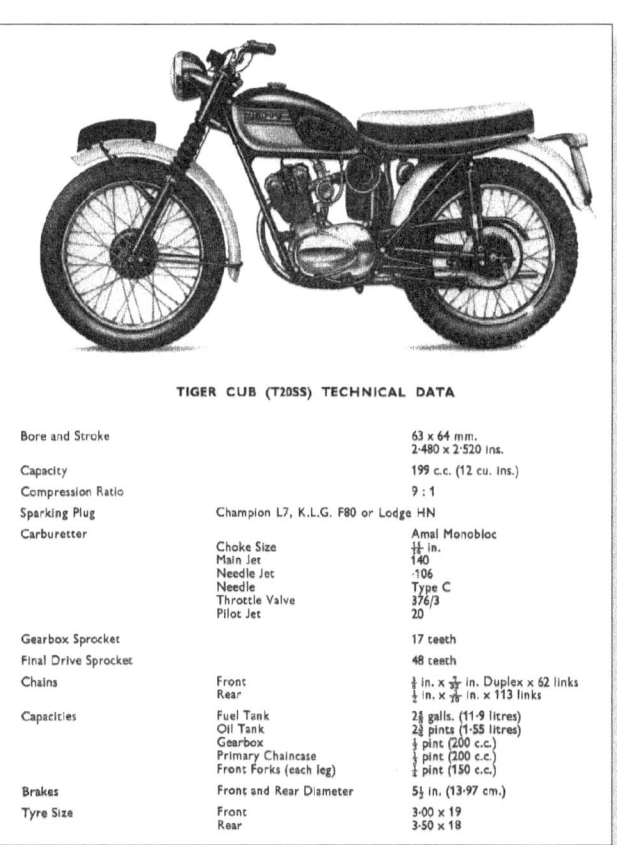

TIGER CUB (T20SS) TECHNICAL DATA

Bore and Stroke		63 x 64 mm. 2·480 x 2·520 ins.
Capacity		199 c.c. (12 cu. ins.)
Compression Ratio		9 : 1
Sparking Plug		Champion L7, K.L.G. F80 or Lodge HN
Carburetter		Amal Monobloc
	Choke Size	1 1/16 in.
	Main Jet	140
	Needle Jet	·106
	Needle	Type C
	Throttle Valve	376/3
	Pilot Jet	20
Gearbox Sprocket		17 teeth
Final Drive Sprocket		48 teeth
Chains	Front	3/8 in. x 7/32 in. Duplex x 62 links
	Rear	1/2 in. x 5/16 in. x 113 links
Capacities	Fuel Tank	2⅝ galls. (11·9 litres)
	Oil Tank	2¾ pints (1·55 litres)
	Gearbox	⅓ pint (200 c.c.)
	Primary Chaincase	⅓ pint (200 c.c.)
	Front Forks (each leg)	⅓ pint (150 c.c.)
Brakes	Front and Rear Diameter	5½ in. (13·97 cm.)
Tyre Size	Front	3·00 x 19
	Rear	3·50 x 18

TIGER CUB (T20SH) TECHNICAL DATA

Bore and Stroke		63 x 64 mm. 2·480 x 2·520 ins.
Capacity		199 c.c. (12 cu. ins.)
Compression Ratio		9 : 1
Sparking Plug		Champion L7, K.L.G. F80 or Lodge HN
Carburetter		Amal Monobloc
	Choke Size	1 1/16 in.
	Main Jet	140
	Needle Jet	·106
	Needle	Type C
	Throttle Valve	376/3
	Pilot Jet	20
Gearbox Sprocket		17 teeth
Final Drive Sprocket		48 teeth
Chains	Front	3/8 in. x 7/32 in. Duplex x 62 links
	Rear	1/2 in. x 5/16 in. x 113 links
Capacities	Fuel Tank	3 galls. (13·5 litres)
	Oil Tank	2¾ pints (1·55 litres)
	Gearbox	⅓ pint (200 c.c.)
	Primary Chaincase	⅓ pint (200 c.c.)
	Front Forks (each leg)	⅓ pint (150 c.c.)
Brakes	Front and Rear Diameter	5½ in. (13·97 cm.)
Tyre Size	Front	3·00 x 19
	Rear	3·50 x 18

The 1961 T20SH roadster Cub, with sports engine but with ordinary coil ignition and battery lighting.

The new models

T20T competition Cub for 1961. Energy transfer ignition, direct lights, straight-through exhaust, and if you didn't handle it forcefully when starting, it would kick you back.

Factory photograph of T20SH roadster model with flat bars, grey-topped seat, and battery ignition.

Triumph Production Testers' Tales – from the Meriden Factory

The Royal Signals machines ready for collection on the front drive. Amal 3T carburettors can clearly be seen, and with no lights or electrics, the bulb horn beneath the saddle was a legal requirement.

sequence suffixed with the letters NA. In the 1962 build, numbered from 28186NA to 28464NA, only some 278 were completed. These were used by the army, navy, air force, and for several other Home Office duties. We all mucked in to get them out as soon as possible, but took care to go home on a standard bike each night. Depending on which section of the Ministry the order was for, they would be finished in khaki matt or khaki gloss, with gold pinstriping for the army. For the Air Ministry, they again would be in air force blue matt or

The 'ladder ride.' This is where you needed steady, even running from the engine, hence the Amal carburettor.

The new models

The military specification TRW on Lucas 4CA twin coil ignition and the dreaded Solex carburettor. Drive-side view.

Timing-side view of the TRW showing the two-into-one exhaust and small Cub-shaped silencer.

gloss with gold pinstripes. Finally, for the Admiralty, navy blue matt or gloss with white pinstriping.

They all had the same nacelle forks, coil ignition systems, and generator lighting, as well as the rigid rear frame and panniers on frames, and a rear top carrier.

The forks were those with the early bottom legs, not the 1957-on type that clamped the fixed wheel spindle. Generally, all had the large section four inch tyre to cushion some of the bumps, and a spring saddle, either Lycett or Terry's.

DIMENSIONS

Overall height (over headlamp)	41 in.	104·1 cm.
Height over saddle	31 in.	78·1 cm.
Overall length	84 in.	213 cm.
Overall width (over footrests)	28 in.	71·1 cm.
Overall width (over handlebars)	28½ in.	72·4 cm.
Wheelbase, static	53 in.	134·6 cm.
Ground clearance	6¼ in.	15·9 cm.

SHIPPING TONNAGE (not dismantled) ... 1·45 tons 58 cu. ft.

PERFORMANCE

Recommended average safe speed (cross-country)	20 m.p.h.	32 k.p.h.
Maximum gradient climbable (firm dry surface)	1 in 2	
Range of action on road (average speed 30 m.p.h.)	250 miles	400 Kilom.
Fuel consumption target (normal road conditions)	50 m.p.h.	65 m.p.g.
	30 m.p.h.	90 m.p.g.
	80 k.p.h.	23 k.p.l.
	48 k.p.h.	32 k.p.l.

TURNING CIRCLE

Left and Right lock	8 ft. 6 ins.	2·7 metres

NETT POWER/GROSS WEIGHT RATIO ... 67 b.h.p. per ton

WHEELS AND TYRES

	Front	*Rear*
Rim Size	WM2. 19 in.	WM3. 19 in.
Tyre Size	3·25 × 19	4·00 × 19

TYRE PRESSURES

Road	17 lb./sq. in.	17 lb./sq. in.
Cross-country	13 lb./sq. in.	13 lb./sq. in.
Road	1·194 kg./sq. cm.	1·194 kg./sq. cm.
Cross-country	0·913 kg./sq. cm.	0·913 kg./sq. cm.

CAPACITIES

	Imperial	*U.S.*	*Metric*
Fuel	3 galls.	3½ galls.	13 litres
Oil	4 pints	5 pints	2¼ litres
Gearbox	½ pint	⅝ pint	300 c.c.
Chaincase	⅓ pint	0·4 pint	200 c.c.
Telescopic forks	⅙ pint	0·2 pint	100 c.c.

ENGINE

Type	Vertical, parallel twin-cylinder, air cooled
Maximum b.h.p. at clutch	16·8
Loss of efficiency at altitudes of:	
5,000 ft.	22%
10,000 ft.	40%
Bore	63 mm. (2·48 in.)
Stroke	80 mm. (3·15 in.)
Capacity	499 c.c. (30·5 cu. in.)
Piston ring gap: Compression Ring	Min. ·010" (0·25 mm.)
	Max. ·014" (0·35 mm.)
Scraper Ring	Min. ·007" (0·18 mm.)
	Max. ·011" (0·28 mm.)
Compression Ratio	6 : 1
Valve Tappet Clearance (cold): Inlet	·004" (0·10 mm.)
Exhaust	·006" (0·15 mm.)
Contact Breaker: Type	Lucas 4CA
Point Gap	Min. ·014" (0·35 mm.)
	Max. ·016" (0·40 mm.)
Ignition Timing	⅛" B.T.D.C. fully advanced
Coil	Lucas MA6
Sparking Plug: Type	Champion L.11.S
Point Gap	Min. ·018" (0·45 mm.)
	Max. ·022" (0·55 mm.)
Engine Lubrication System: Type	Dry Sump
Oil Pump	Twin Plunger

10

FUEL SYSTEM

Carburettor: Type	Solex 26 WH2
Choke	No. 22
Main Jet	110
Correction Jet	190
Pilot Air Jet	2·10
Pilot Fuel Jet	45
Starter Air Jet	3
Starter Fuel Jet	65
Air Filter	Vokes: oil-wetted felt

CLUTCH

Type	Four Plate, cork sheet segments in oil
Clutch cable free movement	⅛"

GEARBOX

Type	Four Speeds, foot operated
Ratios: 1st	2·91 : 1
2nd	2·21 : 1
3rd	1·42 : 1
Top	1·00 : 1
Sprocket ratio	5·80 : 1

OVERALL RATIOS (Engine to Rear Wheel)

1st	16·85 : 1
2nd	12·80 : 1
3rd	8·25 : 1
Top	5·80 : 1

SPEEDS

At engine speed of 5,000 r.p.m.:	1st	25 m.p.h.
	2nd	35 m.p.h.
	3rd	50 m.p.h.
	Top	70 m.p.h.

CHAINS

Primary:	½ × ·335 × ·305 in. 12·7 × 8·51 × 7·75 mm.	74 links
Rear:	⅝ × ·400 × ⅜ in. 15·875 × 10·16 × 9·65 mm.	90 links

BRAKES

Type	Mechanically Operated. Internal Expanding
Size (Front and Rear)	7 in. diameter × 1⅛ in. wide
Pedal clearance (rear)	¾"
Lever clearance (front)	$\frac{3}{16}$"

BATTERY

Type	6 Volt Varley MC.7/12
Capacity	12 ampere/hours

BULBS

	Volts	*Watts*	*Type*	
Head	6	30/24	Prefocus	Lucas No. 312
Pilot	6	3	M.B.C.	Lucas No. 988
Tail	6	6/18	Offset pin	Lucas No. 384
Speedometer	6	2	Special	Smiths No. P.52305

11

The full specification for the TRW military machine, including recommended speeds for cross-country riding.

They all had, unfortunately, the awful Solex carburettor, which took so much faffing about with that we gave up in the end. All we could do was set up the pilot mixture when the engine had reached working temperature, and then set the slow running speed. As the carburettor was of the fixed jet variety, and the specification for that was fixed between Solex and the Ministry of Defence, there was no changing jets or anything to improve matters. There was little anyone could do to improve throttle response and slow running evenness; we were stymied.

There was so much of a problem with the Solex instrument on the Royal Signals Display Team bikes that we found we couldn't perform no-handed tricks as the tickover or slow running speed rose and fell alarmingly. I think it was my old friend, Reg Hawkins in the Repair Department, who came up with the solution for us in the shape of the long inlet tract Amal, separate mixing chamber and float bowl carburettor from the 1946 to 1952 three fifty twin 3T. It certainly cured the problem because the Signals bikes would ticka-tocka along on a closed throttle in bottom gear all day long.

The Team bikes were renewed in the time between Les Williams being a member in 1955-1956, and me going in to replace him as rider team fitter. The TRWs Les rode had the same problems with slow and steady running, and after a lot of experimentation, it was found that the SU carburettor was superior to the Solex, so it was given a try. Although the constant vacuum jobs were okay, in the 1958 season, they were changed on the 6T Thunderbird for the cheaper Amal monobloc as fitted to all other models. Whether this is why the SU was

The new models

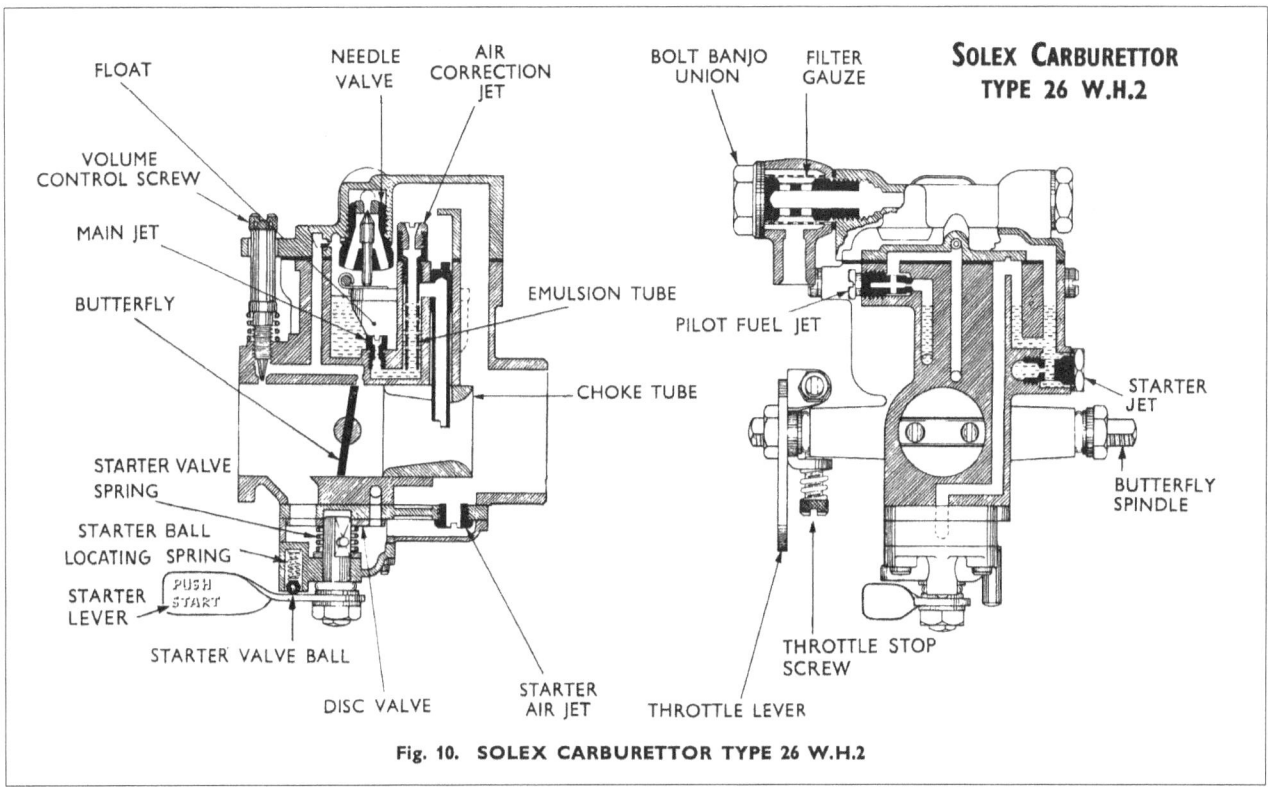

An exploded view of the Solex type 26 TRW carburettor.

not fitted to the new machines, I don't know, but the 3T Amal job proved more than satisfactory, especially as we rode the bikes from show to show. They performed very well, in fact.

I remember being in the Service Repair Shop before being called up in 1956 when Les Williams returned the bikes to us at the end of the season. Reg Hawkins and I had the job of converting them to road-legal machines with a full lighting system.

We had to remove special fittings such as ladder attachments, extra footrests, pillion seats on the front mudguards, etc. We removed the existing top fork covers, fitting in their place a set of TR5 Trophy top covers with headlamp mounting lugs. The new front number plate was sited in its correct position on the front mudguard. We fitted alternators in the primary chain cases, a new seven inch chrome headlamp complete, a battery carrier and battery, as well as a rectifier and a complete wiring harness. With a hole in the headlamp shell, just below the ammeter for a three position lighting switch, a horn and dipper switch together with a new Lucas six volt horn, mounted on the nearside saddle pillar bolt, we were nearly there.

All that was required now was a stop and tail light and a stop light switch. With two of us working on a bike, one each side, we could convert two machines a day, and when we got into the swing of things, we could finish two and make a start on dismantling a third by going home time. I still see these bikes come up for sale in the various motorcycling publications every now and then. It wasn't so long ago that someone rang me to confirm that the 1957 Speed Twin he had just purchased was the one used in my year's Team.

The bikes were offered through dealers who each took three or four and put them in their showrooms. I think Ron Bilton of H & L Motors, Stroud, in Gloucestershire had quite a few. They certainly would have been a low-maintenance going-to-work bike, that's for sure.

Thinking back to when I was in the Team with the 3T carburettors on our machines, I expected a little more from the bikes we were now riding. After setting up everything and putting on our trade plates, I rode out of the factory with Eddie, and turned to go up to the top of the hill. Eddie followed me, and when down the other side on the approach to the village, I signalled to turn left

Triumph Production Testers' Tales – from the Meriden Factory

into Church Lane. Eddie pulled up beside me, and, after lifting his goggles, pulled a bit of a face and said to me, "Wouldn't pull the bloody skin off a rice pudding." I had to agree, the bikes were awful compared to the Team machines. "They just can't be this bad," I thought to myself – but they were.

That thought took my mind back to my training as a Despatch Rider at Ripon, and the BSA M20 five hundred, side valve, girder fork single: what an awful beast. I had to suppress an involuntary shudder. It was a good thing I had JRW 405 to ride at the weekends to alleviate the awfulness. I looked again at the TRW; it was light, compact, and quite stylish, and maybe I wouldn't have minded training on something like this after all.

One good thing about a production run of these side valve twins was that, for us chaps still with our 1950s models, there was a ready supply of cycle parts. The old-type forks with the nacelle and the knock-through spindle bottom legs, the nineteen inch wheel and front brake, as well as the front mudguard and number plate, would all fit directly on my bike. The handlebar assembly complete with twist grip, horn push, dipper switch, front brake and clutch levers were all the same. The gearbox was identical, too, except instead of standard road-going ratios, all Ministry of Defence – or Mindef, as we called it – bikes were equipped with wide ratio clusters in case off-road work was required.

Nothing else on the TRW was any good because

The naked 6T Thunderbird for US markets. Finished in Kingfisher Blue and Silver sheen, with two-into-one exhaust and sports oil tank and tool box.

The new models

The UK Thunderbird, still with rear panels and finished in Black and Silver sheen.

frames, engine, rear mudguard, and all the other ancillaries were peculiar to that machine. I'm not saying we dismantled the TRW when we got it home, but it did mean that, should you be involved in an accident, you could always go cap-in-hand and ask for help. Under such circumstances, if you were an ordinary worker and relied on your bike to get to work on, nine times out of ten you would be. I've still got a brand new front mudguard, in khaki gloss and factory wrapping, that – up to now, fingers crossed – I've never needed to use.

We pressed on with the TRWs but managed to include a couple of the big models in the day's testing to break up the boredom. The Tiger 110 had now disappeared, mainly because the Americans didn't want a so-called sports model looking just like the 6T Thunderbird, and although the home market 6T retained the rear enclosures, the 1962 American market Thunderbird went naked on the back end. It looked good, having the TR6 Trophy oil tank and battery box, and the twin-seat fitted as on the two sports models, not hinged as it had been previously. With its Kingfisher Blue and silver paint job, two-into-one exhaust, downswept on the timing side and high-rise bars, it looked really good. The home market 6T now had an eight inch front brake the same as the American models, but these were finished in black and silver, and still had the rear enclosures as per the previous year.

One of the problems occurring on a regular basis was fracturing of the petrol tank centre fixing band, which was held at the rear with a $5/16$in bolt, nut and

Triumph Production Testers' Tales – from the Meriden Factory

washer, and at the front with an adjustable stirrup fastening, which could be tightened by turning a $\frac{5}{16}$in self-locking nut underneath the steering head adjacent to the steering damper plate and friction disc.

What was found was that, with a full complement of fuel on board, the tank would rock side-to-side under slow running conditions. The rider, in the mistaken belief that tightening the centre band would improve the condition, managed only to overstress the back of the band where it was fixed, so that, on the next long run, it broke. We changed the centre band material and in effect made it more flexible so that it was more forgiving, and not so critical with regard to tension. A large black horseshoe-shaped rubber doughnut with a split in it was forced over the top frame rail, and when the tank was pushed down over this, so that the rubber was up inside the frame tunnel, it reduced the rocking to an acceptable level. The doughnut was such a tight fit inside the frame tunnel of the tank, we had no more problems in that area.

The 1962 models brought more useful modifications, such as with the lighting and charging system alteration to both the TR6 Trophy and T120 Bonneville.

Actually, when I had returned to the Service Repair Shop after my stint on Test, Trophies and Bonnevilles were coming in from dealerships with overcharging problems, and acid spillage over the silencers and frame.

We didn't know what was going on and, in fact, didn't know this was going to happen on the test distance we rode the machines. Even if we rode home in the dark, I don't know whether the problem would have manifested itself as it was only when the lights were generally not in use over a prolonged high speed journey that it did.

The Repair Shop was getting in quite a few bikes under warranty, and if we weren't careful, it could end up costing a lot of money. The batteries on the bikes were what we in the trade call 'cooked,' which is what happens when a current that is too high is pushed into an already fully charged battery. The excess current boils the electrolyte or acid, and causes it to overflow out of the battery case. It looks like just water at first glance, but if it's not immediately washed off with soapy water, it will run everywhere, blown by the slipstream around the bike when riding fast. Once it gets onto paintwork or chrome works, that's those ruined.

This happened on the magneto sparked models only, and not on any of the AC coil ignition jobs.

Joseph Lucas found that in order to reduce generator output with the lighting switch in the 'off' position, a green and white wire can be fitted from the green and white terminal on the rectifier to the number seven terminal on the lighting switch. This only applied to models with the Lucas SA41 lighting switch, so the 1961 Tiger 110, and the two sports models were affected in this way.

When the bike came into the Repair Shop, it was parked on its centre stand, and the headlight switched on to partly discharge the battery. After a while, the bike could be started and taken outside. If the alteration had been satisfactory with no lights on during a high speed run, but a slightly higher than normal charge was being experienced with the headlight in the 'on' position, then a more powerful headlight bulb of 45-40 watt value was fitted. Conversely, if someone wanted to fit extra equipment, such as a couple of spotlights mounted on a front crash bar, which, let's face it, a lot of chaps did, then there may be insufficient output after the modification. What was suggested was a cut-lead switch in the green and white wire, so that breaking the wire via the switch allowed the overcharging to re-occur, which then adequately powered the additional equipment.

The only thing really essential was to have the switch in the correct mode when no lights were being used.

After the Lucas boys had been over to see us, they went back to Great Hampton Street and came up with a complete new wiring harness which cured everything.

The only other electrical problem we encountered on the two sports models was that the headlamp plug where the main harness goes through the back of the headlamp shell could unexpectedly detach, cutting power to the headlight. The main cause was the wiring loom being a little tight on the dimensions when it was made at Lucas. The headlamp unit, comprising the shell, ammeter, light unit and horn-push and dipper switch on its grey four-core lead, was assembled on the lighting section.

This was a long bench similar to our testers' bench, but it was covered with a thick blanket, almost like the one on my army bunk. The headlights arrived from Lucas made up ready to fit, and the QD female plug fixed in the back of the shell. The wiring looms were laid out on the bench, and the male plug on the front of the harness was connected, and the rubber waterproof cover pulled over the join. Apparently, the dimension of the wiring loom was too short by a couple of inches when the headlight was mounted on the fork top covers, and the loom fed around the nearside of the frame head lug.

The new models

The UK market TR6SS. A very nice, fast, unfussy road-burner, but still with dreaded QD headlamp plug.

Traditionally, the wiring loom on all Triumphs travelled along the nearside of the crossbar, exiting between the front of the petrol tank and the front frame head lug casting where the frame number is stamped. It is secured to the frame crossbar by three or four alloy, black-painted cable clips, but before the first clip is fitted, the steering needs to be turned to full right lock, which ensures there is enough slack in the loom when the steering is turned. Further back where the rectifier, battery and cut-out lead comes out of the main woven covering, and all the switch connections go in to the SA41 switch housed on the offside under the twin-seat nose, the loom is very stretched, so a little of it was pulled back to enable proper connection mid-section of the bike.

This, of course, used up some of the slack required round the front of the frame head lug. Turning the bars to full right lock didn't cause the QD plug to come apart straight away, but, out on the road, it could happen at any time, and if this was at night, along a dark country lane, it was not good.

Although this never happened to me personally, two of my colleagues had this very off-putting experience whilst on their way home. Consequently, we all came to know Joseph Lucas Ltd, Great Hampton Street, Birmingham, as Joe Lucas, Prince of Darkness.

My standard procedure, even when testing during daylight hours, was to give the wiring loom a little tug just where it emerged from the front of the petrol tank,

Triumph Production Testers' Tales – from the Meriden Factory

The 3TA was a smooth-running little twin, but suffered with cutting-out problems attributed to the Amal carburettor.

to check there was enough free-play. Later on, a simple remedy was a jubilee clip around the rubber waterproof cover, and later still, the wiring looms were modified after engine number D18419 to do away with the plug altogether. Lucas did go on to remake some harnesses for the Spares Stores, and allowed a little more material at the plug end to battery leads and rectifier connections so that there was more free-play around the steering head. I never met anyone who wanted to remove the headlight completely on their machine, unless they wanted to go racing, of course. Even then, when Percy or anyone was racing a Bonneville, nine times out of ten the headlight would still be in position.

The hole was still in the bottom of the headlight shell where the QD plug fitted, but now the harness passed through a large rubber grommet.

The problems we experienced with the Solex carburettors on the TRW side valve twins weren't the only carburation difficulties. The three fifty 3TA, for so long a nice-running, sweet little thing, developed a problem we called three-tee-itis.

It was an annoying complaint that could also be a deadly one as my friend, Bill Letts, was to discover one night. The problem occurred at tickover, and happened with absolutely no warning whatsoever. The Amal monobloc carburettor, model 375/32, could be set in the twinkling of an eye. After getting the motor warm, to set tickover speed was simply a case of winding in the pilot mixture screw until the engine began to 'hunt,' then slowly winding out the screw until the tickover was smooth and even, at about 650-700 revs per minute.

It was usually after you had done this and were putting your helmet on prior to going out, that there would be a fairly loud spit-back through the carburettor, and the engine would stop. Sometimes you had your helmet and gloves on and had selected first gear ready to move off when this happened. The most peculiar thing was that it didn't happen on every 3TA; some were worse than others, and some were no trouble at all, so there was no rhyme or reason to it.

We found that if tickover was set at a faster speed, it didn't happen so often. Bill was having a job trying to set up the carburettor on his test bike out in the yard. Sooty Price, Eddie, and I had ours running fine, although mine was on a slightly faster than normal tickover. After a while, Bill exclaimed, "Sod it, that's got to do or I'll bloody be here all afternoon." We started out on the test run, and I can honestly say that, once the little twin was up to twenty or thirty miles an hour, all was fine. It was just when idling and coming off the stop with the throttle that the trouble occurred. Sometimes, when the bike had been ticking over for a few minutes, if you put it in gear and started to let out the clutch to move off, there would be this loud 'spit' and the engine would stop dead. This was fine on test, because it either happened outside in the yard or in the lay-by down the Mile if we

The new models

had stopped to check things over, so it didn't matter so much. We made notations on the test card, but apart from increasing pilot jet size from 25 to 30, and fitting a fibre washer underneath the tickler retaining nut to slightly increase fuel height in the float chamber, there was little that could be done. I can't remember how the problem was finally overcome, but I do remember 3TA models coming into the Repair Shop for the selfsame problem.

Where this particular anomaly did have an impact was if there were hundreds of 3TAs that required testing, which meant you had to go home on one. Twelve testers going home on twelve 3TAs equated to another tester on the job, so go home on them we did.

Back in the early 1960s, the new A45 bypass from Coventry to Birmingham completely cut the loop of the old A45, past the front of the factory, Millison's Wood, Meriden Hill and the village out of the mad, going-to-work from Coventry to Birmingham and back traffic.

There was an intersection off the bypass on the Birmingham side of the village where you could join or exit to Meriden, ditto on the Coventry side where again you could join or exit, and go straight across both up and down lanes into Oak Lane opposite. This is the way Eddie and I went home to cut across country along the lanes. Bill, Norris, Westy, and one or two others would cross the up lanes from Coventry to Birmingham, then sit in the centre reservation until it was clear to swing out and accelerate on the Coventry down lane. It wasn't so bad crossing the up lane, then sitting in the centre refuge, it was the pulling out and accelerating to traffic speed that was the worrying bit.

That's when Bill's problem occurred.

We had a long run of 3TAs, so Bill hadn't much choice on what to go home on. It was either a three fifty or a Cub, and Bill was a bit big for a Cub, so he chose the American 3TA with high-rise bars, the sort he liked when he rode either the TR6 Trophy or the T120 Bonneville.

I think Bill must have had another 'silly' one, and as we waited in the yard for Pop Wright to open his window and say, off you go, Bill said, "I'll just keep the bugger wound on." With Pop's wave of the hand, we sped down the drive with a little more than usual noise because we all gave the little motors more gun than usual. Some of the chaps peeled left up towards the hill, and the rest of us right, down to the intersection on the bypass and the right turn into Eastern Green Lane. Jock, Sooty, and Alan Armitt turned right up towards Eastern Green, the remainder continuing to the intersection. Eddie and I,

going straight across, stayed on the inside, and Bill, Norris, and Westy were on the offside.

As soon as the oncoming traffic eased, we would be across into the middle. With a gap coming up, we prepared and, keeping up the revs, waited for the gap. As one, we moved forward with bags of revs towards the central reservation – with the exception of Bill, that is. Just as he moved off with us, the 3TA cut out, leaving him halfway across and broadside to oncoming traffic. All we could do was sit there and watch in horror as Bill paddled his big feet like mad and propelled his bike to the safety of the central reservation. The car in the fast lane must have missed his rear number plate by inches, and as it passed, its horn was blaring. We all sat there although by now, there were more vehicles waiting to cross, but they couldn't move forward because we still occupied the middle. Bill pushed up his goggles onto the front of his helmet; he was a ghastly colour, so we waited until he had gathered his composure, even though traffic was stacking up behind us. After a minute or so, he gave us the thumbs-up sign, and, prodding the 3TAs kickstart, revved the bike so hard, I swear it lifted off the ground for a second. Eddie and I waited for him, Norris, and Westy to pull away in a welter of revs, before we moved quickly across and into Oak Lane.

The following morning we waited for Bill and Norris to bang through the doors, and when they both did at the usual time, we breathed a sigh of relief. Bill rode his bike straight up to Roger Bryant's Rectification section and, while he was taking his plates off, I walked over to him with his mug, full of hot tea that Evvy had made. The thing that struck me first was the stink of burnt clutch plates coming from the bike. Bill looked at me as he took his tea and said, "Poor little bugger, every time I've stopped and had to pull away again, I've given it maximum revs and slipped the clutch so it wouldn't happen again, but I've burnt it out." Then he shouted to Roger, "Needs a new clutch Rog, sorry."

This incident really occurred, and was an eye-opener because Bill was built like a brick you-know-what, and it certainly was the nearest we came to losing one of our number. A sobering thought for us all.

A report was sent to Amal about the problem, and sometime later, after I had returned to the Repair Shop, the problem was eliminated by alterations to the internal drillways in the carburettor body. Ironically, by then, little Stan Whitcomb, the Service Department tester, had come inside on a fitting job, and Bill was faced with testing the modified carburettor models under warranty.

The Tiger 100S/S

Even in March and April it was cold and usually extremely wet, so we were really grateful for our Mr Michelin Men suits. Still a big problem was keeping our hands and feet dry. Leather riding boots were not really up to being out all day in, as they soaked up the water, even though we tried to waterproof them with football boot dubbin.

In the early sixties, with only the ex-army Despatch Rider boots available from Army and Navy stores, or the big navy sea boots, again made of leather, there wasn't that much of a choice. I knew through experience how sodden DR boots could get after long training runs of five or six hours' duration.

There was nothing like the thick, misty rain on the north Yorkshire moors to wet you to the bone, and after a day riding in it, your DR boots were like soggy cardboard. What was worse, if you dried them out overnight in front of a coke pot-bellied stove, in the morning, they had set hard like concrete.

The navy sea boots were certainly a better option, as they were impregnated with a wax-like substance when made and stitched together. Being for use onboard ship, they were supposed to keep your feet warm and dry, but were so cumbersome to wear you had to be careful not to catch the gear lever accidentally. I actually had a pair my dad brought home in 1945 that the crew of motor torpedo boats wore, but when you also had on the thick, white sea boot socks, these were quite unmanageable.

This left us with just the one hundred per cent waterproof option, the humble welly. If you wore a decent, thick pair of socks, your feet certainly stayed dry, but got progressively colder and damper with perspiration as the day wore on. I look now at my modern Belstaff waterproof boots with breathable membrane, Kevlar, and everything else, and try to imagine what it would have been like to have these back then.

Hands were kept dry by the very popular Barbour mitt over a decent, thick pair of grey woollen gloves. Being fingerless mittens, they allowed the air to circulate, which kept hands warmer than standard gloves.

One of the things we used to do was take the right-hand Wellington to the Repair Shop, and get someone to vulcanise a patch on the top, just where it contacts the gear lever when changing up through the gears. You might be surprised at how quickly a gear lever wears through the relative thinness of Wellington boot rubber ...

The T100A, with its rear enclosures, had now gone, and the new, semi-naked rear end T100S/S appeared, really a revamped version of the TR5A/R American model, with Bonneville-style forks and headlamp, but sports-type mudguards instead of the T100A bathtub. It now had smart quarter rear panels, mainly to hide the oil tank and all the electrical equipment under the twin-seat. It had a lovely, two-into-one, downswept exhaust system on the timing side going into one normal, Triumph-shaped Burgess silencer.

The colour settled on was the Kingfisher Blue and silver of the previous year's Tiger 110 and the 6T Thunderbirds. Once again, we had the quickly detachable headlight plug in the bottom of the light shell and on the main harness, though strangely, probably because of different dimensions, there were no incidents of it unplugging itself. Nevertheless, the wiring harness went to that of the bigger models, doing away with the plug on later models.

It certainly was a handsome bike, with the petrol tank top half in Kingfisher Blue, as well as the rear quarter panels, and the centre stripes on the mudguards. These were again pinstriped in gold, and with everything else in gloss black, chrome and polished

The Tiger 100S/S

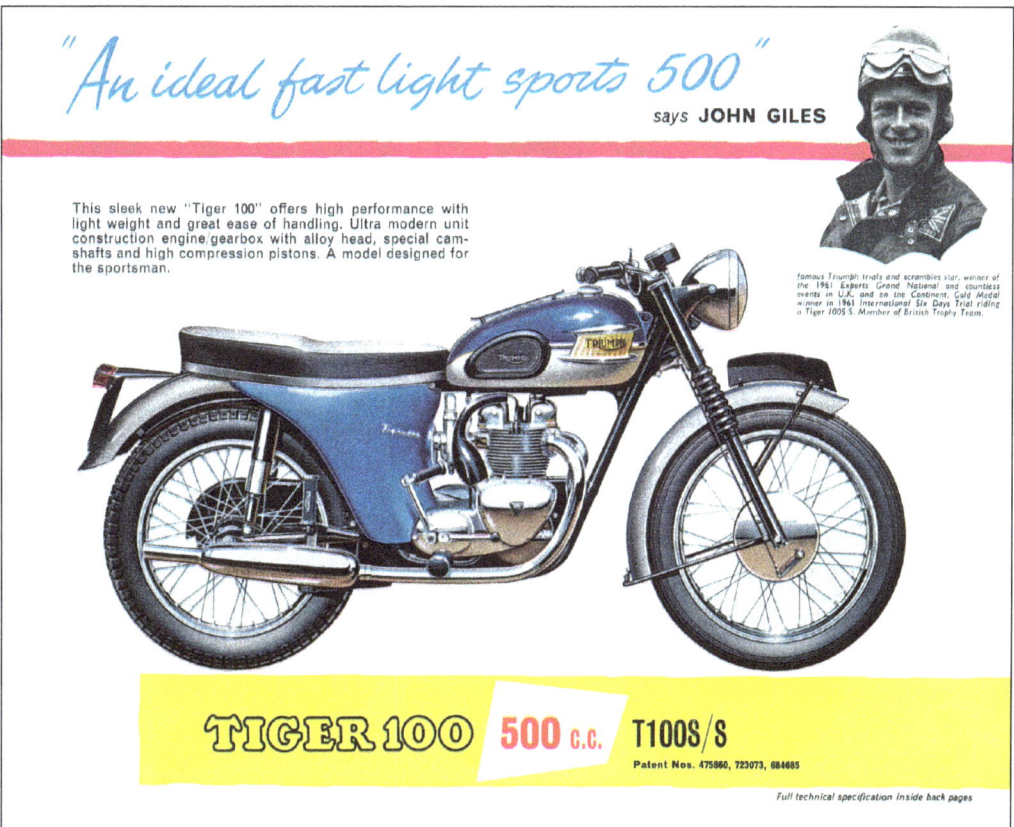

The Tiger 100SS in Blue and Silver made a handsome little sports twin, although some thought it would look better without its abbreviated rear panel arrangement.

Publicity photograph showing Bert Watmore on a T100SS in Showell Lane.

Triumph Production Testers' Tales – from the Meriden Factory

alloy, I do not think it had a rival for looks, in its class, anywhere else in the motorcycling world.

Percy did a lot of mileage on the experimental model, but with the tried and trusted engine that had been used in the Tiger 100A, there were no real problems at all. Good old Bert Watmore did another photo shoot for the Publicity Department, this time posing on the 1962 model in Showell Lane, looking at someone's posh house.

The only problems that seemed to appear on the T100S/S after a few thousand miles, but when the machines were still under warranty, was a persistent oil leak around the bottom of the push-rod tubes. After several attempts to cure this by removing the rocker boxes, then the cylinder head, washing everything and refitting with new seals on the inlet and exhaust push-rod tubes, the problem persisted, though this time fresh engine oil puddled around the base of both tubes after just a few miles, not a few thousand.

After scratching his head, Repair Shop Chargehand Reg Hawkins ordered the top off the engine again. This time, the tappet blocks were removed from the barrel, and after degreasing them and the bores in the base of the barrel (into which they are an interference fit), they were pressed back in with sealant. It was just as the barrel was about to be refitted with a new base gasket it was noticed that although where all the cylinder base joint face on the crankcase was oil-free, there was clean oil around the four cylinder base studs each side of the large tappet block holes in the crankcase.

Removing all eight studs with a ⅜in extractor, it was found that the four outboard studs, the two above the timing chest, and the two on the drive side above the engine number, were into blind holes. The four studs which were inboard, however, were in open holes straight through into the inside of the engine, immediately above the inlet and exhaust camshafts.

On earlier models, the studs had been dipped in sealing compound on these four holes on production before being driven in with a stud driver, so that they were tight. The latest engines had these studs fitted dry, and after a few thousand miles, oil worked its way up the threads and out of the cylinder barrel flange stud holes from underneath the holding down nuts. To all intents and purposes, it appeared to be a push-rod tube oil leak, and it had us fooled for a while.

As mentioned previously, the T100A, in its black and ivory livery for 1960, then black and silver for 1961, was a sporty twin, even if it did not exactly look it. The five hundred unit was very willing, and after the Energy-Transfer system had been thrown over the hedge and standard coil ignition fitted in its place, it became a fast, trouble-free little bike, as the engine was almost certainly the best five hundred as far as performance went.

The 5TA Speed Twin continued, and for 1962 was finished in Ruby Red, becoming a super-smooth little cruiser, with basically the same engine as the T100S/S, but in a softer state of tune, having ramp E3275 form camshafts, requiring a ten thousandth of an inch tappet clearance all round, and the lower 7-1 compression ratio. Where the T100 engine developed around 38bhp at 7000rpm, the Speed Twin gave a more docile 27bhp at 6500rpm.

As I've said, Percy did a lot of mileage on the Tiger 100S/S, and the experimental model that he rode was quite the scruffiest I've ever seen, but Percy said it didn't give a spot of bother at all. In fact, the over-square engine of 69mm bore and 65.5mm stroke was virtually indestructible. Percy had a racing engine early on in the Daytona episode that used the same pistons, and what we called the squish-band head.

In nice weather I used to enjoy riding the T100S/S, especially as you could use the revs. Being over-square, the diameter of the bore greater than the length of the stroke, the engine operated in a higher rev band than the larger models, so you could really buzz it through the gears. All in all, a nice little bike, so much so, that when my son wanted to get off Japanese machinery and go classic British, we got him a beautiful little T100S/S from a chap at Wiveliscombe for the princely sum of five hundred pounds.

Needless to say, it was up on the workbench when we got it home for a quick check over, and we found that it required a complete overhaul to put everything right in the automotive department. After doing this and running it in, Simon went to the Isle of Man on it and had a splendid time. That little motor ran as sweet as a nut and was still doing so when the Vintage Motorcycle Club had it off him for one of its raffle prizes.

The 1962 models of T120 in their various guises were coming down the track, and the weather improved no end. I had seen the Repair Shop Manager talking to Mr Tubb, our boss, and I wondered what was up. It transpired little Stan Whitcomb was ill, and they required the services of a tester up in the Repair Department for customer machines. I suppose I was a known quantity, so they opted for me.

Stan Whitcomb, otherwise known as Mickey Dripping – why, I don't know – was a very experienced tester I'd originally met back in my Coventry Motor Mart

The Tiger 100S/S

days. The dealership I worked at was situated on the main London Road out of Coventry, and coincidentally on the test route for the Francis-Barnett boys, one of whom was Stan. Their factory was situated in Lower Ford Street, virtually in the city centre, and not more than a quarter of a mile away from the site of the pre-war Triumph works.

The test route for them was turn left out of Ford Street, straight up Cox Street, then over the traffic lights at the Gaumont cinema, and up on to Whitefriars Street to the London Road. The main Triumph dealership, Walter Brandish and Sons, was in Whitefriars Street, and where my own Tiger 100, JRW 405, originally came from. At the top of Whitefriars Street, they turned left on to London Road and out past my dealership, towards the Baginton roundabout. Once round the roundabout the route was retraced to Ford Street; about ten miles in all.

There were three testers: Dickie Shade, Stan, and a young chap called Derek, whose surname I didn't know. Dickie was the eldest and Derek the youngest, always in the middle when the three went buzzing past together. I never did see them ride individually like we did, they were always together, line astern.

If I was outside on the showroom frontage when they came by, Stan would sometimes stop and let me look at his new, little 197cc whatever-it-was he was riding.

At this time, a regular scrambles meeting took place on Bayton Farm down Blackhorse Road, quite near to where I live now. On the odd occasion, I would meet Stan there to watch the meeting. I had my old 1938 three fifty AJS, and Stan had a muddy little 197 Francis Barnett competition model. I also met people there who I was destined to bump into again when I got my Meriden job. Thinking back, my life seems to be like a cog wheel, meshing with other people's cog wheels, and coming round again later in life.

Although the dealership I worked at were main BSA and Sunbeam concerns, they were also agents for Ariel, AJS, Matchless, DOT, and Excelsior. We also had Sun and Norman as well as Bond three-wheelers. All – apart from the big four stroke makes – were powered by the Villiers two stroke engine, and I know that Stan was more than a little keen on the Sun trials bike we had.

So I knew Stan, the same as I knew Jimmy Brown, for about twelve months before I left and went to work for Triumph. It was some time before Stan came to Meriden, but it was during my time in the army, when the Francis Barnett factory either closed or moved, and Stan applied for, and got, a job at Meriden. It's funny, but a couple of years later when the Coventry Motor Mart Limited closed its doors for good, another couple of chaps who worked there got jobs at Meriden. Noel Summerfield and Tommy Weir, a salesman and a spares storeman, both looked me up when they arrived, so it was like old times.

As it was, Stan was off sick for only two days, but it was enjoyable being back where I worked before call-up. Bert Carter, the Repair Shop Foreman, and the man responsible for having JRW 405 rebuilt after my spectacular spill the week before I was due to report at Catterick, mentioned there would be a request at the end of the year for me to move off test and back onto the fitting bench in the Service Repair Department. This I did not mind one bit.

Although the Production Test department was glamorous, and very nice in the summer, in the winter on ice and in fog, it was a bugger. It didn't seem so bad in the Repair Shop because in the hot weather, Arthur the labourer hooked open both the rubber doors so that there was a bit of a breeze, and when you had finished working on the job you had been given, you could always run it outside to check things over. Besides, it was another couple of pounds a week due to it being, apart from the Experimental Department, one of the most highly skilled jobs in the factory. These chaps could dismantle a bike down to the last nut, bolt, screw and washer, and if you picked up any individual item, they could name it and tell you exactly where it fitted.

Little Stan came back and I returned to the Production Test, resuming my daily routine.

The four C range machines were the 3TA three fifty, the 5TA five hundred, the new Tiger 100S/S and the T100S/C, so all machines on the range were tried and tested.

Along with the little Cubs, these remained the staple models for the home and general export market which covered Europe and Australasia.

The beautiful TR6SS, TR6SR, and TR6C models were now finished in a very nice polychromatic red and the standard silver, the original silver sheen that Edward Turner settled on to lighten up his slimmed-down Tiger range of sports models, so it had been around for quite some time. The 6T Thunderbird was now the only tourer, and in black and silver, still with its rear panels, was the home market's steady seller.

We had a nice range of machines to choose from for our going home bikes, and only the Cub men continued to use the little models for their evening ride home, while the rest of us opted for either the American Tiger 100 models or a nice TR6 Trophy. Not many chose

107

Triumph Production Testers' Tales – from the Meriden Factory

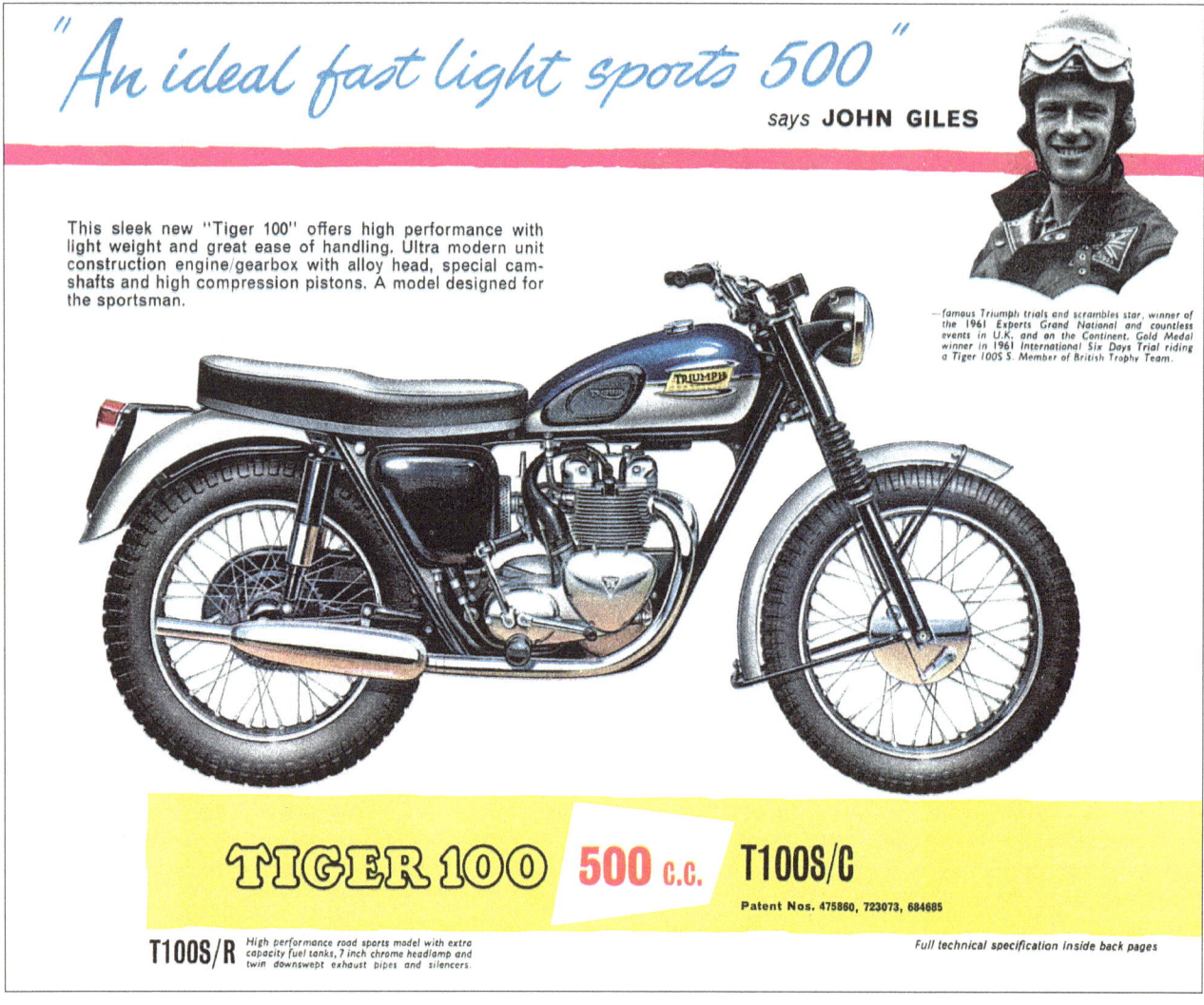

The US T100SC with no rear panels and the small 'peanut' petrol tank.

the Bonnevilles now; they were too much trouble to get ready between 4.45 and 5 o'clock.

The home market Bonnevilles were still in blue and silver livery, but with oil tank and toolbox in black. One of the problems now showing on both of the six fifty sports models was that, under harsh acceleration, when you were really winding it on hard, the gearbox was twisting fractionally on its mountings, even this small movement altering the carefully adjusted primary chain. The power required to try and turn the back wheel made the main chain yank the gearbox on the transmission side backwards, which unduly tightened the primary drive chain, which, if it wasn't slackened off, would stretch, causing damage to the teeth on both the engine and chain wheel sprockets. It could also cause overheating of the chain links, distinctly increasing the chances of a breakage with catastrophic results for the aluminium cases and the Lucas stator housed therein.

No matter how many times the chains were adjusted, after a brisk ride, the primary chain was, nine times out of ten, found to be overtight. The only way to cure the problem was found to be a secondary chain tensioner on the top gearbox through stud, primary drive side. With the two adjusters, it was possible to prevent the gearbox twisting under load.

A while later, however, when I had moved back to the Repair Shop, a new problem materialised concerning all of the six fifty gearboxes, including the 6T Thunderbird and the now defunct Tiger T110. A customer came to the service counter one morning, and made a

The Tiger 100S/S

A very nice 1962 TR6 UK model, restored by the author. In Hi Fi Scarlet and Silver sheen livery, this road-going standard model is highly sought-after. Timing-side view.

This model TR6 had the revised Lucas wiring loom that obviated the dreaded QD plug.

Triumph Production Testers' Tales – from the Meriden Factory

complaint that his gearbox could be felt to move when he blipped the throttle. After Stan the service tester had given it a spin, he rode it straight into the Repair Shop. Stopping the engine, he put the Bonneville on its centre stand before disrobing. Stan called Reg Hawkins, the Chargehand, and Bert Carter, the Foreman, to him and restarted the bike. As he revved the motor, he told them to place their hands on the gearbox outer cover. Reg looked incredulous as Stan revved the motor again whilst Reg had his left hand on top of the gearbox. Bert nodded his head in agreement before switching off the motor off by pressing the magneto cut-out button situated in the middle of the handlebar between the mounting clamps.

We'd all been looking on and wondered what they had found. Maybe a faulty bearing causing a roughness that they could feel being transmitted through the casing, or, as one wag remarked, "They've found one of the Great Train Robbers trying to get out."

What they had discovered, in fact, was that the whole gearbox was loose, and was moving with the pull of the primary chain. After explaining to the customer that he would have a couple of hours' wait, the bike was put up on a bench and the transmission completely removed, leaving engine and gearbox completely isolated from each other.

By introducing the wooden shaft of a hide mallet between the gearbox and the rear of the engine, and then exerting some force, using the mallet handle as a lever, it was noticed that the whole of the bottom of the gearbox case, through which passed the half inch diameter bottom gearbox clamp bolt, moved. Trying to tighten the clamp bolt nut further made no difference, it still moved. This meant that even with two top gearbox adjusters, the whole plot was practically jumping around in the frame.

It was no good, to investigate further the engine had to come out, so I was asked to work with Joe Bosworth, the chap whose bench the machine was on, because the customer needed to go home on the bike, if possible before the factory closed at end of play.

With the engine out and the rear engine gearbox plates off, everything was now free for the four of us to see the problem more clearly. With the gearbox still mounted by its bottom bolt in the frame, you could grip the gearbox and wiggle it about in its entirety. The bottom pivot bolt was supposed to clamp the gearbox solidly in the frame, only being slackened when primary chain adjustment was required, then retightened afterward. Having the gearbox held in its mounting plates, as well as the top clamping stud and twin adjusters, you assumed that, as the bottom clamp was tight, so too would be the gearbox in the frame.

Due to either a mistake about the distance between the machined side faces of the bottom main mounting lug, or the frame bottom lugs inside face dimensions, the job wasn't being clamped as it should have been. There was quite a gap, and Joe introduced his feeler-gauge blades, increasing their collective value until he could barely force them into the gap. Making a note of the figure, he then slackened off the bottom pivot bolt nut and checked the gap again. Subtracting the first figure from the second gave Joe the amount of pinch when the bottom pivot bolt nut was tightened to its correct torque. What had to be done now was to find a half inch plain washer of the appropriate thickness, and introduce it into the unclamped gap. By withdrawing the bottom bolt a few inches so that it cleared the gap, the washer could be tapped carefully into place and the bolt pushed back and through it. Now when the bottom nut was tightened, the gearbox was rock solid on its bottom mounting.

Working quickly, Joe and I got the engine back in and bolted up before refitting the transmission and adjusting the primary chain. After fitting the petrol tank and exhausts, and carrying out some final adjustments, we dropped the trestle and little Stan Whitcomb started it up. Revving the motor, he declared there to be no movement, but would reserve judgement until after he had given it a good run down the Mile.

After Stan had gone, Joe and I cleaned and degreased our tools. It was the first time I had worked with Joe since the day I started in the Repair Shop in January 1954, and my first job was helping him rewire a 1953 Speed Twin.

It wasn't long before little Stan was back. Putting the bike on its stand, he left the engine running while he took off his helmet and gloves. Bert and Reg came down the Repair Shop central gangway toward him just as he revved the motor and placed his hand on the gearbox. He stopped the motor, and declared, "It's fine." He told us he'd stopped down the Mile and checked it, and all was well, so Bert gave him the all-clear to take it out to its owner waiting in Reception. He had finished in plenty of time so I asked Reg for a job for the following day.

Since that incident, one of the things I've always paid special attention to when restoring a duplex framed model is ensuring that the gearbox is being held tight in the frame by its bottom mounting lug. I even made a special frame-spreading tool, that when introduced in-between the two bottom runs of the frame and wound

The Tiger 100S/S

open, can make the gap slightly bigger in order to insert a decent thickness washer. I always liked to feel the gearbox was tight after the spreader was slackened off, even before the bottom pivot bolt nut was tightened.

Stopping the gearbox jumping about certainly cut down the vibration transmitted through the rider's footrests, and that's got to be a bonus.

Eddie and I were testing away merrily, mainly on the nice Tiger 100S/S models, but also on the American S/C types, as with the wider bars they were comfortable. The weather warmed up so we changed back into our Belstaff waxed cotton riding suits, and almost felt as if we'd removed a suit of armour.

Bill and Norris had a place they went to for a break from the rest of us, up on top of the banks in Church Lane. It also offered a commanding view of all the traffic using the hill in both directions, which gave them ample warning should Stan Trowell decide to go for a ride-out to make sure we were all on the job and on route, and not sitting in the cafe.

I spoke to Charlie Wallace quite a lot because he was a keen ornithologist, and what he didn't know about birds, the feathered variety, wasn't worth knowing. He wasn't into the exotica, just the ordinary, common or garden birds we usually take for granted. I had always been interested, so sometimes we would sit on the grass bank leaning on the fence to Billy and Bonneville's field, watching Lapwings performing their fantastic tumbling flight. Charlie used to call them clowns of the sky.

Once, down Pikers Lane, one of the roads Eddie and I used on the way home, at the bottom of which is a little brook with a wooden plank footbridge over it, Charlie did his stuff and talked to a flock of crows. I sat watching, amazed really, as he jumped up and down on the little footbridge, making cawing noises and flapping his arms up and down. I swear they were answering him as they flew around above him in a big circle, or maybe not. They could have been saying to themselves, "Look at that silly bugger down there." Just then Charlie missed his footing. He hadn't noticed how near he was getting to the edge, he was so excited jumping up and down, then 'splosh,' over he went. I almost fell off my bike laughing, and as I helped him out of the brook, I could tell Charlie wasn't amused.

Sitting having a mug of tea the next day, we were treated to a story by Jock, my old army mate. It had rained the night before just as we were about to knock off. As we all shot off down the road, Jock and Westy went down the A45 towards Coventry on a pair of 5TA Ruby Red Speed Twins. As usual, going down the Holyhead Road towards Westy's home on the outskirts of the city, they were larking about. Coming up close behind Westy on his offside, Jock reached over and flipped Westy's helmet forward so that it was almost over his eyes. The front edge of his helmet had pushed his goggles down over his nose, and whilst he was frantically fiddling one-handed to straighten his helmet and get his goggles back to where they should be, a Findus frozen food van stopped at the traffic lights in front of him. I reckon Jock must have been wetting himself at Westy's predicament, and even though Westy was sitting with us whilst Jock related the full goings on, there was no animosity whatsoever because they were good friends. I suppose it would have been the same if the shoe was on the other foot.

Anyway, Westy looked up too late and grabbed all the brakes, sliding off in the pouring rain. Thankfully, he didn't actually hit the van, but the bike was on its side, and Westy had rolled into the gutter, where he lay moaning. Jock stopped, and putting his bike on the stand, walked back to Westy and began kicking water from the gutter over him, shouting, "Come on, you silly sod, get up, you're not hurt."

What Jock didn't see was the little old lady who now came up behind him and hit him over the crash helmet with her umbrella, shouting at the same time, "Leave him alone, you big bully!" We all laughed as we imagined the scene, and both Jock and Westy had a good laugh. too. Mates. It was just larking about as Westy put it to Mr Tubb as he was trying to explain the marks on the 5TA ...

It does happen, you can't ride all those machines for years without some sort of accident. All you can hope for is that the accident with your name on it isn't a serious one, as I was about to find out one night on my going home bike.

I hadn't been on test long, and had only been on the six fifties for a day or two, when I came unstuck good and proper. It was the year before, 1961, and we were on a run of Kingfisher Blue and Silver Tiger T110S models when it happened.

On my way to work that morning, roadworks signs had been put out, warning of tarring and chipping resurfacing on our stretch of the old A45 from its lead off from the bypass, up past Millison's Wood, and on up to the top of Meriden Hill at the Showell Lane junction.

I had elected to go home that night on a Tiger 110. We had all pre-checked our bikes after the four o'clock tea break: brakes, lights, tyre pressures, controls, steering, etc, started them and initially set the

Triumph Production Testers' Tales – from the Meriden Factory

carburettor. At five minutes to five, we rode out to our start positions outside Pop Wright's office. I remember sitting there, feet up, bike on the centre stand, fuel on ready to kickstart and rock off the stand in first gear at Pop's 'away you go' signal.

Pop slid his office window back and gave us the go signal. As one, we fired up and sped down the drive to the road. We had done this so many times before, each rider in his usual position, that we didn't have to think about it.

The chaps to the left of the bunch turned up toward Meriden Hill for Birmingham, whilst I and the others turned right down to the A45 intersection, Sooty and Alan Armitt turning right up to Eastern Green Lane. Whether I was asleep or on auto pilot, I failed to notice that the road had been sprayed with tar, and then spread with chippings. The road menders had used a road sweeper wagon to get the worst of the loose chippings up, but where they had gone down to the A45 bypass intersection, the sweeping action of the big wide rotary brush on the wagon had left a wash of chippings in the middle of the road. We didn't know this because, all through that day's testing, we had turned out of the factory and gone left up toward the hill.

As we roared down to the left-hand bend that took us to the intersection, I got on to some of the loose gravel, and, with the bike banked over, before I knew it the back end started to go. Even as I was going down, the penny dropped why Sooty and some of the chaps had taken a funny line when they turned off. It was, however, too late for me. The Tiger 110 went down on its driveside as I slid off and kicked the bike away from me. It was one of the things you were taught as a Despatch Rider, if the bike is going down and there is nothing you can do about it, get off and kick the bike away from you, because if it hooks you and you get dragged or, worse still, end up underneath, it will do you serious damage.

I rolled quite a few times but leapt to my feet as the others stopped and came back to me. The bike had carried on and had come to rest against the opposite kerb of the little slip road leading down to the intersection. Bill and Eddie pulled up and lifted their bikes onto their stands. "Wotcha doin', Hughie, one of your old Signals tricks?" asked Bill. "I'm alright, I'm alright." I said. "You bloody look it, your eyes are going round like Catherine Wheels," Bill replied. "You'd better wait here and I'll nip back and tell Tubby," he said, and shot off back up the road.

Jock must have seen my bike go past him without me on it, on his nearside as he was turning up Eastern Green Lane. He and Westy came back, and with that, the mickey-taking started. Jock said, "Bloody hell, been on the job ten minutes and he's writing off Tiger 110s like no bugger's business." Westy just looked at me and smirked; he didn't need to say anything, I knew what he was thinking.

Bill arrived back, and pulling up, shouted, "Tubby said you've got to ride the bike back cos he wants to kick your arse personally." Eddie hadn't stopped giggling all the while this was going on, but at least he had picked up the gravel-rashed Tiger 110 for me. Slowly, owing to the fact I didn't know if anything was broken (on me, not the bike), I climbed onboard. The clutch and front brake levers had moved so I twisted them to roughly the right position, checked that the fuel was on, gave her a quick prod and away she went.

Gingerly, I wound my way back through the still exiting factory traffic to be met with some strange stares as I pulled into the Finishing Shop. Mr Tubb was waiting, but not for the reason Bill had said. He asked how I was, and then said, "Well, if you're sure you're alright, put your plates on a tiddler and go home, we'll sort it out in the morning." I think he was relieved I wasn't a hospital case and he'd not lost another tester to the Triumph ward at Coventry and Warwickshire hospital.

The following morning, sore and stiff, I rode to work with Eddie. He was on a Tiger 110, so rode behind me, the slowest we had ridden together for a long time. After a nice hot mug of Evvy's tea, I got on with the job. Mr Tubb didn't even ask to see me, and the chaps didn't mention it; as far as all were concerned, it was forgotten.

So, that's the story of my big prang in 1961, nothing to be proud of, but, as I said, riding the number of bikes we did day after day, the law of averages are bound to catch up with you, sooner or later.

My mind went back to my old friend, Alex Scobie, who, from 1946 to 1948, road tested all the racing Grand Prix models from the factory, down the A45 to the Blue Boar cafe, then back again at speeds of well over a hundred miles an hour. In all the years I knew Alex, right up until his death, he never mentioned whether he had had any accidents. This also applies to Percy, as I never heard of him, in all the time I was at Meriden, coming off in any shape or form when he was out on the road. I know he had a few prangs when racing, and indeed was on intimate terms with a notorious wall on the old Aintree circuit. He had that many pins in him, as well as walking with a limp to starboard, he used to set scanners into orbit at airports. At the speeds that those pair rode at, accidents don't bear thinking about.

The Tiger 100S/S

The famous square barrel and head Grand Prix motor, also used in the TR5 Trophy models up to 1951. Restored by the author.

The two greats – Percy Tait and Alex Scobie, specialists in covering large distances at very high speeds. Seen here on the author's stand at the International Classic Bike Show.

The Grand Prix engines were all tested on a dynamometer before being installed in the frame to ensure they met requirements. The test report and data sheet was very thorough, with a little more to it than the one's we had to fill out.

When a bike had been put through its paces on the road by Alex, it was despatched together with the full report so that the customer could see just how everything performed.

Fitted to the motor on assembly was a decompression plate, in-between the cylinder base and crankcase joint, which allowed the motor to be used on the low octane, seventy-plus stuff that was all that was available in the immediate post-war years.

When the engine had been run in, this plate could be removed, and special, higher octane racing fuel used. If the bike had been taken out on the road by Alex on low octane post-war petrol, a lot of detonation in the combustion chambers would occur with resulting damage to the pistons.

Triumph Production Testers' Tales – from the Meriden Factory

```
                    T R I U M P H.

              "GRAND PRIX" RACING MACHINE.

               Test Report and Data Sheet.

                                    Gearbox No. 97169 N

Date. 23 Apr 50   Engine No. T100    R    Frame No. TF

Bore 63 m/m       Stroke 80 m/m     C.C. 498   C/R 7:85
Valve timing : Inlet opens... 38          Closes... 53 ) with 0.030"
               Exhaust opens... 53        Closes... 29 ) clearance
Valve clearance, cold : Inlet... 0.002"   Exhaust... 0.004"
Ignition timing : 42 degrees         Magneto points : 0.012" gap
Sparking plug : KLG 689 / Lodge R49 / Champion LA15
Carburetter.  Type : 1" Amal Type 6
              Setting for 70-75 octane fuel
              Needle jet 109           Needle setting... 2
              Throttle valve... 4      Main jet... 200 approx.
Reductions in gearbox :   1.095    1.44    1.73
Gear ratios : 22T -       5.00    5.48    7.20    8.67
              23T -       4.78    5.24    6.88    8.26
              24T -       4.57    5.01    6.58    7.93
Oil. Mineral oil of grade : Engine SAE 50  Gearbox SAE 50  Front forks SAE 20
```

TEST BED REPORT :
Barometer 29.76   Jet 150 (Test bed)   Plug R.49   Date 14 Apr 50
Run in for 3½ hours at .... R.P.M.

R.P.M.	Power Curve. lb. pull	B.H.P. Corrected to N.T.P.
4000	–	–
4500	26.8	26.9
5000	–	–
5500	29.4	36.00
6000	28.8	38.5
6500	28.3	41.4
7000	27.9	43.6

Signature..........................

ROAD TEST REPORT :   Date 17 May 50
Steering...... ✓ roller bearing H/Shaft   Oil bath
Brakes........ ✓ Pistons E190X   Kick starter
Carburation... ✓ Tappets E1478   Cork Central
Performance... ✓ Front brake cam W856

Signature... J. A. Scobie

Safe maximum R.P.M. 7200
Always state both engine and frame No's. when writing for
information or spares.

TRIUMPH ENGINEERING CO. LTD., Meriden Works, Allesley, COVENTRY.

An original Grand Prix test report and data sheet that was routinely compiled by Alex Scobie after high-speed testing on the open road.

The Tiger 100S/S

Scobie on one of the high-speed Thunderbirds in France, being refuelled by Allan Jeffries, with HG Tyrell-Smith attending to oil, and Coventry rider Len Bayliss standing behind in a white helmet.

Up until a couple of years ago, I had the complete file of Grand Prix machines, their individual test reports, individual specifications they were built to, the dealer or customer they went to, all signed by dear old Alex. It was only when we moved house that they came to light in a cardboard potato crisp box in the loft, left with me by Alex for safe keeping all those years ago. Now, they are with the Triumph Owners Club of Great Britain, but to be honest, I couldn't help myself, and I have great delight in sitting and reading through the photocopies I made of these, seeing Alex's comments and signature on each one.

Alex was a remarkable rider in his day, and when he and I used to go and give talks to the various Triumph Owners Club nights, I marvelled at his car-driving ability also. I've always maintained you will be a better car driver in this day and age if you have been a motorcyclist first. I am sure if Alex is watching, he will not mind me saying that Percy seamlessly took over his mantle.

I stayed on T100S/S models for going home for a few weeks. To tell the truth, it wasn't until a couple of days later that I started to stiffen up, and even though I was only some three to four years older than when I was training on the G3L Matchless over the North Yorkshire moors every day, and riding in the Display Team, I said to myself, "It never used to hurt like this."

Practice every day and you will get better, that's what we were told, and on the football pitch behind the barracks at Ripon, riding the G3Ls, you never gave it a second thought when you came off. Believe me, learning to ride backwards, no-handed, you were off more than you were on. When we started to ride as a team, and not as individuals, we had to learn the multiple rider and machine tricks, such as the six-bike fan, or pyramid, as it's often called, and as another well-known display

Triumph Production Testers' Tales – from the Meriden Factory

team at the time was doing this same spectacular trick, we were determined to be better.

The other armed forces team used later model bikes. and these had special bracketry to hold the bikes together, and ladders, held vertically, for the pyramid riders to hang on to. The Signals, on the other hand, would not use any artificial help of this kind, and had great delight in proving so at the end of the ride, the top-most rider jumping down followed by the other fan riders, then the six bikes peeling off to show that no aids were used. Mind you, when we were on the football pitch practising on the Matchless singles, we were down more than we were up, but we got there in the end, knowing that if we could do it on the three fifty G3L machines, it would be easier on the five hundred Triumphs.

When you get all the chaps onboard and the fan starts moving, you could bet it was going to come down, and if you happened to be one of the six riders, as I was, you ended up underneath a lot of blokes. My greatest joy was performing at the 1958 Meriden Gala on the top football pitch in front of my old bosses and Gloria, my wife-to-be. Afterwards, I could walk around in my splendid blue uniform and show her the various departments in the factory. It was certainly a splendid day.

One day, at a show in the London area, we were visited by one of motorcycling's greatest journalists, Vic Willoughby. He was a splendid chap, game for anything on a bike, so we persuaded him to take the top-man spot on the six-bike fan. It went off splendidly, and from the smiles on some of the chaps' faces when performing the trick with him on board, they enjoyed it, too.

I think it was the best thing about my time in the army, even better than when I was posted for my last few months to the then War Office on the embankment. It was a part of the Royal Signals I had not known about previously, and having had to submit to the then Military Secrets Act, I was a courier, operating out of the War Office, and billeted at Hounslow with the SIB. Travelling on express trains in reserved compartments to Salisbury, Chester or Waverley Street, Edinburgh, with an armed escort was a cushy number.

Weighing everything up, though, it wasn't as good as the freedom to ride every day over the north Yorkshire moors in the companionship of good mates, getting back on the road and stopping off at our favourite cafe in Thirsk. I count myself a very lucky chap indeed.

When I was back in the Repair Shop, the other Display Team riding on Meriden-supplied and maintained machines was that of the Royal Marines. They did not use the TRWs, however, but rode specially-modified T100S/S models with no lights, finished in gloss

A proud moment. The author, third from right, collecting new team machines from Meriden in 1958.

The Tiger 100S/S

The 'fan' practice on G3L Matchless machines going all wobbly. The author is on the machine second from the right.

The fan practice, still on Matchless models. The author is second from the right on 27YB08.

navy blue. They had low compression pistons and lower than standard gearing overall, but with wide ratios in the gearbox. With the normal downswept separate exhausts and, if I remember correctly, scrambles tyres, not the Dunlop Trials Universal that we used, they were not a bad set of lads. They did what we did and brought their bikes to the Repair Shop at the end of their season for overhauling during the winter month. One of their chaps, Gordon Matthews, a jovial Cornishman, secured himself a job on the engine bench when he was demobbed.

I often wondered how they got on riding the T100S/S. Being an over-square engine, it thrived on revs and didn't have too much torque. On our taxi bike, Martin 'Desperate Dan' Swindon would start off entering the arena with a chap sitting on his shoulders, a pillion rider with someone on his shoulders, and collect additional

Triumph Production Testers' Tales – from the Meriden Factory

Performing at the Triumph works gala day 1958, on the top football pitch. The author is the third rider from the left.

Notable journalist Vic Willoughby joins the team for a spot of practice. Being the motorcycling journalist who took the 1952 Vincent Black Shadow to its top speed, this was a 'cake walk' by comparison.

passengers placed at strategic points around the circular course without stopping until there were twenty two on the bike. That TRW motor just kept on chugging away until Dave Race and I, the twenty first and twenty second passengers, were safely on. Coming down the pitch, the taxi TRW was leaving tyre tracks in the grass three to five inches deep. I couldn't see a similar feat being performed on a Marine Display Team T100S/S.

The T100S/S engine was calling out for a high performance list, so in conjunction with Experimental, the Service Department issued Technical Information Bulletin Number 13, which listed modifications that

The Tiger 100S/S

The author out on the army range, riding his Matchless 27YB08.

could be carried out to make the C range engines more competitive.

It proved very popular with owners, and especially with a quick little job prepared by Experimental for Percy to ride. It would only be a few years before the Daytona was to come along.

That reminds me of a telephone call I received one day while I was working on a little job in my workshop at the bottom of my garden. The caller's name was Julian Amos, and he had been asked to road test the new Hinckley Daytona model. I'm not afraid to say I have never been too interested in the Hinckley marque. I've always looked at the beautiful alloy engine in my Tiger 100, and thought to myself, "No factory will ever make anything as pretty as that again." Amos asked if he could talk to me and so I invited him over for a coffee while he asked his questions.

When he arrived, it was a bright day, even though a little on the chilly side, and I must say that the new Daytona he was riding looked rather splendid in its livery. It reminded me a lot of the old British Racing Green, popular back in the fifties among the racing car fraternity.

Over coffee in my workshop we talked, and I said, "Well, you know where Daytona comes from." He naturally said America, and I replied that it was also the name of a Triumph twin carburettor model back in 1967. He was interested in this ancestral line from modern day to 1967, so after showing him photographs and specifications, I took it back further to the Tiger 100 and its introduction in 1938. He was amazed, and, being only a young chap, had never seen any of the early models. As this was 2002, I said, "Interestingly, I've got your modern model's grandfather in my garage, want to see

Triumph Production Testers' Tales – from the Meriden Factory

it?" He couldn't believe that 50 years separated my bike and his, and then his eyes lit up with an idea. How would I like to participate with him in an article that featured both our bikes? Obviously, the answer was yes!

As he had ridden this modern thing a fair few miles, when we had finished our coffee, I took him by the arm and introduced him to a proper Triumph. He was really, really interested, and after a while and a few questions, I suggest we go over to the Meriden site, then along the old test route and finish up down the Mile. This we did, and after a long photo session, we rode back up the Mile and stopped in the old lay-by at the end of Somers Lane. I explained about Production Test and the machines we rode, and then asked him if he would care to take JRW 405 for a spin. His eyes lit up with delight – until he got on the bike, that is. Where's the start button? No, you've got to kickstart it and the gear lever is on the proper side, too. Never mind, after one or two attempts, he was away, giving JRW some welly up toward the top of the Mile and the village. I must say, she never sounded better, especially on the down run, passing me at about eighty miles an hour. I thought "I hope he adjusts his braking distances." As he came back and pulled in to the lay-by, he was grinning from ear to ear. He pressed the ignition cut-out and took off his helmet and gloves, looked at me and said, "The brakes are a bit poor." I thought to myself, "Well, riding modern stuff with discs, they would seem a bit ... spongy."

I must say, he wrote a marvellous article with photographs of the bikes, and in the write-up, admitted to the thoughts that had flashed through my mind as he hurtled toward the roundabout at the village end of the Mile. The difference between JRW's brakes and those of the new Daytona had caught him on the hop. He wrote in the article how he thought he'd never be forgiven, if he hurtled headlong into a national monument riding a national treasure.

The technical information bulletin number 13, dealing with the preparation work to obtain the maximum performance from 350 and 500 mint engines.

Summer of '62

My wife, Gloria, was pregnant with our second child, expected sometime at the end of the year, so this concentrated my mind on the subject of transport for my family. Simon, our son, was already four years old, and, thus far, we had travelled in either father-in-law's car or by bus. The latest addition to the family meant that JRW had to go.

One of my old friends in the Repair Department, Benny Marshall, knew a young chap just starting a one-man business as a plumber who wanted a reliable bike to put a box sidecar on for transport in his work. It nearly broke my heart, but he duly came round to the house, coin of the realm changed hands, and away he rode on my JRW 405, all for the princely sum of sixty pounds.

As I had already passed my driving test in the army, in a Bedford three-ton lorry in Leeds on a Saturday morning, all I had to do was find a car. Reg Hawkins, the Repair Shop Chargehand, was going to sell his Morris Eight, four door saloon deluxe so he could buy a more modern Morris Minor. He asked how much I got for the bike, and when I told him, he said I could have his car for the same price, sixty pounds. So there we were, a little family with a car, and the insurance was only four pounds twelve and sixpence a year.

Although I currently had a company bike, I knew that when I returned to the Repair Shop at the end of the year, I would be driving to work every day, instead of riding. This did not appeal, but I thought that maybe something might come along in the future and I would be back on two wheels with the car for family use only. The important thing was to have a car for Gloria to travel in with little Simon.

It was a lovely little thing in gloss black, a dark red pinstripe coachline along the side, and real leather seats. When you opened the door, that smell of leather hit you. I was really pleased with the thing – until the winter. It only had a six-volt electrical system, you see and, on a cold morning, you might as well try and start the thing with a torch battery. It was out with the starting handle, choke out, in neutral, handbrake on, ignition on, then contact. It was like starting up a bloody Tiger Moth.

Eddie and I continued on the 1962 models, each day virtually the same as the previous one. The other chaps had their own way of working, some going quite quickly before lunch, getting eight or ten bikes completed, and leaving just a couple for an easy afternoon in the heat, laying on the grass bank inside Somers Lane.

It was on one of these lazy afternoons that Eddie brightened things up by telling us about the little incidents that he got up to on HMS Broadsword.

For some misdemeanour or other, he was given cookhouse duty, which meant standing at the big stainless steel sinks washing, rinsing, and draining all the big tins and containers the hundreds of meals had been cooked in. The washing up was horrendous, to say the least. At this particular time, the ship was heading down the Bay of Biscay, which is pretty notorious for rough weather at the drop of a hat. Due to the heat of the galley and the motion of the ship, Eddie decided to let in some air, so opened a porthole and pushed out the air scoop induction tube, a round section of curved ducting, just slightly smaller in diameter than the porthole. This operates on a push-pull hinged fitting so that it can be pulled in and stowed, and the porthole closed against bad weather. The forward motion of the ship forces air into the scoop and thence into the galley.

Of course, this air scoop should not be used in seas with a big swell, but as Eddie didn't check first before he pushed it out, all he managed to do was scoop damned great amounts of sea straight into the galley. He was chortling all the while he was telling us the tale, even the

Triumph Production Testers' Tales – from the Meriden Factory

A 1962 T120 UK model restored by the author. Timing-side view.

1962 UK T120, drive-side view.

Summer of '62

bit about being put on close quarter confinement until Gibraltar where his charge would be heard. It made matters worse when he tried to go ashore the next night – as he put it – incognito, dressed in a large waterproof top coat and light grey American cowboy Stetson. Needless to say, he didn't make it ...

While Eddie had been going on about his escapade, Jock was sitting astride the top rail of the wooden fence that bordered the lane and corner field, which happened to be the home of two very fine, heavily built rams. We used to feed them, and when they trotted across the field and came up to the fence to see us, they actually seemed tame. The old chap who owned them did warn us they were unpredictable, and even he, on one or two occasions when in the field with them, had had to make a quick dash for it.

Anyway, we were laughing at Eddie's story and Jock was swinging the leg on the field side of the fence backward and forward, backward and forward. The rams – Billy and Bonneville, as we had named them – came trotting across, because, we assumed, they had heard our voices and were expecting to be fed. The biggest of the two, Billy, had stopped about a yard from the fence and was staring at Jock's swinging leg. He began to sway from side to side ever so slightly, at the same time seeming to pull himself back on his haunches. Then, with the speed of a striking cobra, he lowered his head shot forward, butting Jock's leg with a resounding crack. Poor old Jock yelled and fell off the fence on to the grass bank, shouting, "My bloody leg's broken!" It really was an awful crack we heard, but it wasn't his leg, it was the middle horizontal fence rail that had fractured. We had to lift Jock on to his bike and follow him back to the Finishing Shop to make sure he was alright. We all felt sorry for him, he really was in agony, but we couldn't help laughing all the same, except Eddie, who just guffawed! Poor old Jock, it was weeks before he stopped limping.

The 1962 models we rode that summer included the American five hundreds, the T100S/C, and the T100S/R, along with the T20S/R and T20S/C Cubs. The ignition system on the S/C Cub and the T100s was still the Energy-Transfer, direct lighting setup. I suppose it made sense, because if you were off-roading somewhere, you didn't want an acid-filled battery jumping around beneath you.

These little bikes certainly went well, and I recall the popular American magazine *Cycle World* giving them quite a favourable write-up. With the home market T100SS in Kingfisher Blue and silver sheen, and the American models finished in Burgundy and silver sheen, the rows of completed machines awaiting our attention looked really splendid. In the mornings, when you first banged through the rubber doors, the overhead fluorescent lights really brought out the colours of the machines lined up, row upon row..

As well as being on the Energy-Transfer system, the T100S/C now had both inlet and exhaust camshafts with the E3134 cam form, which gave slightly more power, though the motor had to be revved more to obtain it. The other models retained the previous year's arrangement of the E3134 cam form on the inlet, and the E3325 on the exhaust, the same as the TR6 Trophy and the T120 Bonneville, which made the little motors more tractable.

For 1962, the Duplex frame for the B range six fifties had a slight change to the steering head angle from 67 degrees to 65 to improve handling. Apart from those frames made after 1962 production ceased, the new, stiffer, single downtube frames for the unit construction models would be coming through. I think after Duplex model production finished, about a hundred frames were made for spares, but if more were required, I'm sure they would have been available.

To improve the smoothness of the bigger engines (and I've actually done this on my son's Bonneville) the crankshaft was changed from the straight-sided, bell crank type to the later pear-shaped version, and the balance factor altered from 71 to 85 per cent. My son's T120 exhibited very annoying vibration at about 55-65 miles per hour, just where you didn't want it, so we changed the crank to a later type, and went to the unit motor balance factor using 689 grams per journal weights: bingo! a nice, rideable Duplex Bonnie.

One of the things I could never understand was the really small increases in retail price of the bikes, year-to-year. In some cases, I thought it hardly worthwhile, but I suppose, back in the 1960s, with us selling anything with two wheels as fast as we could make it, to make six pounds' clear profit over and above the previous year was good. I think there was a law, then, called retail price maintenance that prevented profiteering in industry; oh, how I wish it was still in force today.

The two week summer holiday was nearly upon us again, but this year I wouldn't be volunteering for the maintenance stint. With Gloria pregnant, as she was, and now being the proud owner of a little car, we thought we might have a proper holiday.

Eddie was looking for somewhere of his own now that he was romantically involved. We didn't know much

Triumph Production Testers' Tales – from the Meriden Factory

about the lady, except that her name was Florence and that she came from the neighbouring town of Nuneaton. It was funny, really, because all the chaps on test were really keen to get home each evening in time to see the children's programme currently on the television called *The Magic Roundabout*, which had, as one of its characters, Florence. Anyway, Eddie was prepared to go the whole hog with this lady, which would mean a mortgage, and everything that goes with it. I don't know whether Eddie was ready for domesticity, but he seemed to be getting closer to it after all his years of carefree bachelorhood.

Eddie and I talked a lot during our test runs, and he also spoke to the other married chaps, asking about building societies, and such. He was such a devil-may-care sort of bloke, I think he was a little worried about the enormity of the step he was about to take, so we did our best to reassure him.

During our morning tea break, he told us he wanted a day off, but thought that, if he asked, he would lose a day's pay. A few of us talked it over, and came to the same conclusion; the only way to get Eddie his day off with pay was if the boss told him to go home as he was unwell. You couldn't go to the boss and say "I want to go home, I'm not feeling well," he had to send you home. It was company policy in those days to allow two days' sick leave, after which a doctor's note and form for the DSS (Department of Social Services) was required. The trick was how was Eddie going to persuade the boss he was so ill that he needed to be sent home? Sometime later, when he began to chuckle to himself, we knew we were in for an 'Eddie special.'

The following morning, sometime after testing our second bike of the day, Eddie positioned himself where Mr Tubb and Stan could see him from their glass-sided office, and began moaning and holding his stomach. I actually thought there *was* something wrong until he gave me a quick wink, and I knew this was part of his master plan. For the next half an hour, making a big song and dance about getting his bike ready, he made sure he was seen grimacing and clutching his stomach. About every ten minutes, he would scurry off to the toilets, only to re-emerge a few minutes later with a pained expression on his face.

Jock, Westy, Norris, and Bill were all in on this, pretending to attend to their next test machine, but crouched down by the bikes, and almost wetting themselves with laughter at Eddie's antics. What we hadn't noticed, was that Fred – obviously pre-arranged with Eddie – had placed his bucket, half full of engine oil and the big, brass syringe he sucks it out of the oil tank with, just by the toilet entrance. While Eddie was play-acting again, making sure one of the bosses could see him, one of the chaps quickly took the bucket and syringe into the toilet and put them in a cubicle.

We were all intrigued and looked at each other, wondering what the blazes was going on, as Eddie, this time ran into the toilets and the cubicle where the bucket and syringe were, slamming and locking the door behind him. I can't remember who it was that poked their head into the office to let Mr Tubb know that there was something wrong with Eddie, who'd locked himself in the toilet. Sure enough, the boss went marching into the toilet, calling out, :"Eddie, are you in here, are you alright?," only to be met with the disgusting noise of someone really suffering an incredibly loose bowel movement, followed by a low moan. By now, we were beside ourselves with glee, and, as Mr Tubb emerged from the toilet, looking a little shaken, he called over to us "Tell Eddie to get off home." :"Yes, Mr Tubb," crowding into the toilets to see if Eddie really was alright. I think it was Jock who said, "It's alright, you can come out now, he's gone." With that, one of the cubicle doors swung open. Eddie was sitting there, fully clothed, with the oil bucket between his legs, and the big brass syringe in his hands, plunger fully extended. With a grin, he placed the suction pipe end in the oil and slowly depressed the plunger. The noise was disgustingly awful. I understood why Mr Tubb had come out of the toilet straight away after hearing it; it really turned my stomach. Eddie sat there and chortled, and the rest of us laughed until we were fit to burst.

As he put his helmet on to go home, Eddie feebly lifted his hand to the office, as if to say, "I'll be alright, thanks," then turned to us and said, "There's nothing like it when a well-oiled plan pays off!" And off he went on two days' 'sick' leave. We could hardly believe it. Roger Bryant from the Rectification section got the bucket and syringe out of the way, and as Eddie cleared off, we all marvelled at his ingenuity. Even now, at the gatherings we periodically meet up at, you can rely on someone coming out with, "Do you remember old Eddie and the bucket of oil?" We loved him, and he is still remembered as the nicest of all those we worked with.

A run of TR5AC models at the end of the 1961 build suffered with frame flexing problems, which had a less than desirable affect on their petrol tanks. It was found that rough terrain in America caused a degree of flexing in the swan-neck portion of the front frame. The forces being exerted by the front forks caused the main head lug to bend backward just a little, but as the petrol tank was bolted to a fixing point at the back of the front frame, and at the front, behind the steering head casting, the distance between the two fixing points was altering quite rapidly when the machine was ridden off-road.

This applied undue stress to the petrol tank fixing ears, and, of course, fractured the petrol tank where the mounting ears were welded on to the main body of the tank. You didn't want a petrol tank leaking fuel on to a hot motor out in the baking heat of the American desert, oh no!

A modification was put through in the form of a bracing bar, which reduced flexing of the front frame to an acceptable level that didn't affect the petrol tank front or rear mountings.

Thinking about a leaking petrol tank and fire, one lunchtime we were sitting outside on the front lawn, talking, eating, and generally watching the world go by, when we heard a bike coming down the hill, going hell for leather toward the factory gates. From its flat exhaust note, we could tell it was a TRW side-valve twin. It was being ridden by my old friend Stan Truslove, and – why, I don't know – it was on fire. Stan was wearing his long riding coat, and, as he pulled to a hurried stop on the opposite side of the road to the main gates, he leapt off and let the bike fall onto its drive-side on the grass verge. The fire must have started under the seat somewhere, and had burnt through one of the fuel pipes from the petrol tank to the carburettor. Stan had obviously felt his bum getting warm, and high-tailed it back to the yard where the fire extinguishers were.

The 'frame-stiffening' strut introduced after reported petrol tank leakages in the USA. Frame head-lug flexing during fast off-road use caused tanks to split and leak.

Triumph Production Testers' Tales – from the Meriden Factory

We all watched old Stan in wonderment as he proceeded to do a fair imitation of a war dance, trying to beat at his smouldering coat-tails at the same time. Two chaps had seen him coming toward the factory down the hill past Millisons Wood, looking like a fiery comet, and had dashed into the packing bay to grab a couple of extinguishers. Running across the road, they covered the bike and Stan's rear end in foam. We had all stopped eating and simply sat there, staring at the scene unfolding in front of us. I looked at Bill, his face a picture of astonishment. I don't think he had finished his mouthful of sandwich, as his mouth hung open, but he turned to look at Eddie and me, and said "Christ, these things are determined to get us one way or the other."

The testers were the factory bosses' gophers: go for this, go for that; there was always some errand that we were asked to do during our daily routine, be it collect a new car, fetch a loaf of bread from the village bakers, or go to the specialist tobacconist at Leamington Spa that supplied the Company Secretary, Mr Charles Parker, with his pipe fodder.

It was a special blend, and Charles Bud Parker would not have his pipe tobacco from anywhere else, so it befell to one of us to fetch it whenever he was getting down to the dusty remnants in the bottom of his pouch. He would get one of the office girls to ring though and order the stuff, and then send the money down to Mr Tubb who, while not liking it, would send one of us off on the errand.

The shop was some ten miles away in Leamington Spa. As this was the home ground of Bill and Norris, it was usually one of these who were detailed to go, although, on this occasion, for some reason or other, Jock got the job.

The tobacco was always nicely wrapped by the shop, and it was brought back on the petrol tank parcel grid, secured by one or two of the many Dunlop rubber bands we carried in our riding suit pockets. As was the norm, as soon as the rider banged through the rubber swing doors with his front wheel, he would shout the nearest tester to him and throw the packet. The tester, whoever he was, would then quickly take the packet to the office and put it on Mr Tubb's desk so that a quick internal phone call could be made to let Mr Parker know it was there, and he could send someone down to collect it. Now, you might say, okay, what's so special about that? But it was the throwing bit that was relevant.

A couple of days later, Mr Tubb asked Jock to go to the village bakers and get him, ready to take home that evening, one of Tuckey's freshly baked and sliced loaves. Back then, it was an ordinary, old-fashioned tin loaf, baked on the premises and put through a machine that sliced it whilst you waited, then lovingly wrapped in greaseproof paper with a parcel fold at each end which somehow stayed done up. The greaseproof paper kept the bread really fresh, not like today when, after a couple of days, it starts to go mouldy.

Anyway, just after the break at four o'clock, Jock set off on a Thunderbird to do his test run, and stop at the village shop on the way back for Mr Tubb's loaf. Whether there was a queue and he was kept waiting we don't know, but it wasn't until around quarter to five that he banged back through the rubber doors. Bill Letts was the nearest to him, and expected – as we all did – that when Jock shouted, he would catch the loaf and put it on Mr Tubb's desk. Thankfully, Mr Tubb wasn't around to witness the farcical events which followed, but hearing Jock's stentorian shout must have startled Bill, and as he straightened up and spun round in surprise, all he saw hurtling toward him through the air was a long, white package. Bill was a good footballer in his day, so he didn't hesitate for a second, and fetched the loaf a full-blooded, on-the-volley kick. We looked on in amazement as, suddenly, it was raining bread.

Jock screeched to a stop, and putting the bike on the stand, shouted, "You bloody great lump, I'll have to go for another one now!" Bill, smiling, said, "You worry too much, we'll soon put it back together; c'mon." Well, there were four of us on our hands and knees, searching under bikes, with each slice found, trying to pick off the black bits. We had almost managed to get the whole loaf together and in its wrapper, when we saw Mr Tubb walking down the main gangway toward his office. "Bloody hell ..." said Bill, "the little bugger's back and we've still got an end crust missing!"

As luck would have it, that very crust had lodged on top of a Thunderbird petrol tank, right down at the front, partially under the back of the nacelle. Not having actually hit the floor, no foreign bodies blemished its whiteness, so, quick as a flash, Jock popped it in the end of the packet, and with his back turned to the approaching Mr Tubb, neatly folded the ends of the packet, using the original creases as a guide. Waiting for Mr Tubb to enter his office, we all looked at one another, wondering what to do. Jock, seeing that he had picked up his phone, quickly walked up to his open office door and, without saying anything, put the re-wrapped loaf on top of the filing cabinet next to the desk. I don't think Mr Tubb even looked at Jock, so we all put our heads down and got on with preparing our going home bikes.

The new unit twins

Just before the summer holiday began, there seemed to be a lot of activity, and people dashing about clutching sheaves of papers in their hands, especially chaps from the drawing office. We could only assume that final preparations were being made for production of the new unit construction six fifties. We had all seen the strange-looking engine in the bike that people from Experimental had been riding, and Percy had been thrashing around for a fair while on a gloss black bike with nacelle forks. Thinking back, it must have been a Thunderbird, one of two that ultimately turned out to be 6TP police machines, forerunner of the TR6P Saint. On one of my visits to Experimental, I remember seeing a rather ugly-looking lump of a power unit, the engine, gearbox, and transmission housed as one unit, just as the three fifty and five hundred twins already were.

A run of our favourite model – the TR6 Trophy – began coming down the line in its various guises; a lovely bike. We always felt happy when we knew the TR6 was about, there was something comforting about this not-so-glamorous brother of the Bonneville. It was nice to ride, unfussy, and, believe me, plenty powerful, even if it did only have one carburettor. Whether in home market spec or one of the more exotic American adaptations with knobbly tyres and upswept exhausts, it endeared itself to us.

Some TR6C models – build specification I can't remember, though I seem to recall knobbly tyres and upswept exhaust systems – were built for the Swedish army. What made them unusual were the ski attachments each side of the bike. These particular models were very, very fast, hitting almost seven thousand revs per minute in fourth gear, which was approximately 110 miles per hour. The American versions, the TR6C and TR6R models, were on 8.5-1 compression ratio pistons, the same as the T120. They didn't have the E3134 inlet cam of the T120, but the E3325 camshaft on both sides of the motor. I was always amazed at how much power these camshafts produced, and they gave it lower down in the rev range, allowing a wider torque band than engines equipped with the E3134 type.

My own Tiger 100, when rebuilt in 1982, received a pair of these camshafts instead of the standard items, and it really did make a difference to performance and general all-round pulling power. They were originally designed for the first Tiger 110 in 1954, and, prior to being allocated a part number, were christened the Q cam.

Mention that the TR6 had only one carburettor has reminded me of the combination of Amal Monobloc carburettors tested out on the Bonneville between 1959 and the end of 1960.

The 1962 West Coast TR6R with rev-counter kit, two-into-one, downswept, high-rise bars, and a strap over grey-topped seat.

Triumph Production Testers' Tales – from the Meriden Factory

The first spec T120 (which looked like the twin carburettor Tiger 110) had the 376/204 chopped monoblocs with the type 14 remote float, top-fed and rubber-mounted on the saddle downtube. In 1960 when the new Duplex frame was introduced, the chopped monoblocs remained, but now a float chamber was suspended by a threaded rod off a metalastik mounting incorporated in the rear engine steady plate, between the inlet rocker box main through bolts and the frame lug.

Although chopped monoblocs remained in production use, several combinations of instrument were tried out in an attempt to do away with the remote float setup.

A standard floated right-hand monobloc on the timing side was fitted, then a chopped instrument on the driveside which was fed fuel by a crossover pipe from the floated item. This did work, but the flow of fuel under load at high revs was found to be inadequate, which resulted in faltering at high speed. Amal then supplied a handed pair of floated monoblocs (they had their controls on the outside, making tuning access easier), but it was decided that it would complicate spares or track supply if one or the other side was out of stock.

So, in 1961, the Bonneville went to the standard right-hand type, and all that was required when tuning was a longer-than-usual screwdriver to reach the pilot mixture screw on the driveside instrument.

In the Experimental Department, carburettor tests were being carried out on a Bonneville with the mix'n'match carburettors, when it was found that blasting one down the Mile caused misfiring and hesitation. There were two reasons for this: firstly, the rider was wearing a long riding coat which was obstructing the carburettor intake bell-mouths, so a change of garb was the order of the day. This reduced the problem though it was still there at a higher speed, so both fuel taps were turned on, not just the single right-hand one, increasing fuel flow and curing the missfire. I think a modified full-flow tap was used on production after that, and in one of the high performance publications, the use of both taps was suggested.

Behind all of this chopping and changing was the then head of Experimental, Mr Frank Baker, who could be seen out and about, mostly doing fast runs up and down the Mile on a Bonneville.

In-between the big glamorous twins there were always the more mundane Cubs and TA models to test, and if, like me, you wanted something quiet to ride once in a while, it was nice to hop on either a 3TA Twenty One or a 5TA Speed Twin.

On one of my test runs on a 3TA, I had the misfortune to experience piston seizure. When this happened, if you were quick enough with your left hand, as soon as you felt the motor momentarily tighten just prior to locking up the back wheel, you could whip in the clutch lever and shut off the motor. Usually, if you sat for ten minutes while the engine cooled a little, and then removed both sparkplugs, you could turn over the motor on the kick-start, which would bring the oil up the bores. You could then refit the plugs, start the motor, and ride carefully back to the factory. By noting on the test card what had happened, Roger Bryant, or one of his men, would check inside the bores and take the bike out into the yard, where it would be run for some time and the exhausts checked for smoke out of the silencers. This would usually save the expense of renewing the barrel and pistons.

Suddenly, however, every 3TA began tightening up: obviously, something was amiss. "The little buggers," as Bill called them, began nipping up pistons with a vengeance, and no matter how experienced the rider, there was little you could do about it. They seized anywhere and under any conditions, and could even go on the over-run and coasting down toward the bottom of the hill on a closed throttle.

As soon as Stan Trowell and Mr Tubb became aware of how many bikes were being rejected for the same thing, investigations were immediately begun.

Whether it was incorrect piston skirt to cylinder bore tolerance, or a problem with the material the pistons were actually made of, I don't know, but it was sorted out in double-quick time. It didn't happen again on the little twin, and the Service Repair Department got a whole load of re-bored barrels for the service exchange scheme.

We had another seizing problem, this time on the larger 5TA model and the Tiger T100A. The problem manifested itself almost immediately the bikes started on the test run from the yard outside. Once down the drive and out on to the road, the gearbox would lock up solid. It was really awkward because the bike could not be moved; it wasn't possible to select neutral and move the bike, nor could you pull in the clutch and move it.

In the gearbox section, the sleeve gear, or high gear as it's known, has a long bush pressed into its bore, in which runs the gearbox mainshaft. Apparently, the phosphor-bronze bush had been made with too tight a bore, and when the bush was pressed into the gear, the bore of the bush tightened slightly. The fit of the bush when in gear has to be good, otherwise the clutch assembly on the driveside of the main shaft would be jumping around due to too much play. On the other hand, there had to be a certain amount of clearance, otherwise oil could not get between the shaft and the bush, causing these components to run dry and overheat. On the inside of the bush bore is an oil scroll that should take oil down for a certain way, just for lubrication, but, for some reason, the bushes were too tight and, as soon as load was put on to the gearbox at this point, a seizure occurred.

With the bike being run in the outside yard, it was just about ready to lock up as the bike began to accelerate up the road, and, when it did, it stopped you dead in your tracks. There was nothing to do but manhandle the bike to the side of the road, put it on the stand, take off your helmet and gloves, and walk back to the Finishing Shop to report.

Usually, one of the fitters from the large bike Rectification section would grab one of the little steel, low trolleys that supported the bikes on their stands as they came down the production track, and walk back to the bike with you. Whilst you lifted the back end of the bike in the air, the fitter would place the trolley under the back tyre. This allowed the bike to be carefully held upright and pushed back up the drive and into the Finishing Shop for the attention of the Rectification chaps. This little ritual was played out quite a few times until the problem was rectified on production. Even now, whenever I overhaul gearboxes of either the pre-unit or unit construction type, I always ensure that the gearbox main shaft to high gear bush clearance is adequate.

The new twins began coming down the production line with their big unit construction automotive units, the engine, gearbox, and transmission all in one lump. Remembering the weight of the pre-unit cast iron engine of the Thunderbird, which, on its own, was enough to make you talk with a high-pitched voice for a week after you had struggled with it out of and into the frame, I thought "This one is going to cause some problems amongst the fitters in the Repair Shop." I would be heading back up there in a few weeks or so. All of the men there were ten or more years older than me, and I reckoned there were going to be a few double hernias ...

The little three fifty and five hundred unit engines were heavy enough, but these were taking the mickey. On the track, they had an overhead electric hoist with which to sling the motors into the frame, which I knew the Repair Shop didn't yet have.

Unit 650 T120 Bonneville engine undergoing a total overhaul by the author, prior to the fitting of heads and rockers.

Unit 650 Bonneville engine completed.

Triumph Production Testers' Tales – from the Meriden Factory

All those years later, in my own restoration business, if an engine job involved a big six fifty, I would usually get the customer to deliver the unit in the boot of his car, and at the workshop the two of us would lift it out and place it on my workbench. There it would be dismantled, overhauled, and rebuilt, with him helping with the lifting again when it was time for collection.

If I had a unit construction Bonneville in for complete restoration, with the bike on the hydraulic workbench, I would dismantle the engine down to the cylinder base joint still in the frame. Then the complete transmission would be dismantled and removed, followed by the gearbox and all its workings. This would leave just the crankcase and crankshaft, camshafts, and a few other bits, making the whole job lighter and easier to lift out. Then, when the machine was going back together, the reverse of the procedure was applied. I've got to the point now where I would rather not take on a big unit if I can avoid it. Give me a pre-unit T120 anytime!

The 1963 line-up included a new little three fifty called the Tiger 90, which had the same frame, forks and running gear as the Tiger 100SS, but with a sports three fifty engine finished in Alaskan White with gold pinstriping. It reputedly gave as much power as the 5TA Speed Twin, but at a very much higher rev range of 7500rpm. It was a buzzy little bugger; you really had to use the gears and rev the nuts off it to get anywhere. Still, it seemed to sell well enough.

New for 1963, the sports 350 Tiger 90, now with twin contact breakers in the timing cover instead of the distributor.

The new unit twins

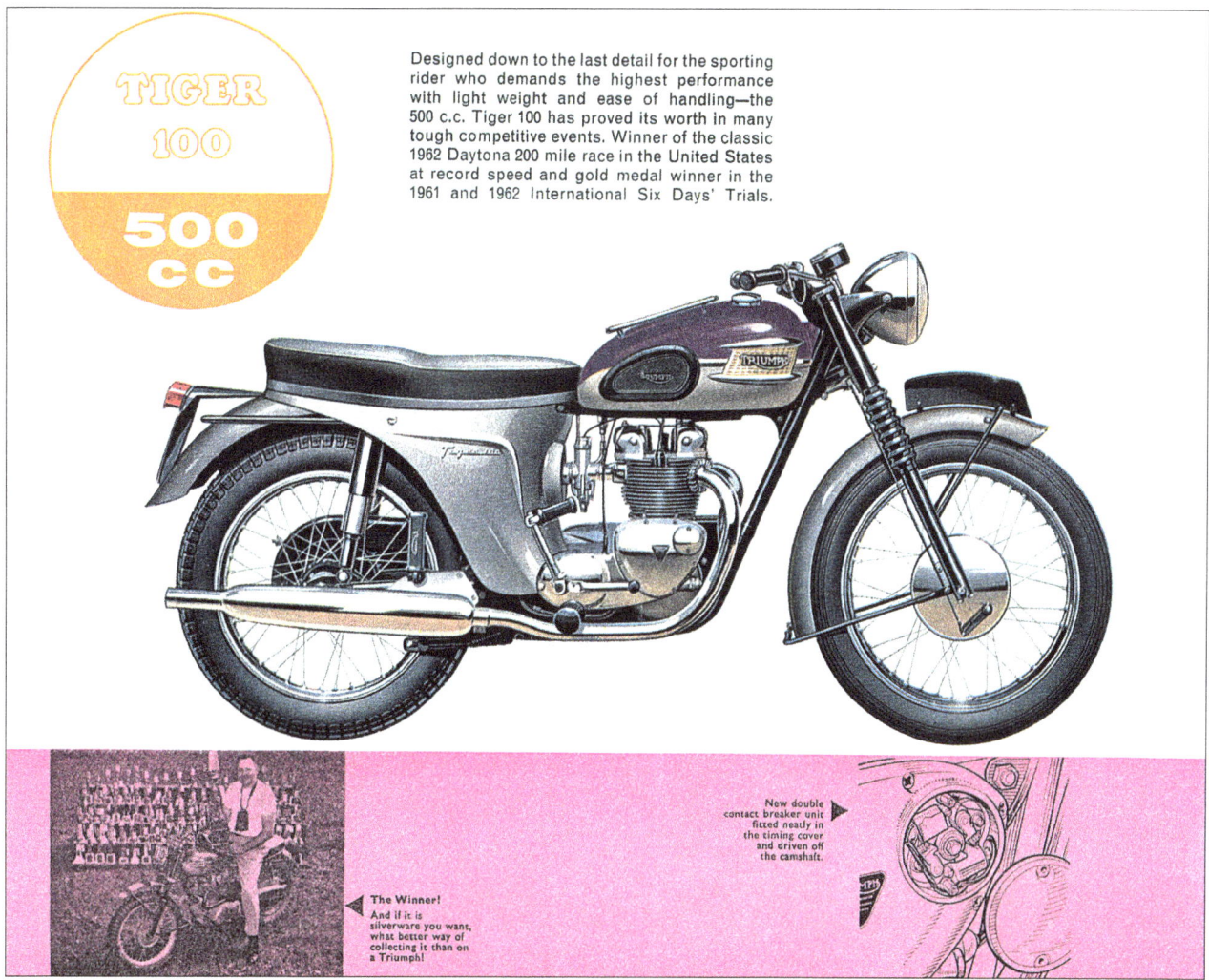

The 1963 Tiger 100. A new crankcase and twin Lucas contact breaker, but the running gear was the same as 1962.

All the new models now had the Lucas 4 CA contact breakers housed in new shaped timing covers in place of the vertically-mounted distributors of the Cubs and C range. The magnetos of the sports twins had also given way to the new coil ignition systems.

On the six fifties there was also a change to the cylinder head rocker box bolt arrangement. The pre-unit models had the eight stud configuration, but the new models now had a ninth bolt positioned in-between the cylinders. The main eight 3/8in diameter bolt positions had been moved fractionally to eliminate the cracking from the inboard bolt holes to the valve seats commonly seen on the earlier eight stud models. The ninth bolt was to eliminate distortion of the cylinder head and prevent blow-by between the combustion hemispheres.

The primary transmission went from single row chain as on the pre-units, to 3/8in duplex chain drive as on the C range models. The gearbox internals were almost identical to the 1962 needle-roller lay shaft specification, but the frame went to a much beefier single downtube version, and when the big lump of an engine was bolted in, it served to stiffen the whole lot.

The front forks, front wheel, headlamp, mudguard, and wheel remained as the previous year. For 1963 only, rider footrests were bolted to the bottom rails of the front frame; the following year, they were fixed to the swinging arm outrigger rear engine plates, a better arrangement altogether.

The motors were fitted with a six volt AC generator via a 12 amp, 6 volt battery, and this remained the same

Triumph Production Testers' Tales – from the Meriden Factory

A 1961 T120R engine rebuilt by the author for an Irish gentleman in June 2011. This one has the eight-stud head machined out of the nine-stud casting, and correct rocker boxes.

until the end of 1965 when the twelve volt electrical system was introduced.

There were two conditions of rear wheel: the ordinary bolt-up (which had wheel nuts at each end of the rear wheel spindle), or, for an extra few pounds, the quickly detachable wheel, whereby the sprocket, brake drum, etc, were left in place, and the wheel could be detached by simply removing a dedicated spindle and withdrawing it from its splines. It wasn't until 1964 that the front forks were updated and the external spring types introduced.

The weather was warm and the bikes kept rolling by; irrespective of model, we kept going. At about this point, I seem to remember a change to the brake shoes in an effort to improve the stopping power of the forty cubic inch twins, as the Americans called the B range models. Apart from the Cub models, the 5.5in diameter brakes front and rear, the other models all had 7in stoppers, and, in the case of the 3TA, 5TA, and T100S, these had 7in diameter front drums, too. It was only the six fifty models that had the 8in unit, though this was not considered a good brake. Indeed, all these years later, given modern materials and technology, I still cannot get my son's 8in front brake on his Bonneville to work as well as I think it should.

The new shoes were not anchored at the pivoting end on a fixed round peg in the brake plate. The reasoning was that if you made this fixed point flexible or floating, the shoes would self-centralise when the brake was applied when the actuating cam expanded them in the drum. Theoretically, this would allow more of the brake lining to come into contact with the drum surface, hopefully, improving efficiency. Whether or not it worked, we didn't notice until the wide shoes were introduced on the unit models, but then the twin leading front brake came along, and braking took a turn for the better.

The models were improving, the new six fifty twins especially so now that the TR6 Trophy and T120 Bonnevilles had gone to coil ignition and used the new Lucas 4 CA twin contact breaker assembly housed in the timing cover, and driven off the end of the exhaust camshaft. This also applied to the new Tiger 90 and Tiger 100 models, but with the 3TA and 5TA having to wait until the following year.

The Lucas 4CA twin contact breaker assembly required the use of a stroboscope and degree plate to ensure the engine ignition timing was accurate, and set at the correct, fully advanced figure. Whereas on the Lucas K2F magneto models you could set up a degree plate on top dead centre, then wind the engine back to its before top dead centre figure to set the timing, knowing that it would be correct for the opposite cylinder, this could not be relied upon with the new setup.

Due to there now being double points in the timing cover, the engine had to be run up to a minimum of 1800-2000rpm, and with the stroboscope gun connected to the timing side plug, the spark occurring figure could be seen when the gun was pointed at the spinning degree plate.

The fully advanced figure for the T120 Bonneville, TR6 Trophy, and variants of the Tiger 100 models was 38 degrees before top dead centre with the automatic advance and retard mechanism in the fully advanced mode. The auto unit had two bob weights which were flung outward against spring tension via centrifugal

The new unit twins

Offering the ultimate in road performance, the famous 650 c.c. Bonneville 120 is the choice of the really skilful and experienced rider. Specification includes new unit construction twin carburetter engine, completely new frame, new twin coil ignition system, duplex primary chain and a considerable reduction in overall weight, for safe and easy handling.

The first of the unit construction Bonnevilles for the 1963 season, with new large bore tubing frame. Front forks, wheels, etc, as for 1962.

A model with an unequalled sporting reputation in all parts of the world, the new 650 c.c. Trophy embodies all of the improved specification details common to the 650 c.c. range, the new engine/gearbox unit, twin coil ignition, new frame, etc. The reduced weight will undoubtedly appeal particularly to the sporting rider for its contribution to easy handling.

The TR6 Trophy, again unit construction, and the same running gear as the T120 Bonneville.

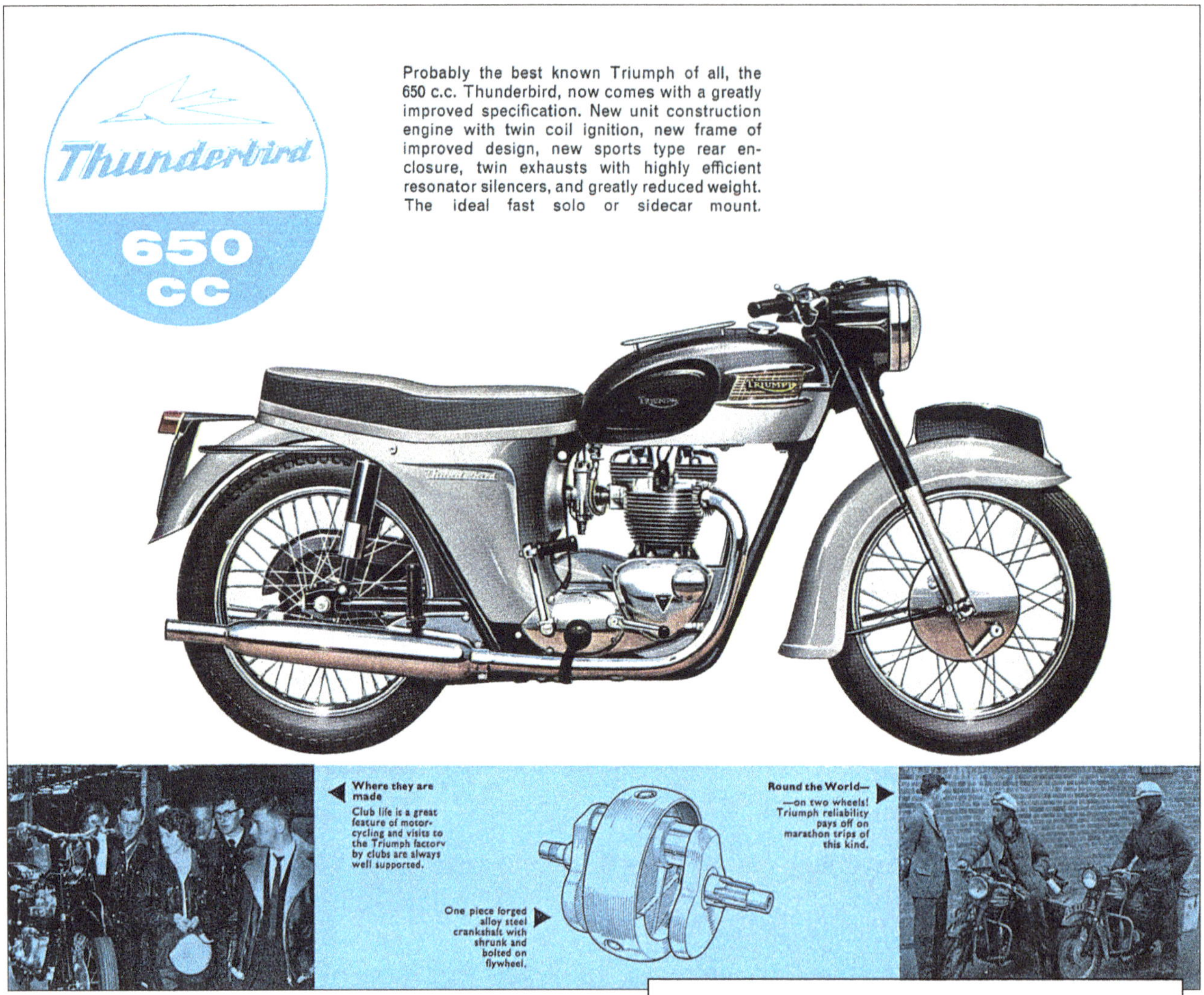

Triumph Production Testers' Tales – from the Meriden Factory

> Probably the best known Triumph of all, the 650 c.c. Thunderbird, now comes with a greatly improved specification. New unit construction engine with twin coil ignition, new frame of improved design, new sports type rear enclosure, twin exhausts with highly efficient resonator silencers, and greatly reduced weight. The ideal fast solo or sidecar mount.

The 6T Thunderbird for 1963 was to remain virtually unchanged until its phase-out in 1966.

force, thus advancing the ignition. This is why timing could only be set with the engine running in excess of the figure previously given.

To avoid any engine problems due to a timing discrepancy between cylinders, the procedure we applied was as follows.

Set up the engine with the degree plate at top dead centre, and pointer set at zero on the plate. Hook up the strobe gun to the timing side sparkplug, and

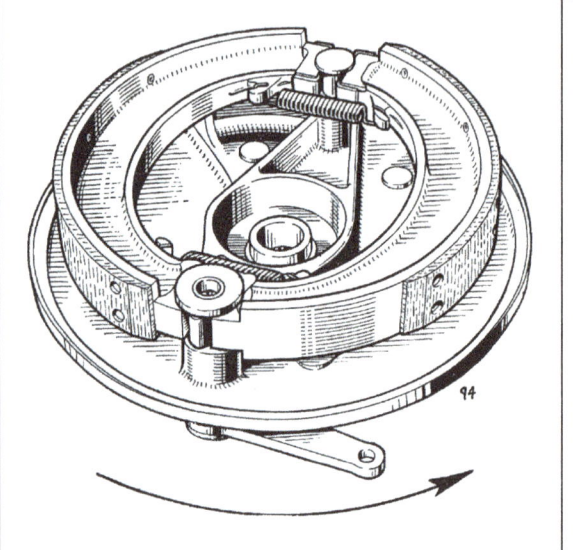

Showing the correct assembly for the single leading shoes on the brake plate. Mix up the leading and trailing shoes, and they would jam into the 'on' position when applied.

134

connect the strobe to a separate power source (usually a spare six or twelve volt battery). It wasn't advisable to connect the strobe to the machine's battery, as this sometimes caused a random spark, which showed up on the degree plate, giving a false reading.

With the contact breaker points set at 0.015in, start the machine. Shine the stroboscope gun onto the degree plate and rev the motor to between 1800 and 2000rpm, at the same time reading the figure highlighted by the strobe beam on the degree plate adjacent to the pointer. If the figure is not the 38 degrees required, loosen the back plate by backing off the pillar bolts, and adjust the back plate until the figure is obtained at the rpm specified. We could establish accurately the fully advanced figure for the timing side of the engine, it was only when the strobe was swapped to the driveside sparkplug, did problems sometimes occur.

It was drummed into us it was absolutely imperative that the fully advanced figure had to be exactly the same on both cylinders, there was no margin for error. Obviously, if the second reading on the degree plate when the engine was revved was not 38 degrees, it was not possible to adjust it as this would, of course, upset the first cylinder timing. It was found that the second cylinder timing could be satisfactorily achieved by either opening the points gap to advance, or closing it to retard.

The machined tolerances in the manufacture of the fibre-heeled points, and the grinding of the automatic advance and

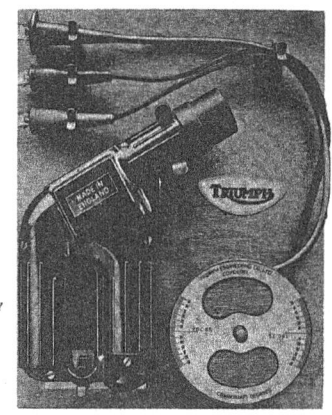

A most valuable bit of kit for correctly setting the timing on both cylinders.

retard mechanism cam profile, could not fully guarantee that if you set the first cylinder timing correctly, the second cylinder timing would be automatically correct also.

We found that with the new M1 motorway, customers were doing some seriously high speed riding from one end to the other, à la Percy. If, by chance, the advance ignition figure was wrong on one or the other cylinder, especially if it was retarded by a few degrees, then the cylinder affected would generate a much higher temperature within the combustion chamber, which usually resulted in a nasty seizure.

The Lucas 4CA twin contact breaker assembly, showing the points gapping procedure.

Triumph Production Testers' Tales – from the Meriden Factory

Much worse, if the machine continued to run after this, blowing a hole through the piston crown was a distinct possibility.

Usually, when a machine had been set up correctly by a Repair Shop fitter, it ran beautifully, with no problems at all. But an owner, carrying out a spot of routine maintenance on a nice sunny Sunday morning, might spot that one set of contact points had a different gap to the other, and alter it, thus causing a whole lot of trouble for himself. It wasn't long before the Service Department liaison man from Joseph Lucas, Mr Frank Bartlett, was spending time in the Repair Shop, examining machining tolerances on the cam profile and the differences in between the points assemblies' fibre 'heels,' and listening to our tales of woe.

It was realised that the 4CA unit wasn't any good as it was. The points assemblies mounted on the main back plate had to be individually adjustable, which meant that both sets of points could be gapped to 0.015in, and then adjusted forward or backward on the back plate independently of each other to get the correct timing on both cylinders. It worked like a charm, and, provided the timing on the big twins was set up correctly with a stroboscope, we experienced no further problems with pistons.

The obvious thing to do was to educate dealers to use the strobe kit correctly on customer machines in their own workshops. We thought that if the dealers' mechanics were also unwittingly altering points gaps, this compounded the problem, and the poor customer would be the one to suffer.

A dealer convention was arranged at the factory, and yours truly was chosen to set up a 6TP Thunderbird police machine with the degree plate and pointer, then demonstrate the correct setting and adjusting of the timing on both cylinders. It all went off very well, and it seems that the boss of the Service Department must have seen how I talked to people and handled myself, and decided to keep an eye on me for other things.

The following year, the TR6P was born, a much modified Trophy, simply because the 6T Thunderbird was soon to cease production, so another model had to take on police work.

We kitted out a TR6 in the Service Repair Shop, and I was told to ride it down to New Scotland Yard and meet the Metropolitan Police liaison officer, Maurice Hedlum. It all went swimmingly, and from that meeting big orders ensued for many years to come. Other police forces throughout the country, seeing the Met's lead, also took on the TR6P, and in different specifications for different

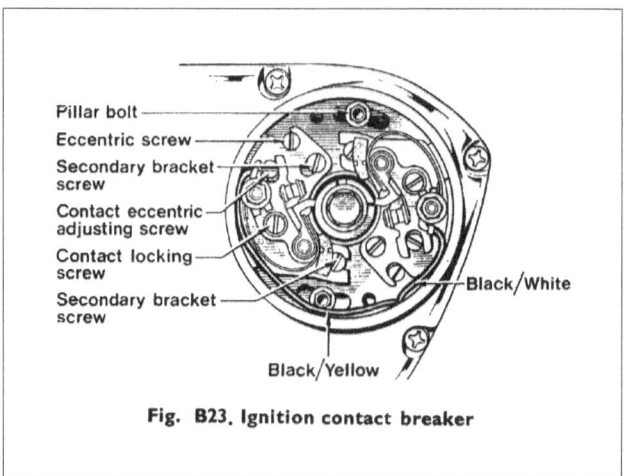

Fig. B23. Ignition contact breaker

The later modified Lucas 6CA twin contact breaker with separately adjustable contact point assemblies.

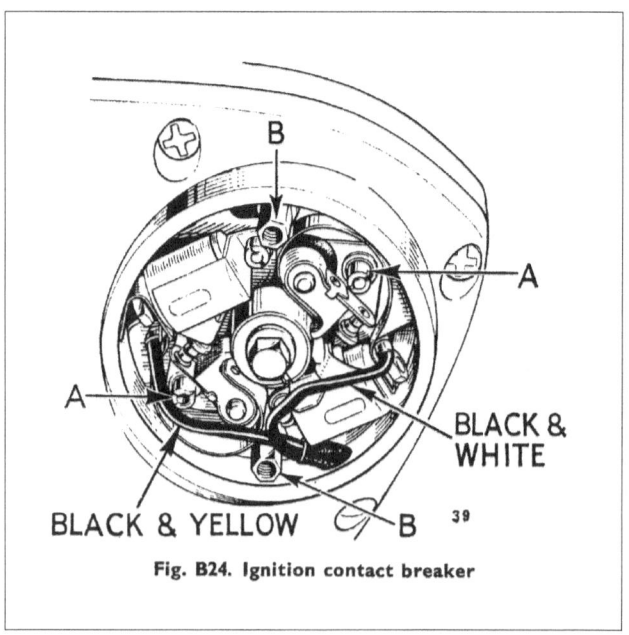

Fig. B24. Ignition contact breaker

Lucas 4CA setup.

uses. The TR6 Trophy, in its new livery of Motorway White, took on a new role.

Many years later in the early 1990s, I had a chap call me and ask if I could totally restore a police bike. After a short talk on the telephone, establishing that the job was a complete bike and not, as I so often found out, a 'bitsa,' I said I could, but would have to see the job first. He gave me his name and address in Surrey, and, on a mutually convenient day, I travelled down to meet him.

When I arrived, his home, set in a private road, was

The new unit twins

The author (in overalls) at a dealers' convention, demonstrating how to use the stroboscope correctly.

like something out of a posh magazine. He came out to meet me and showed me the bike in his garage. His name was Rodney Timson, a big, lean chap, he was, ex-Lancashire police, and this was the actual bike he used to ride when patrolling the M6 motorway. It wasn't a normal TR6P, but one of only a few we built as fast pursuit machines to go after high-speed merchants. It was a T120P, and with its special gearing, there was nothing that could outrun it in its day.

I had taken my trailer with me, so, after agreeing terms, we loaded it up. He invited me into the kitchen to wash my hands and have a cup of tea before I set off back home. His wife was preparing their evening meal with her back to me when I entered, and, as he introduced me, she turned. I nearly fell over, it was Penelope Keith, the actress, star of *The Good Life* and *To the Manor Born*. What a lovely lady, dead normal, and not at all like the characters she so often portrayed. Obviously, her name was Mrs Timson, but in a blind funk at meeting someone like this unexpectedly, I called her Mrs Keith. They both laughed at my being so flustered, but by the time I had drunk my tea and used their loo, we were

chatting normally about the bike. She didn't want Rodney to do too many miles on it, saying, "He hasn't ridden for years," so he did agree to take things easy when he got the bike back. They asked if they could come along to the workshop when the rebuild was under way to see how things were going; of course, I said yes.

Some months later, when the engine had been rebuilt and installed in the rolling chassis, I rang Rodney and he said they could come along the following Saturday, arriving about lunchtime, which they duly did, in a big Mercedes Estate car. They brought with them a Fortnum and Mason hamper, and while we talked about what had been done to the bike and what was yet left to do, Penelope, Rodney, and I enjoyed a nice lunch.

When the job was completed, I agreed to take the bike to them and, after unloading it, started it and generally explained things, after which, Rodney leapt aboard and shot off up the private lane. He was ecstatic, to say the least, more so than Penelope, anyway, who came from the direction of the garden, to rollock him after I had left, I think. It was one of my more enjoyable restorations, I must say.

Triumph Production Testers' Tales – from the Meriden Factory

The very quick T120P, as used by Lancashire Police on the M6 motorway.

The drive-side of the T120P ex-Lancashire M6 motorway machine.

The new unit twins

The Lancashire Police T120P M6 fast pursuit bike. A Bonneville in police spec.

The other nice little touch we noticed inside the new six fifty contact breaker timing cover was that the oil nose on the timing side end of the crankshaft no longer relied on the fit of a phosphor-bronze bush in the cover for oil pressure. It's strange how a soft material like phosphor-bronze lay shaft top hat bushes in the gearbox could wear away a hardened shaft surface. We found this was the same with the bush in the pre-unit engine timing covers, used since before the Second World War as a revolving pressure joint. This is where engine oil is forced under pressure into the crank and then fed to the big ends. Any wear in the main bearings or flex on the crankshaft at high speed that allowed the oil nose surface of the crankshaft to contact the bush creates wear and extra clearance. Any undue clearance at this revolving point allows engine oil pressure to escape, thus depriving the big end assemblies. Therefore, a proper housing for a garter lipped oil seal and circlip groove were now the order of the day. With an oil seal in the cover, retained by a circlip, the crankshaft oil nose was no longer subjected to undue wear.

Not much could outrun this in 1969-1970.

Triumph Production Testers' Tales – from the Meriden Factory

Pre-unit timing cover oil seal conversion, with original bush, then with E4568 oil seal and circlip, ensuring no oil pressure loss at this juncture.

The running tolerance between the crankshaft oil nose and timing cover bush was critical, because it was this that prevented oil pressure loss at this revolving point. Even now, after all these years, you would be surprised at the number of people who ring me for advice after totally rebuilding their twin cylinder engine, only to find after a twenty to twenty five mile run, the oil pressure button indicator on the relief valve has slowly receded, indicating low oil pressure. What they've not realised is, if there is any distortion on the oil nose, or if it is below its standard diameter of 0.624in, then pressure will be lost when the motor gets hot and the oil becomes thin due to engine heat.

Us young chaps in the Repair Shop thought this oil seal modification was a brilliant idea, and it wasn't long before we had devised a jig for holding the covers on the milling machine so that they could be suitably altered. After removing the old bush, setting up the cover on the jig, and centering the bush hole, we cut the housing for the Triumph unit construction oil seal, part number E4568. Then, using a special tool we had persuaded one of the Tool Room chaps to make for us, we cut a circlip groove. The unit oil seal and circlip could now be fitted, and the chaps riding their pre-unit models, no matter what year or model, suddenly found their engines had an increase in oil pressure.

It's such a lovely idea that, over the years since starting my business, I have carried out this modification process to customers' engines I have overhauled as a matter of course. I also offer a service whereby someone can send me their timing cover and it will be modified, fitted with the new bits, and on its way back to them in forty eight hours.

The other modification that can be carried out on pre-unit engines using unit parts is fitting the nine-stud cylinder barrel, cylinder head, and finned rocker boxes. It's not unusual to see a nicely restored or rebuilt pre-unit Bonneville or Trophy engine, fitted with the later top end, which ensures the bike can be ridden hard and there will be no cracking of the cylinder head.

With the gearbox internals the same as the last of the pre-units, and the transmission mainly the same except for the ⅜in duplex primary drive chain, the unit comprised mainly tried and tested parts, so there was no expectation of any serious problems.

Obviously, not being able to move the gearbox to adjust the primary chain tension as was possible on the earlier models meant that a new method of adjustment had to be devised. This took the form of a spring steel, rubber-faced tensioner blade housed in the base of the primary chain case casting. A threaded tie-rod, which compressed the blade and bowed it upwards, was accessible through an aperture at the bottom rear of the chain case after removal of a blanking plug. By inserting a long, flat-bladed screwdriver, a threaded tubular trunnion could be turned which would either increase or decrease the amount of bow in the blade, thereby applying tension to the duplex chain. It also meant that the rear main drive chain tension was not affected by the adjustment, which took re-adjusting the rear chain and re-tracking the wheels off the menu. Generally a good idea all round.

We found that having the big engine bolted so rigidly into the new frame, and the large section tubing swinging arm supported at each end through out-rigger plates really did tighten everything up, and gave the whole bike a feeling of togetherness. As we headed toward winter once again, I began to think more and more about my new job in the Repair Department, and was glad I wouldn't be going through another four or five months of bad weather, and perpetually wet kit.

One afternoon, Eddie and I were at the testers' bench sorting our respective bags, lunch tins, and whatever else prior to getting our going home bikes ready, when one of the chaps suggested a pre-Christmas, testers' and wives' night out. Without exception, we all thought it would be a good idea. And not just our wives, but all associated with the test: knacker gangs, Evvy, Billy, and Little Jock, the cleaners, plus anyone else who wanted to come. It should be a good do.

We talked about it for a day or two, batting the idea around, discussing suitable venues, and finally settled

The new unit twins

The best of both worlds – a 1962 T120 engine with late nine-stud barrel, head, rockers, and transistorised ignition system.

With ignition set at 37°, E3134 inlet cam and E3325 exhaust cam, and 7.5:1 CR pistons, this ran smoothly on unleaded fuel.

on a pub not too far from the factory called The George in the Tree in Balsall Common. One of the chaps decided to detour off route on a test run and nip off over there to get some idea of costs. It was all very favourable, so after we had acquired a little book and got down the names of all who intended coming, we started collecting deposits, and told the pub roughly how many people would be requiring chicken and chips in a basket.

With the cold weather upon us, we were stopping off down Somers Lane to fill in our test report cards, check the bikes over and, at the same time, warm our hands and Barbour mitts on the warm engines. It was Jock and Westy who first noticed there was something wrong with Billy the ram; he was coughing, and sounded just like an old man with bronchitis. After getting back to the factory and talking things over with the rest of the lads, we gave serious thought to how

we could help him, even down to tying a woollen scarf around his neck coated in Vick ointment. Whoever did it would have to be a volunteer, but no one came forward. After further talks, we decided on a tin of cough pastilles from the chemist shop in the village.

That afternoon, in the early dusk of a winter's day, we all met down the Mile, twelve new bikes, all parked in a line in the lay-by. As usual, when Billy heard the bikes, he trotted over to the fence to see if it was sandwich time. Bonneville stood aloof in the little lean-to in the corner of the field, watching. He seemed to know it wasn't the time of day for food scraps. We wondered whether Billy would take the cough pastilles, but we need not have worried at all, he scoffed the whole bag full. Over the next few days, his cough definitely got a lot better!

Christmas '62

We were having a laugh one dinner hour, all sitting on the testers' bench or on chairs pinched from the canteen, listening to Westy and Eddie. When the two ex-sailors talked, it was a different language, which contained words like 'oggie' and 'goffers,' but generally we got the gist of things and usually were falling about with laughter as the stories got better and better.

It was just as Westy was finishing off his tale of how he walked across the sea bed at the bottom of Sliema Creek in Malta. He was a navy hard-hat diver, but he was also on salvage, clearing stuff left over from the Second World War when Malta was continuously bombed. He described the murkiness of the water and said he couldn't see his hand in front of his helmet-covered face.

It was during a lull in Westy's story, that Eddie chimed up with his most unlikely yarn yet. Back in the 1950s, when England still had a navy and ships, on odd occasions, two of them would meet on the high seas. Sometimes at such meetings, personnel, stores, fuel, or whatever were transferred from ship to ship. On this particular occasion, Eddie's ship, HMS Broadsword, encountered a vessel that contained a Rear Admiral of the Home Fleet, according to our intrepid storyteller. Apparently, he had to be transferred as quickly as possible, and so that both ships did not have to come to a dead stop in order to make the transfer by boat, it was decided to use the Bosun's chair. Broadsword was heading back to Blighty, which is why the Admiral was changing buses in the middle of the Atlantic. According to Eddie, something was afoot, my lucky lads!

As was standard practice, the two ships turned onto the same heading, holding station at the same speed next to each other, thirty to forty yards apart. Next, a light line was shot across from one vessel to the other, on the end of which was tied a heavy line which was then pulled across and secured by a team of five or six ratings. The line was supported by davits, pulleys on which the line would run, about five or six feet above the decks, and on this line was a travelling pulley. Suspended from this was a light canvas and wooden seat – the Bosun's chair – with arms and back, and a safety bar across the front to prevent its occupant from falling out. Each side of this there was a pulling line, one going to each vessel. On the end of each, three or four ratings stood ready to pull the chair and its cargo across from one vessel to the other, above the surging, crashing waters below.

With lines up and across, Eddie on Broadsword was the end man on his team. The object of the exercise was to keep the suspension line in constant tension, compensating as required for the motion of the fast-moving ships so that the chair's high-ranking passenger didn't get dunked in the briny if the ships involuntarily moved closer together.

Well, the Rear Admiral was secured in the chair, and, as Eddie told it, the boat was moving about a fair bit. Consequently, they were working overtime, letting the line out when it was required and pulling it in when it went slack.

We all sat eating our sandwiches and listening intently to Eddie's story, which he punctuated with guffaws because he knew what was coming and we didn't. It didn't matter, anyway; his laugh was so infectious, we found ourselves joining in in anticipation.

The Rear Admiral was now halfway across the chasm, at the very moment that Eddie decided to tie his end of the suspension rope around a cleat to give his arms a rest. This was fine, said Eddie, until the vessels moved quickly apart for an instant. His crew, because the end of the rope was tied off, couldn't let out the slack to compensate, and so, with a twang, the rope violently

Christmas '62

tightened, causing the Rear Admiral and the chair to perform an almost perfect loop-the-loop. The lieutenant in charge quickly appraised the situation, and, giving Eddie an awful dressing down, ordered him off deck. Anyway, Eddie was put on another charge and had several days' pay docked, then it was back in the galley and the washing-up. Our laughter at his antics when relating the story echoed around the Finishing Shop, causing people on the other sections to look up, but it was the way that Eddie told the story; we could almost see the acrobatic Rear Admiral. As a section we were usually very quiet, moving amongst the bikes doing our job: some even claimed we were standoffish, so found this outburst of raucous laughter a bit strange. I know I was tittering to myself for a good while afterward thinking about Eddie's antics, and wondering how on earth the good ship Broadsword stayed afloat.

The George in the Tree is a rather large, sprawling public house situated on the Balsall Common to Kenilworth Road. It has a nice atmosphere, and the grills are always very good, so Gloria, myself, and friends have eaten there on several occasions since the testers' Christmas get-together, mainly, I suppose, in an effort to make amends for the fiasco I am about to recount.

At the event in question, Jock Copland, my old army mate, and his lovely wife, Valerie, sat with Gloria and me as we enjoyed that special, happy atmosphere that a bunch of mates generates. The order of the evening was dancing, which Gloria and I didn't participate in (because of my two left feet), laughter, and good spirits. But something happened that evening which threatened to wreck the night, and not one of us saw it coming.

One of the chaps who came along with his new wife was Johnny Bugsy Douglas, who worked on the Tiger Cub assembly line. He was the most fantastic rock 'n' roll dancer I have ever seen, and with Maureen, his wife, gave a demonstration to the catchy beat of Bill Haley's *Rock around the clock* rang out. During this, some sort of disturbance started at the door to the room where our party was being held, and it registered with us that something was wrong.

It was an awful commotion, but, being in our best suits, and with our wives in tow, we were also on our best behaviour, so all we could do for the moment was sit and watch. The music died away and Bugsy, standing with Maureen, was suddenly forgotten as we watched the Manager of the establishment, trying to prevent someone or something gatecrashing our private party.

The individual was a burly, horrible-looking tramp, pushing a dilapidated pram laden with rubbish of all kinds, and he was locked in a monumental scuffle with the Manager. He had managed to get the pram inside, and now the tramp struggled violently to follow it.

Westy was up out of his chair, grabbed the pram by its handles, and pushed it to one side away from the struggle, which by now had made it into the room, with the surly tramp getting the upper hand. Finally, the Manager, realising he was slowly but surely being overwhelmed by the smelly apparition, suddenly gave up and decided to go and get help to eject the unwanted, unwashed personage that had gatecrashed our party.

Several of us were now standing, and I was aware of Gloria holding my arm. I looked down at her and she shook her head, as if to say, "Don't get involved."Westy was now grinning evilly at the tramp, and all of us stared in disbelief at the awful person wearing odd, scruffy shoes with no laces, dirty trousers and raincoat, and a trilby hat that looked as if it had been home to a nest of rats, shuffled up to the bar and asked for a pint of bitter. You could have heard a pin drop as the lady that had looked after us all evening, said, "I'm sorry, I can't serve you, you will have to leave immediately." We waited with bated breath, and I said to Jock, "Now there'll be trouble." The tramp said nothing, just concentrated on rummaging in the depths of his disgusting trousers, obviously looking for some form of payment.

The two girls, Jock and I just couldn't take in what was unfolding in front of us. Apart from the violent tussle at the door, this stinky personage had not offered any more violence, and was now quite calm. We looked around: Westy and now Sooty, both very hard men who I wouldn't like to meet down a dark alley, were closing in, ready to grab and eject him forcibly into the car park, his junk-laden pram, too.

Finding no money in his trousers, the tramp began feeling inside his raincoat, the little drama seeming to unfold in slow motion. Bill Letts and Norris were so helpless with silent mirth that Beryl, Bill's wife, was hitting him to try and shut him up, perhaps seeing a farcical humour in the situation that us young chaps, full of indignation, couldn't. The tramp slowly produced a small package, roughly wrapped in newspaper, and said, "I'll give you this bacon sandwich for a pint, my dear, it's nice and warm, I've had it under my armpit." We watched various expressions flit across the poor woman's face, as she, trying to come to terms with what was happening, struggled for something to say, but nothing would come. Jock looked at me, his eyes bulging with suppressed

Triumph Production Testers' Tales – from the Meriden Factory

At the 1962 testers' Christmas get-together. Left to right: Jock Copland; the author; Valerie Copland and the author's wife, Gloria.

Jock and Valerie in 2009 at a Ripon reunion for the display team.

Christmas '62

mirth; Westy and Sooty, now both more relaxed, had half smiles on their faces, too. Bill and Norris were gently sliding under the table with laughter.

Suddenly, we heard a chortle and the penny dropped. The 'tramp' was, in fact, Eddie, up to his best ever prank, played on us, his unsuspecting audience on our annual night out!

After removing some of his awful attire, we found he had on a decent suit and pair of trousers, and after producing his proper jacket from the depths of the pram, he accepted the drinks now lined up on the bar. He even managed to elicit a rueful smile from the lady behind the bar.

By the time the Manager returned with reinforcements to help eject this undesirable, we were all gathered around Eddie, slapping him on the back and trying to buy him more drinks. He was in his element, chortling and chuckling uncontrollably. When the Manager realised what was going on, he joined in with good nature. I don't think I ever went to such a wonderful night out again.

It was with these, the happiest of memories, amongst the finest bunch of blokes, that I took my leave a week before Christmas. A quick word and a handshake was all that was required, because I could always come back down in the lunch hour; a short walk down the main gangway from the Repair Shop would take just two or three minutes, and if I needed cheering up, well, Eddie would be there.

The Repair Shop Foreman, Mr Bert Carter, wanted me up there, settled in before Christmas so that I would be straight into harness when we started back in the New Year after the break.

That night, Eddie ran me home on the pillion of his going home bike after I had handed in my set of trade plates to Stan, and shook hands with him and Mr Tubb. I went over to Evvy and gave her a cuddle, then the two shillings and sixpence I owed her for the week's supply of tea I had consumed. As my enamel mug was a fairly new one, she told me to take it with me to my new department.

After the four o'clock tea break, I said cheerio to the lads on the Rectification gangs, and thanked them for putting up with me. Roger Bryant said, "Don't worry, Hughie, you're not the worst we've had," which made me feel great. I thought I had better go along to Pop and Joan in the gatehouse and warn them I would be turning up early on Monday morning in my little Morris, loaded up with toolboxes, and would be driving straight round to the back of the Repair Shop to unload before driving back and round into the main car park. No more riding up through the throng of workers in the morning, and banging through the rubber doors on my company bike. I would be like everyone else now, parking and walking from the car park in the rain, snow, or whatever. Never mind. At least I would be inside in the warm for the rest of the working day. Although I was sure I would miss the test, I knew the warmth of the Repair Shop and its fitters from working in there prior to my call-up, so it wasn't as if I was going in amongst a load of strangers.

I was sad, though, when I got off the back of Eddie's bike at home and walked around to the back garden instead of riding round on a new bike. I looked down the garden at my empty shed, knowing JRW 405 was now pulling a box sidecar, loaded up with plumber's tools and equipment, ridden by some young chap instead of me. And I knew that when spring and summer came round, I would be envious of those black-suited riders. Still, my mind was one step ahead, and even though JRW had to go to make way for the Morris, I thought that if a little bike presented itself fairly cheaply, maybe it wouldn't be too long before I was going to work on two wheels again ...

www.velocebooks.com / www.veloce.co.uk
All current books • New book news • Special offers • Gift vouchers

Reflections

On the Sunday afternoon before I was due to start my new job, I loaded my toolboxes into the back of the Morris, and promptly discovered that the boot wasn't big enough, so my large wooden box had to go on the back seat. These boxes I had had since my time in the Repair Shop with Reg Hawkins, which I took home with me when I left to go into the army. Then, after demob, they came back in to Experimental, going home again when I transferred to Production test. Now, they were going back to where they had started, the Repair Department.

I had used some of tools whilst in the Display Team, small, special ones, peculiar to the TRW side valve twins we used. On the back of each Team TRW, behind the pillion pad, was a rear carrier, and these tools, wrapped in a canvas bag, were held to the carrier of my bike with Dunlop rubber bands. As both a riding member of the Team, and also the Team fitter, I was always Tailend Charlie when we were travelling from show to show in convoy, in the event someone dropped out with mechanical problems.

We didn't have a 52-seater coach and a huge articulated lorry in which to transport the bikes as they do now, just a Bedford three-tonner for the kit, and we rode the bikes everywhere we had to go to fulfil our display bookings. I must say, despite all the miles we did, only two breakdowns ever occurred out on the road: a broken throttle cable and a BTH magneto problem that was rectified very quickly.

Monday morning saw me arrive at the factory a little early so that I wouldn't be battling the crowd coming in. I drove straight round the back after pipping my car horn to Pop, and pulled up outside the back doors of the Repair Shop. These opened onto the concrete drive that came from round the back of the factory and ran down the right-hand side of the site, joining up with the main front drive, then ran past the front of Experimental and on down to Pop's office.

After grabbing Arthur Ashley's two-wheeled barrow, I took the toolboxes up to the workbench I had been allocated, then parked the Morris in the main car park. I could now walk up the testers' ramp and through the rubber doors that had made a fool out of me on a Cub, through which I had banged a few times on a bike.

I was now on a different time clock, so had to walk up the gangway that the office girls used, turning left at the top and on into the Repair Shop. Our time clock was on the left-hand wall, and, finding the time card with my name on it, I dinged in for the first time in my new department.

This would now be my workplace until 1966, when I would again be transferred, but this time, because of my experience, to the staff in the front Service Office, where I would become a technical writer, service adviser, technical author, and, in-between answering letters and the telephone, meet customers at the Service Reception counter, discuss their problems and, if required, book their vehicle a workshop appointment. I generally did anything and everything to do with service and warranty, which also included making a right pain in the arse of myself to higher management if I thought there were wrongs to be righted.

It was the week before Christmas and, as things were a bit slack in the Repair Shop, I was given a couple of menial tasks to help me get my hand in, I suppose.

Firstly, there were some accident-damaged fork assemblies of different years and models that required dismantling. This wasn't piecework, so there was no working against the clock, and I could take my time and think about what I was doing.

Various scrap metal boxes were placed on the floor next to my bench by Arthur Ashley: one for phosphor-

Reflections

The author at his desk in the Service Office, 1972.

bronze fork bushes, one for steel, and one for any damaged tinware that had to go for repairing. After dismantling, the component parts had to be washed and inspected before the various bits were thrown into the appropriate box. The crown, stem, and head lug, the main parts that both hold together the fork assembly and fix it to the frame steering head lug, go down to the bottom of the shop where Jimmy Davis had his workbench, where test stanchions are fitted and the component tested ready for re-enamelling. The amount of twist that occurs with these very robust components in an accident is quite amazing; they could also become twisted out of true if the machine they came from had pulled a sidecar for a few years.

I reckon I must have dismantled around fifteen sets of forks that first morning using dodges taught to me by Jimmy, which I've been able to employ ever since, and especially during the years I ran my own restoration

John Surtees' signature on the back of my picture.

business. There were all sorts of forks, from the early nacelle type, through the sports forks with the headlamp mounting top covers, to the little standard Cub ones. Some of the damaged stanchions were so bent, I had

Triumph Production Testers' Tales – from the Meriden Factory

to put the forks under the hydraulic press, resting the bent and distorted parts on wooden blocks spaced apart, then applying careful pressure to straighten them enough so that they could be dismantled.

Jimmy was responsible for all of the service reconditioned items such as forks, frames and petrol tanks, and could supply a dealer with any year, model, colour, or whatever, as a service item. With de-dented top covers, nacelle parts and bottom legs that had been re-enamelled, re-jigged crown, stem and head lug that had been repainted, then new stanchions, bushes and seals, all reassembled, you had a pair of forks as good as if they were made of all-new components, but at a fraction of the cost.

Complete sets of forks from Jimmy's rack were only about £15, and repaired and repainted petrol tanks ranged from £4.10s to £6. A five hundred or six fifty re-ground crankshaft and flywheel assembly, dismantled, cleaned, rebuilt and rebalanced, would only set you back £5.10s, all of which was very handy, especially if you were a young chap on a very tight budget.

Tuesday morning I was given a Tiger Cub that had been tested by little Stan Whitcomb, which, for some reason or other, had to have a new barrel and piston fitted under warranty. I had experience of working on Cubs dating back to when I was previously in the Repair Shop, training under the eagle eye of Reg Hawkins, now the Chargehand and responsible for dishing out jobs to the fitters. He was the chap who chased me all the way round the back of the factory back in 1956, because I had left the ignition switched on when he was changing a set of timing gears, and the engine had fired as he turned it over using his Britool Tee spanner, whipping round the tommy bar and cracking him over the knuckles. With a bit of a jaundiced look, he handed me the job card and said, "You know your way around Cubs, do this one, and don't forget to switch off the bloody ignition."

As I reached out for the card, he half-smiled. I see Reg on a regular basis, and only a couple of years ago, he invited Gloria and I to his eightieth birthday bash.

Finishing on the Friday afternoon for Christmas meant we had a couple of days of cleaning up the department. Each fitter was responsible for his workbench, vice and floor space in front of his bench and trestle, on which complete machines were placed to be worked on at a more convenient height. These, though not hydraulic, could be wound up and down to floor level via a large crank handle. When down, you could wheel a Bonneville onto it, put the bike on its centre stand and, using the crank handle, wind the trestle back up. Reg, being ex-RAF, remarked it was like winding up the undercarriage after take-off, then down again for landing on an Avro Anson trainer. Never mind, they worked, and this meant you didn't have to sit down on a box like the chaps on the knacker gangs, but worked standing up, and could get at both sides of the bike more easily by simply walking round it. Better still, if the operation was a rush job, two fitters could work together on the same bike, one each side, as Reg and I used to do in my pre-army days.

After wiping down your steel-topped workbench on which the engine work was done, you could sort out your toolboxes, tools, and accumulated rubbish on the two shelves beneath your workbench. It was surprising how much useless stuff congregated because you thought it might come in handy one day, but hardly ever did.

On the Friday we finished for Christmas, Bert Carter, the Foreman, brought in two bottles of scotch whiskey and two tins of Players cigarettes. Those who smoked helped themselves to the fags, but the whiskey was left to Arthur Ashley to measure out by the capful into everyone's mug of tea at ten minutes to ten, then again at ten minutes to four in the afternoon. Old Arthur had a big wooden tray with three inch sides, with everyone's mug place marked by a numbered circle, which denoted how many spoonfuls of sugar for that particular mug. A drop of whiskey in each mug really gave a Christmassy feeling.

After the lunch break, Harold Dixie Dix went to his Hillman Minx in the car park and brought back an electric Dansette record player with a few 78 black vinyl LPs. I remember one of them was a Cliff Richard and the Shadows album, and the other, good old Bill Haley and his Comets. As soon as the music got going, the people from the Spares Stores next door came round, and who else should appear, but Johnny Bugsy Douglas and his wife, Maureen, who had treated us to an display of rock 'n' roll dancing at The George in the Tree. Soon, the whole place was jumping, and little Stan Whitcomb, sitting on the next bench to me, was in earnest conversation with big Bill Letts, who had walked up from the Finishing Shop. I knew later from Stan that he had asked to come in from the cold and go onto fitting, at the same time suggesting that Bill come up off Production Test and take his place.

Thinking back to these times makes me realise just what a superb place it was to work; a privilege, really.

In my little workshop at the bottom of my garden, to where I am sometimes banished by Gloria, I look at

Reflections

my workbenches and the two toolboxes sitting there, daydreaming and remembering how my father made me the big, beautiful, wooden toolbox when I knew I had got the job at Triumph. The exterior is gloss black enamel, the interior varnished, with internal trays to keep the tools separate. There's a brass mortice lock and a chromium-plated, hinged lifting handle at each end. These, I later discovered, were internal pull handles from the inside of Rover car doors. That toolbox was with me in 1955 in the Repair Shop, then in 1959 in Experimental, and again in the Repair Shop in 1963. Finally, it's here in my little workshop, on my workbench in 2011.

It wasn't too long before an opportunity to re-acquire two-wheeled transport came along in the form of a Tiger Cub and registration documents, offered to me by Harry Woolridge, for the princely sum of £7.10s. It required a spot of work, but, as ever, if you had the chance of a bike to use for work transport, Repair Shop management helped you out with service exchange parts. It wasn't too long, therefore, after taking bits home in the car, and bringing stuff back to go through Jimmy's system, before my little black Cub was ready to go.

As Mr Tubb had let me keep my Belstaff suit, I had the riding kit already, so was back on the road on a bike. Although it was twelve miles from my home to the factory, even in bad weather I knew that when I got there, I wouldn't be going out in it again until going home time, so it wasn't as bad as on test. At least there was another bike in my shed now, and the Morris could be used for family duties. On the plus side, the Cub was returning over ninety miles to the gallon, so I was saving on fuel and money, something Gloria welcomed.

We had a restless Christmas Day with Gloria going into labour, and finally presenting little Simon and me with a lovely baby girl on Boxing Day. We called her Sarah Jane. I explained to Simon, who was four, that he was her big brother, and would have to keep an eye out for her as she was growing up. Standing next to his mum holding the baby, he suddenly looked quite grown up. Little did I know what the pair of them would be getting up to in four or five years' time.

Simon had a little two-wheeled bike called a Pave Master with blow up tyres and a carrier over the back mudguard, rather similar to the ones we had on the Display Team bikes. One day, while working on my car – incidentally, I should mention that we lived on a fairly steep hill – I saw the pair of them hurtle past the end of the drive. I frantically ran but was too late; they were halfway down the avenue, him pedalling like mad, and Sarah, happy as can be, sitting on the carrier, holding on to the back of him with one hand and clutching Mr Ted with the other. They thought it was great fun.

Going back over the years that I have been associated with Triumph motorcycles, I consider that I have been very lucky, very lucky indeed. To have worked in a leading factory in its heyday as I did, amongst the best of friends, has been an honour. The real benefit from my time at Meriden, however, has been the ability to run my own business for twenty five years, using the practices and disciplines that were instilled in me all those years ago.

To be able to answer the telephone correctly and talk coherently to someone on the other end, who, in all probability, is very upset because they have problems with their new machine, I consider to be essential, and to a large extent, lacking in today's scheme of things.

Going out to the Service counter, meeting customers and dealers, sorting out their problems face-to-face, stood me in good stead when I had my stand year after year at the International Classic Bike Show. The years of part numbers and technical information I held in my head gave me the ability to answer and resolve any query asked by anyone with a Triumph.

It was part of my job on the Service staff – even though you didn't get paid for overtime as the hourly-paid workers in shop floor jobs did – to go on occasion to a regional Triumph Owners Club and give a talk. Sometimes I went with another of the Service chaps, but usually it was with Alex Scobie. We would turn up at some club or pub, the monthly meeting place of that particular branch, and after a talk by both of us, would answer technical questions for an hour or so. All very enjoyable, even if it meant getting home in the early hours of the morning. Looking back, I wish we could do it all over again!

With some of my old Meriden friends also running their own businesses, we could sometimes complement each other and use one another's services. If, for instance, I had restored a machine for an overseas customer, I would call upon the services of Jim Lee, the Production Development mileage tester, who now runs his own shipping and export company. Jim knows how to pack and crate a Triumph properly so that no damage is sustained on its journey, sometimes for thousands of miles. He packs them the way we used to do it at Meriden.

Les Williams started his own business originally from his home, and then, as he expanded, moved into larger premises at Kenilworth selling spares and building beautiful Triumphs to his own specification. He

Triumph Production Testers' Tales – from the Meriden Factory

Jim Lee, UK Exports Ltd, shipping a 1947 Speed Twin restored by the author to Sarasota, Florida.

specialised in the seven fifty stuff, something I never got into, my latest year interest being 1969/1970, and four speed gearboxes, not five.

My restored machines were as good as I could get them using the spares and services available to me at the time. To restore a pile of bits, and turn it into a machine that is as near as possible how it was when it came off the end of the production line at Meriden was rewarding, especially when I pulled the covers off the finished job and watched the customer's face as he saw his pride and joy for the first time.

Sometimes I asked customers if I could borrow their finished bikes to put on my stand at the Classic Bike Show, and usually they were only too pleased to agree. My restorations were so good back in the 1990s, specialising in Triumph and with the distinct advantage of having worked there, that, after winning the top award for the third consecutive year, I was told by the organisers that due to complaints from other restorers, I could no longer enter my bikes for competition. Neither me or my customers were best pleased about this, so I displayed a sign to this effect on my stand just to let the public know why my exhibits no longer had large show numbers in front of them.

This decision by the show organisers did more for my business than all the adverts you could wish for, because it made known the fact that my Triumphs were too good; consequently, the waiting list for one of my restorations grew from six to eighteen months. I didn't mind, really, because it took away the stress of wondering whether I would win anything, and, if I didn't, what my customers might think of that.

The organisers must have realised this, because, the following year, I was invited to join the panel of judges. I agreed and that was that, the problem was shunted sideways.

Last year I went to the show as an ordinary punter with my good friend, Graham Bowen, builder of extraordinarily beautiful unit-construction Bonnevilles. We had a good day, meeting lots of our old mates and

Reflections

The author looking smug as he gets the award from Geoff Duke at the International Classic Bike Show.

Outside the workshop with restored machines. The author's two – MTG 190 1952 Speed Twin, and JRW 405 1952 Tiger 100 – are in the background.

Triumph Production Testers' Tales – from the Meriden Factory

looking at the other Triumphs being exhibited with critical eyes. It's sad, really, that when you are, or have been, a builder of beautiful bikes, you look at others and tend not to see how good they are as you're always looking for the things that are wrong.

Being into hi-fi equipment as I am, with extremely expensive, top-of-the-range kit, you get to a point where you are no longer listening to the music, but straining to hear imperfections in the system. When it gets you like that, it's time to pack it in.

While Graham and I were walking round the show, I chanced upon a 1947 Grand Prix Triumph, and, whilst it had the obligatory square barrel and head, I wasn't convinced it was genuine, although the owner said it was. I offered to check his engine and frame numbers against the copies of the Alex Scobie test reports that I have, and if I found the relevant report, I would send it to him. He declined: maybe he knew something I didn't.

My father has been gone a long time now, long before Jack Wickes, in fact, but I still remember his stories about motorcycle racing just after the war. He had a little motorcycle diary that he gave to me, and in it was listed all the Junior, Senior and Sidecar first, second and third finishes in each class.

Names like Collier, Frith, Daniels, Woods, and a host of others painted pictures in my young mind, and when Dad's friend called round on his new 1947 Tiger 100 in silver and chrome, I was hooked.

One story that stuck in my mind was that of a big Irishman called Ernie Lyons. Riding a factory-prepared machine, he took part in the 1946 Manx Grand Prix. The bike was probably road tested by my friend, Alex, along the A45. The 1946 race on the Isle of Man was to seal the fame of Ernie Lyons in the annals of motorcycling forever more, especially with Triumph owners.

I can still see the serious expression on my father's face as he related the story to me yet again, much to my mother's annoyance. The conditions that year were atrocious, dark, and with misty rain and fog on the mountain. Dad and two of his friends went over on their bikes, and witnessed the howling apparition that was Lyons as he flashed by in the gloom.

The other riders had decided to ease up, but not Lyons, who went quicker still. How he could see was anybody's guess, but even many years later in the early fifties when I was at Meriden, brave men paled as they spoke of this awesome performance. I think Dad was at Union Mills and said you could hear the wailing of the prototype Grand Prix on full chat long before you could see it. Then, in a flash, it was gone with only the fading exhaust note of the twin megaphones as proof that it was ever there.

The actual Ernie Lyons machine factory publicity shot.

Reflections

Meriden's old managers circa 1951. Left to right – back row: Mr Masters, Service Department; Jack Wickes, Drawing Office; Mr Holland, Overseas Sales; Mr Tubb, Finishing Shop; Mr Hedlum, Sales; Mr McDonnel, Stores; Sid Shilton, Police Sales; Tyrell-Smith, Experimental; Frank Baker, Development; Ivor Davies, Publicity. Left to right – front row: Bert Coles, Machine Shop; Mr Fearon, Works Manager; Edward Turner, Chairman and Director; Alf Camwell, Managing Director; Charlie 'Bud' Parker, Company Secretary; unknown; Jack Welton, Home Sales.

Poster signing at the Bonneville 50th celebration. Left to right: JR Nelson; LP Williams; John Bloor, and the author.

It's been fifty seven years since I first entered Meriden's doors, and looking at my toolboxes and the tools they contain, bring back memories of the very enjoyable day when I was given a chitty by the then Foreman, Mr Jack Fields, of the Repair Shop, just after the start of the new year in 1954.

You took this insignificant scrap of paper down to the tool stores on the other side of the huge Machine Shop, and gave it to a chap called Cal Gilbert. In

A light-hearted moment during the signing.

Triumph Production Testers' Tales – from the Meriden Factory

exchange, he gave you a huge cardboard box, and while you waited with it at the Stores counter, he would disappear into the bowels of the Stores and periodically return with handfuls of tools. King Dick tee-spanners, open-ended and ring, from ⅛ to ½ inch Whitworth. There would be hide mallets, rubber mallets, hammers, screwdrivers, pliers, bull-nosed, pointed-nosed, side cutters, everything. On top of all this, there were the special service tools for use only by the factory fitters, special instruments for all sorts of operations on any model of the Triumph marque.

It was so heavy I could hardly carry the box back to the Repair Shop, and had to keep stopping and resting it on my knee. But what joy, sorting all the tools and stamping them with a double aitch borrowed from Jimmy Davis.

These are the spanners I have looked after, and still use very lovingly, for every one has a special memory for me. For instance, the beautiful little flat ring spanner supplied in the Triumph tool kit has painful memories due to a trick that backfired on me. This particular spanner is ideal, and the fitters used them for getting on to the awkward nuts holding the three fifty and five hundred unit twins cylinder barrels to the crankcase at the base joint.

One of the older fitters had the old half-crown joke played on him. At the bottom of the Repair Shop was a small, free-standing bench. It had a gas supply, and a Bunsen burner was permanently connected and lit by Arthur Ashley every morning. On a stand above the flame was a cast iron pot containing solder which was left to heat up and turn molten. This was used by the fitters to either make or repair control cables.

By gripping the coin in a pair of pliers, and holding it in the gas flame, it would heat but not discolour. Then, when the victim had his back turned, the hot coin was gently placed on his workbench. As soon as the coin was noticed, a furtive glance around would be followed by quick concealment of the coin in a hand. There would be a count of one, two, three before the shriek, which would be answered by hilarity all down the line of workbenches. The hapless victim saw me laughing along with the older chaps, and, being the youngest one in the department, I should have kept my wits about me, but I didn't.

I was tightening the base nuts on a T100S/S engine when I had to answer a call of nature. Toddling off to the toilets, I had no idea of what was to come, but whoever did it must have acted very quickly, heating up the spanner, and then replacing it exactly where I had put it down. On my return, I swear I picked it up and half-tightened another nut before the pain registered, and I threw the spanner to the floor. There was a chorus of laughter and, with a rueful look round, I could see all the grinning faces. I must have cursed but, after a few minutes, all was forgotten and I had been initiated. A happy, if somewhat painful memory.

I carried on restoring bikes until the lease on my workshop expired in 2002. Since retiring, I have kept myself busy working on engines, crankshafts, and other little jobs in my hidey-hole at the bottom of the garden. It's in the blood you see, you can't stop.

I remember the managers of the various departments back then, real managers, not the lightweights that were to come along in later years. If one of these chaps spoke, you listened, they had gravitas and were much respected.

I found myself looking at John Bloor when we did the poster signing photo shoot at Hinckley in the boardroom, and wondered how he would have fitted in with the illustrious bunch that were in charge at Meriden when I started there. I don't think he's like Edward Turner was; he would fly off the handle, shout, and swear no matter who he was talking to. Jack Wickes told me that as he had the office next to Edward, he could hear him when he erupted at someone, who might be an ordinary draughtsman or one of the managers.

John Bloor seems to be more of a quiet authoritarian, pleasant on the outside, but tough as nails on the inside.

The factory site is now a housing estate, used in I don't know how many photo shoots and videos to do with Triumph motorcycles. People visit from all over the world on their Meriden models, just to sit in front of the Daytona Drive or Bonneville Close road signs and have their photograph taken. It's like history repeating itself as they used to come and sit opposite the main gate back in the 1960s to watch us testers come and go on the new machines.

There was a small ceremony that us old 'uns attended a couple of years ago. A small stone plinth, with a rider on a Triumph depicted on an aluminium plaque, was unveiled on the grass verge in front of where the factory was.

A fitting tribute to possibly the greatest motorcycle in the world. I'm not ashamed to say that, even after all these years, I still occasionally dream that I am back there. Maybe one day I will be, who knows?

My old boss, John Nelson, said last week, "The only trouble is, Hughie, by the time we get up there, all the best jobs will have gone."

Reflections

The Bonneville Close sign at the bottom of what used to be the main drive up to Pop Wright's office.

TRIUMPH MOTORCYCLE FACTORY MEMORIAL, MERIDEN.

Meriden Parish Council was given Planning Permission in April 2004 to erect a memorial on the grass verge near the original entrance to the Meriden Triumph Motorcycle Factory, which was based on this site from 1942 to 1983. Where great models of motorbikes were produced:-Tiger, Trophy, Thunderbird, TRW, Terrier, Bonneville, Daytona and Trident.

The model aluminium rider on a 'Bonneville' motorcycle was sculpted and finished by Frances Firth.

The setting of the model into the granite, inscription, positioning and completion of the memorial was by J E Hackett & Son.

In October 2005 the memorial was unveiled by Mr John Nelson an MD of the Meriden Co-operative factory.

MPC/JN – October 2005

The brochure given at the unveiling of the Triumph factory stone, and the stone as it is today.

Triumph Production Testers' Tales – from the Meriden Factory

American airman Ken Monk on his restored 1959 6T Charcoal Grey Thunderbird. As happy as can be.

The author and Gloria in 2011 on a Hinckley Triumph belonging to the president of the Triumph Owners' Club, Mr Roy Shilling.

Also from Veloce Publishing –

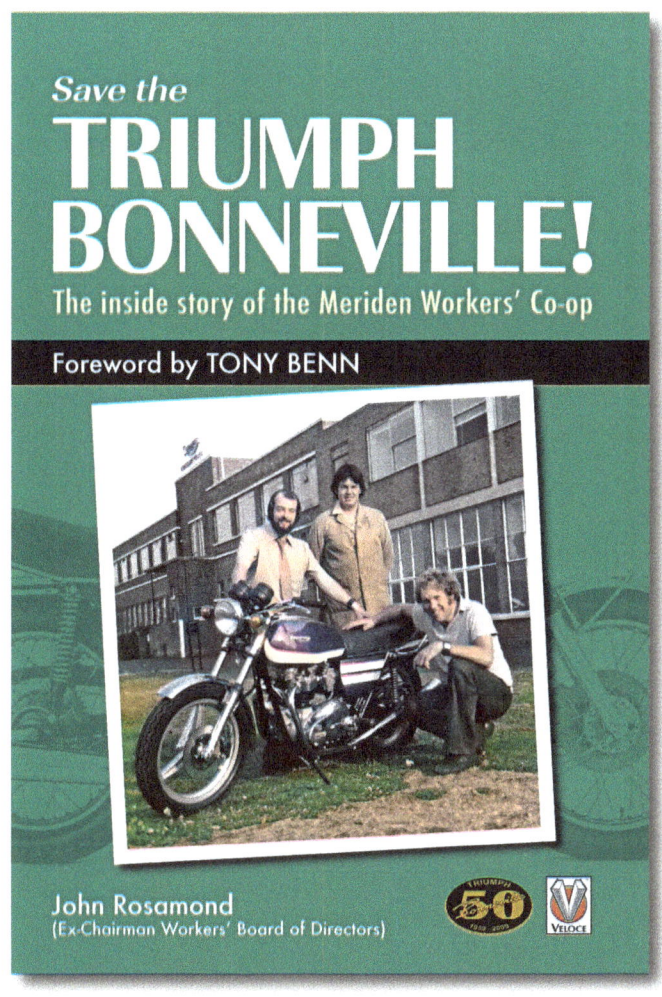

"Any devotee of the British industry must read this book ... a landmark publication that will no doubt be studied by scholars and students for many years to come."
inter-bike.co.uk

Written by the ex-Chairman of the famous Workers' Co-op, this is the real story of the last bastion of British motorcycle production following the collapse of the industry. It's also the tale of a workforce's refusal to let the Triumph Bonneville die ...

• A unique account of a workforce taking over the factory to save the world's most famous motorcycle, the Triumph Bonneville
• Written by the welder who became chairman of the workers' board of directors
• The most controversial chapter in the history of Triumph and the British motorcycle industry
• The most famous of Labour's/Tony Benn's workers' co-operatives
• John Rosamond was at Meriden under BSA, Triumph, NVT and the Triumph co-op until the bitter end
• An integral part of the decision-making process, John witnessed the final negotiations to save Triumph
• John was the public face of Meriden, often featured in the contemporary press
• This part of Triumph's story has never before been written firsthand
• Previously unpublished photographs from the personal collections of the Meriden workers
• 2009 coincides with the 50th anniversary of the legendary Bonneville

ISBN: 978-1-845842-65-9
Hardback • 22.5x15.2cm • £12.49* UK/$24.95* USA
• 448 pages • 122 colour and b&w pictures

For more info on Veloce titles, visit our website at www.veloce.co.uk • email: info@veloce.co.uk
• Tel: +44(0)1305 260068
* prices subject to change, p&p extra

Also from Veloce Publishing –

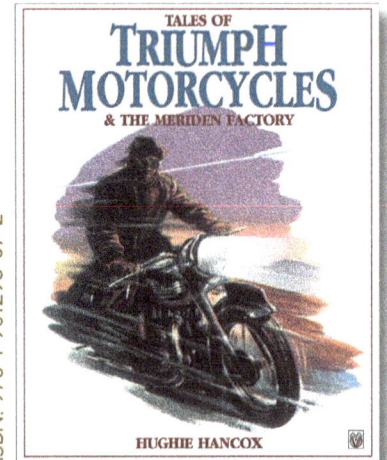
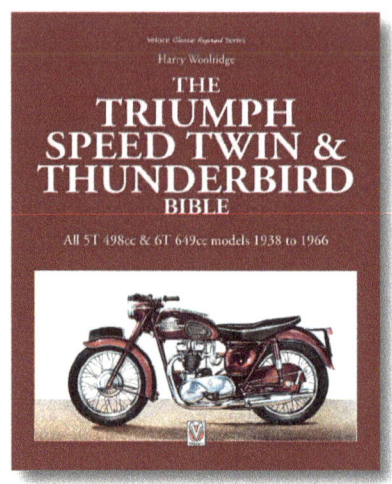

ISBN: 978-1-901295-67-2

- Paperback
- 25x20.7cm
- £24.99* UK/ $39.95* USA
- 144 pages

ISBN: 978-1-845849-82-5

- Paperback
- 25x20.7cm
- £35* UK/ $60* USA
- 144 pages
- 150 colour and b&w pictures

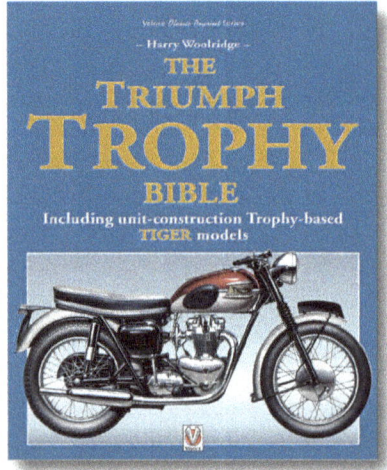

ISBN: 978-1-845849-74-0

- Paperback
- 25x20.7cm
- £35* UK/ $60* USA
- 144 pages
- 130 pictures

ISBN: 978-1-84584-134-8

- Paperback
- 19.5x13.9cm
- £12.99* UK/ $19.95* USA
- 64 pages
- 127 colour pictures

ebooks from Veloce Publishing –

ISBN: 978-1-845844-82-0

ISBN: 978-1-845845-05-6

For more info on Veloce titles, visit our website at www.veloce.co.uk
- email: info@veloce.co.uk • Tel: +44(0)1305 260068

* prices subject to change, p&p extra

Index

Technical

Brochures
T20 21
T21 11

3TA 41, 102, 40
5TA 11, 50, 48
6T 12, 98, 99, 134

TR6 11, 64, 101, 133
T120 11, 63, 77, 133
T100A 48
T100S 105, 108

Tiger 90 130
Tiger 100 131

T110 12

Price lists
1959 24
1961 48
1968 13

Service bulletin
No.21 (energy transfer to coll T100A) 49
No.221 650 performance parts Feb 1962 89
No.13 350/500 performance work 120
No.262 strobe use 135

Lucas
4CA contact breaker DIA 135
4CA set up 136
6CA contact breaker DIA 136

Specifications/schematics
Jomo (West Coast) tech spec 135
T20 General spec 37-39
T110 Technical data 12
T20 COB Schematic 10
T20, T20 SS, T20 SH Tech data 92
TRW Military spec sheet 96

Single leading shock assembly DIA 134

Parts list/DIA
T20 fork assembly 32
T20S 1960 front forks 33
Exhaust system 6T, T1RO, TR6, T120 61
Solex type 26 TRW carburettor 97

Test report
Grand Prix test report (ACEX Scobie) 114

General

A.C.H HELMET 7
A45 74
Accident 112
Agincourt 63, 69
AJS 39
Allen, Jonny 57, 87
Amac 32/1 91
Amal Monobloc 34, 37, 49, 66, 82, 84, 102
Ariel 39
Armitt, Alan 33, 40, 46
Arthur (village policeman) 16, 24
Austin, Dennis 74
Auto advance unit 132
Aztec Red 76

Bagington RD 57
Ballard, Reggie 15, 19
Barbour mitts 19
Barnett, Francis 31, 39, 107
Bedworth 15
Belstaff 8, 28, 31, 32, 44, 69
Berkswell Lane 16

Big ends 49
Billy and Bonneville 26
Birmingham 16, 62
Birton, Ron 97
Bloor, John 154
Bonneville Celebration 44, 71
Bonneville Close 14
Bonnevilles 28, 33, 66, 70, 82, 141, 128
Bore sizes 49
Bostocks Farm 16
Brake drums 132
Brando, Marlon 32
Brown, Jim 5, 14, 12, 41
Bryant, Roger 5, 10, 103, 128
BSA Bantam 31
BSA Motorcycles 14
Burgess Silencers 61

'Chubby' Cub 32
Canal Basin Heritage Centre 44
Carburettor problems 102
Carter, Bert 110

Cashmore, Dougie 90
Cashmore, Tom 65
Comp Shop 37
Con rod 49
Concentric 82
Cooper, Peter 8, 24
Copland, Jock 5, 42, 65, 68, 143
Corker helmet 7
Corley Rocks 80
Cornets End Lane 16, 26
Covehithe 62
Coventry City Council 44
Cub, police spec 24
Cubs 28, 91

D.O.T. 39
Dakota, Douglas 65
Davies, Ivor 30
Davis, Jimmy 147
Degree plate 136
Delta head 80
Delta splayed head 66
Dent, Eddie 5, 15, 42, 44, 46, 80

Despatch Rider's coat 16
Drawing Office 57
Duke, Geoff 7, 151
Dunlop factory 31
Dunlop Trails Universal 77
Duplex frame 70

E3059R camfollowers 84
E3134 camshafts 49, 84
Earles forks 37
Electric rollers 19
Ellis, Scott 37
Ellis, Tom 7
Elmdon airport 65
Energy transfer ignition 21, 23, 36, 37, 49
Engine timing 132
Evelyn, Evvy 42, 86
Experimental Dept 16, 46, 74, 90

Face mask 88
Felixstowe 44

159

Fiddler, Vic 37
Fillongley 16, 57
Finishing Shop 8, 15, 17, 19, 28, 42, 44, 61, 63, 70, 88, 90
Fletcher, Peter 7
Founders Day V.M.C.C. 72
Fred's Cafe 17
French 67

Gauge, Fred 90
Gaydon 60, 70, 72, 87
Gillingham, Allan 72, 74
Grand Prix report 114
Griffin, Dennis 5, 10
Gulson Road Hospital 9

H.M.S. Broadsword 42
Hampton Lane/ The Mile 16
Hancox, Dad 57
Hancox, Gloria 5, 44, 62, 121, 143
Hancox, Simon 5, 72, 149
Harrison, Norris 5, 16, 62, 65, 68
Hawkins, Reg 97, 106, 110, 121
Hawkins, Stan 10
Healey, Tony 70
Hedcom, Maurice 136
Hemmings, Bill 5, 33, 40
Henry V 67, 68
High Perf Kit 66
Hitler 42
Holbrook Lane 55
Hollyfast Lane 80
Hyde, Norman 58

Ipswich 42

James 39
Jefferies, Allen 56
Jefferies, Tony 56
Jinks, Stan 86
Johnson Motors 60
JRW 450 7, 8, 44, 98, 107, 120, 145

Kawasaki 44
Keith, Penelope 137
Kenilworth 57

Lampkin, Arthur 7
Lancashire Police 139
Lee, Jim 5, 70, 150
Leicester 82
Letts, Bill 5, 8, 16, 26, 41, 62, 63, 65, 66, 143
Longbow 69
Lucas
  15DI distributor 34
  4CA 131, 136
  88SA switch 91
  Ammeter 47
  Headlamp 54
  K2FR MAG 84
  Magneto 19
  SA41 switch 101
Lucas, Joseph 36, 39, 100, 136
Lyons, Ernie 152

M.I.R.A. 46
M1 motorway 66
Mac, Bob 7
Magic Roundabout, The 124
Manx Norton 22
Matchless 39
Matthews, Gordon 117
Meriden 14, 16, 25, 42, 44, 62, 70
Meriden Hill 8, 47, 65
Meriden Memorial 16
Meriden Mile 16, 24, 65
Metropolitan Police 30, 136
Michelin Men 69, 104
Miller, Eric 5, 10
Monoblocs 128
Monster 66, 74
Motor Mart 14, 59
Mute 61

National M/C Museum 57, 87
Nelson, John R 5, 58, 70
Nine-stud cylinder barrel 140
Norman James 39
Norton Dominator 15, 42, 44
Nuneaton 16

Oak Lane 80
Oil pressure indicator button 54
Oil seal conversion 140
Olivier 69
Oulton Park 22

Packing Department 65
Peacock, Dennis 5, 15, 41
Peplow, Roy 37
Perth 82
Petrol bowser 14
Pikers Lane 80, 111
Pinfold, Dick 8
Power and the Glory, The 72
Price, Geoff 5
Price, Joe 'Sooty' 17, 22, 24, 25, 30, 33, 40, 46
Primary chain tension 140
PRS8 switch 28, 33, 47
Publicity Department 46, 51
Pye of Cambridge 24

Q cam 127
QD headlamp 101
Queen's Head 65

RAC A.C.U. Riding Scheme 31
Rectification Sections 17
Repair Department 140
Repair Shop 90, 100, 103, 107, 145

Ripon 7
Robin Hood Cemetery 41
Rock Lane 80
Royal Navy 15, 42, 43
Royal Signals 36, 96

Saint, The 31
Scobie, Alex 5, 31, 112. 149
Service Bulletin 84
Service Dept Repair Shop 16, 31, 36, 38, 44, 46, 49, 68, 82
Service Office 56
Shilling, Roy 5
Shilton, Sid 31
Showell Lane 47
Signals 16
Signals Display Team 7, 43, 45, 116
Silverstone 22
Six volt AC 47, 50
Small end 49
Smith, Adam 38
Smith, Anthony 38
Smith, Colin 45
Solex 102
Somers Lane 16, 26, 66, 144
Southworld 62
Speed Twin 40, 41, 47, 61
Stanford Hall 72
Stone 8, 36
Stoneleigh 58, 62
Stroboscope 132
Suffolk 62
Sun 39
Sunbeam 39
Surtees, John 72, 147

6T Thunderbird 30, 51, 70, 76, 80, 82, 84, 99, 104
T120C 60, 66, 86
T120P 137
T120R 60
T20 S/C 123
T20 S/R 123
T20 STD Cub 19, 21, 23, 24, 33, 36
T20J 36
T20S Sports 21, 23, 24, 33, 36
T20SL 31, 36
T21 Three Fifty 34, 40, 41, 42, 47, 49, 60, 61
T2OT 36, 91
T5A Triumph 19
Tait, Percy 5, 20, 37, 58, 66, 72, 74, 86, 106
Tamworth Road 57, 80
Terrier Cub Track 26
Tiger 90 130
Tiger 100A 8, 36, 47, 49, 50, 51, 76, 106
Tiger 100S 46, 51, 82, 106, 123
Tiger 110, 66, 99
Tilley, Pop 74

Time Office 16, 42
Timson, Rodney 137
Tooth, Fiona 5
Torrey Canyon 16
Torrington needle rollers 80
TR5 97
TR5 AR TR5AC 51, 60
TR6C 65, 107, 127
TR6P 136
TR6R 65, 66
TR7 60
TR7A 60
TR7B 60
Trade plates 18
Transport and Gen Wkrs Un 41
Triumph Corp Baltimore 60
Triumph Engineering Co 42
Triumph nacelle 52, 55
Trophy TR6 33, 70, 74, 77, 80, 84
Trowell, Stan 15-17, 42, 44, 45, 128
Truslove, Stan 90, 125
TRW 43, 96
Tubb, Sid 15, 16
Tubbs' Office, Mr 44, 112, 124
Tubby's Cafe (The Thatch) 16, 17, 51
Twelve volt electrics 132

Vace, Henry 37
Vicciers 39
Vincent, Chris 51

Wall Hill RD 80
Wallace, Charlie 16, 65, 68, 80, 111
Wallis, Mike 71
Wangford 62
Warner, Billy 90
Warwick Castle 69
Waterproof 104
Watmore, Bert 5, 16, 20, 46, 106
Watson, Fred 10, 19
Wesco Oil Can 80
West, Pete 5, 42-44
Whitcomb, Stan 5, 62, 103, 148
White and Poppe 55
White Helmets 30, 43
Wickes, Jack 15, 51, 55, 57, 70, 80, 154
Wild Ones, The 32
Williams, Les 5, 36, 42, 43, 96
Willoughby, Vic 118
Wilson, Jack 57
Wrentham 62
Wright, Joan 9, 28, 42
Wright, Pop 16, 28, 42

Zenith 91
Zenith 18 MXZ 19